AMONG THE SUPPORTING CAST

AMONG THE SUPPORTING CAST

Reminiscences and Reflections
on Three Careers by

Tim Sainsbury

BARBRECK

First published in 2020 by Barbreck Publishers
Copyright © Tim Sainsbury, 2020
This edition © Barbreck Publishers, 2020
Foreword copyright © Michael Heseltine, 2020
Edited by Eleo Carson

ISBN 978-1-9995891-1-0

A CIP catalogue reference for this book is available from the British Library

All rights reserved. Published in the United Kingdom by
Barbreck Publishers, 50 Albemarle Street, London W1S 4BD
and distributed by Penguin Random House UK,
20 Vauxhall Bridge Road, London SW1V 2SA

Typography and typesetting by Peter B. Willberg

Printed and bound by CPI, Moravia

For Susie, James, Camilla, Alexander and Jessica

CONTENTS

FOREWORD

The three weeks I spent walking the streets of Liverpool in the summer of 1981 made a profound impression on me and, I believe, on all those who were part of my team. The late Lord Armstrong, then Cabinet Secretary, described me as a man possessed by an experience. Tim Sainsbury was my Parliamentary Private Secretary at the time and he was able to play a critical role in one of the highest profiles of the events.

The invitation to become a PPS to a senior Cabinet minister is often the first step on the ladder of political promotion. It is best described as an invitation to act as that minister's eyes and ears in the parliamentary corridors. MPs will talk candidly to a PPS, who has to deploy tact and timing to pass on warnings of trouble on the back-benches, with a firmness of touch, while preserving the essential good relationship. Tim was a model much to be admired. I had taken a chance in inviting thirty captains of the financial institutions to join me in a bus trip round a city that had rioted, but in which they had major investments. Their reluctance to accept was understandable, but Tim's relationship with Robin Leigh-Pemberton broke the log-jam. They turned up and spared me unfortunate headlines. Our ways parted when I became Defence Secretary in 1983.

Tim's subsequent climb up the political ladder took him through the Whips' Office, the Ministry of Defence, the Foreign Office and the Department of Trade and Industry, where I rejoined him after the 1992 election.

He had had significant experience as a director of his family firm and knew at first hand the complexities of the relationship between the public and private sector, and had long left behind him any instinct to simplify and sloganise. He was a most sympathetic colleague, although no one could have foreseen that he was to step into my shoes and run the Department in my absence following my heart attack.

One of the most exciting projects that fell within our shared experience was the rescue of Somerset House from a prolonged period of institutional isolation. Tim was the obvious choice as chairman of the trust which I set up in the 1990s to mastermind its conversion from courtroom and taxation office into today's popular cultural centre, so clearly suited to its majestic buildings.

The Sainsbury family has been associated with this country's cultural inheritance for generations. Tim himself has followed in that tradition. His generosity, particularly to the Ashmolean Museum in Oxford, was critical to its evolution to its renowned role in modern Britain. Earlier, the Sainsbury Wing addition to the National Gallery is a conspicuous tribute to private patronage.

Tim and I shared the philosophies of One Nation Conservatism. The drift to the right after 1997 persuaded both of us to contribute to Conservative Mainstream, a political group designed to provide a home for like-minded Conservatives and, particularly, give a home to Ken Clarke as he carried the One Nation flag in his bid for the party's leadership.

Of particular interest to the political student will be Tim's reflections on the changes he lived through in Parliament itself. The working conditions there are unacceptable, there are too many MPs, and the increasing social pressures particularly from the internet are making it increasingly difficult to attract men and women of the calibre ministerial responsibility demands.

It is often said of politicians that they are only in it for what they can get out of it. This brief story of Tim's political life carries the lie to so trivial a generalisation. His service to political life offered no gain to him, save that of public service itself, and the satisfaction of a job well done. It has been a privilege to have known and worked with him in so many aspects of our shared careers.

Michael Heseltine

PART I

My mother with her three sons, *c.*1937: John on my right, Simon on my left.

1

EARLY YEARS

Born in 1932, my memories of the pre-war years are fragmentary. We lived in Chelsea in London and had a holiday cottage in Suffolk, near Bures. There, my brothers and I played shops, unaware of our retailing future. I recall fields that seemed full of mushrooms and picking blackberries. The cleaning lady who came in was called Hetty; I was later told that she had never married because she had lost her young man in the war, the Boer War. There was a gardener, Baldwin. He had an interesting back story, having been taken on by my father after he was sacked as a farmworker. He had broken an arm, falling off a haystack, and went to see his union in Colchester to ask if he could claim compensation. For that, he lost his job and his home. When my father employed him, he gave him a fortnight's holiday a year. There was a protest from local farmers about that, on the grounds that if Baldwin got a holiday, all their farmworkers would start wanting two weeks' holiday. When the war came, Baldwin joined the Home Guard and announced that, 'If Hitler comes to Bures, he will meet his Waterloo.'

There were several domestic staff at our London house, 27 The Vale, Chelsea. They were headed by Cook. She was always referred to as 'Cook'; I never knew her name. The lower ground floor was her domain, where she was assisted by a scullery maid. When I was very young, we had a nanny who was assisted by a nursery maid, as Nanny was not expected to clean the nursery floor, or even apparently boil a kettle. In 1940, Cook was in the lower ground floor kitchen, sorting out a hamper of soft fruit sent up from the cottage in Suffolk, when a bomb dropped very nearby and there was the noise of much broken glass. She thought she had better go upstairs to assess the damage. She later said, 'Then I thought I had better go outside first to see if there was an upstairs to go upstairs to.' There was, but the bath she would normally have been in at that time was full of broken glass. Irritated by all this, she looked over the garden wall and saw the senior RAF man, who lived next door, catching a moment of rest. She shouted at him, 'Why don't you go and bomb Berlin?' And, she said, 'Next week they did.'

I can just recall a holiday in St Moritz, Switzerland, in a large and grand hotel, Suvretta House. Plenty of snow but no skiing for my age group – I must have been about four and a half. Then there were holidays in Brittany, lots of sand and lollipops. Finally, a holiday at Le Touquet, which ended early: it was August 1939. There were no flights involved in these holidays; all travel was by car, train and ferry. My mother decided that as she was nervous about flying, she would try doing it herself. She went to Croydon and qualified to have a pilot's licence.

When I was four, Nanny was replaced by a governess, Muriel Fox Hill, known as Foxy. She taught me the early stages of reading and writing. When I went to the first of my three pre-prep schools, I was ahead of my fellow classmates in these skills, so I came top of the form in my first term as a schoolboy, a feat which I never managed again. The prize was a book, *Whitefoot the Woodmouse*. We still have it. The figure missing from most of these early memories is my father; my parents were divorced in 1939.

Like many others, expecting an immediate start to bombing, my mother and her three sons left London at the end of August 1939 and we all went to live with my paternal grandparents. They had quite a large twentieth-century house near Bexhill. There was a tennis court and what seemed to me then an enormous garden. My grandmother, who was a Van den Bergh, from a Dutch Sephardic Jewish family, was so upset at the behaviour of her elder son (my father) that she told him he could only come to the house if my mother agreed. She was known as 'Little Granny' because of her diminutive stature; sadly she was diabetic and died in 1942, but I did get to know her quite well, living in her house for nine months, during which time I went to my second pre-prep school.

The fall of France came in June 1940 and, as we lived on the south coast, we could hear gunfire across the Channel. Enemy aircraft started to fly overhead and brought about another change to my life. We abandoned Bexhill and, after a short stay in a hotel near Weybridge, moved to my maternal grandmother's house just off the A4 between Maidenhead and Slough. This became our home for the next fifteen months. This grandmother was a widow. Her husband, Leonard Adams, who had died aged fifty before I was born, had been a wine merchant. Daisy, who was always known to all her grandchildren as Lil or Lilly, had run the business during the First World War when Leonard was away in the Army and did the same in the Second World War, when her two sons were away. In the autumn of 1940, I went to my third pre-prep school. It was on the A4, just before the Thames Bridge into Maidenhead. It was primarily a girls' school. During the First World War, the headmistress, who was also the owner, had opened the school's two lower forms to boys as her contribution to the war effort. She did the same again during the Second World War. The two lower forms, which were mixed, joined with the rest of the school for morning prayers. When they were over, two sliding doors to separate us off from the senior school were shut and locked. The headmistress seemed to think it essential to keep those dangerous seven- and eight-year-old boys away from the older girls.

It was while living with my grandmother that I had my closest encounters with enemy action. During the Blitz, which started in September 1940, air raids on Slough were quite frequent and resulted in a lot of noise, both of bombs and of anti-aircraft fire. On one occasion, when there was a lot of activity, my mother sat me under the stairs, wrapped in her fur coat with her jewel box on my lap, saying, 'Now I know where the three most precious things I have here are located.' In the event of a bomb hitting the house, under the stairs was always regarded as the safest place if you weren't actually in a shelter. As our shelter was an Anderson shelter out in the garden, with no light or other amenities, it was not a popular place to be alone in the dark at night. One night, an aircraft, perhaps wanting to get rid of its bomb load having missed its target, dropped a stick of very small high-explosive bombs, one of which fell on one side of the house and the next on the other. The first dropped only some ten yards from the house and blew out a few windows but caused no other damage. More frightening to me were the whistling bombs which were once or twice used in the raids on Slough. They made a very audible whistling noise as they came down, so loud that they made you think they would land very close to where you were.

In the autumn of 1941, I became a boarder at a preparatory school for boys called Sandroyd in Wiltshire, following my two brothers, who had been there. By the time I got there, my eldest brother, John, had moved on to Stowe, so I was only Sainsbury Mi rather than Sainsbury Min. The school had been located at Cobham but had, like many others, left the London area at the beginning of the war and relocated in a house at Tollard Royal in Wiltshire. Its owner, a member of the Pitt-Rivers family, was detained under Section 18(b) of the Emergency Powers Act as he was a fervent supporter of Oswald Mosley. He never returned, and the school remains there to this day, having greatly expanded from the ninety or so pupils who were present during my time. My memories of the school are not happy ones, mainly focusing on the food, which got steadily more unpalatable, the cold which was ever present in the winter and the chilblains from which I and a number of other boys suffered. I was also ill on several occasions, once with the measles like many other boys. I was in bed in a dormitory with the curtains drawn because of the risk to our eyesight when the Assistant Matron came in to announce that Russia had invaded Germany and taken sixty cities. She had got her facts slightly wrong! We soon became aware of the actual situation and, while at Sandroyd, one of my favourite activities was following the course of the war both in Russia and in the desert and later, in Europe. We were all very keen on watching the maps and seeing how the battle lines moved across the desert and to and fro seasonally in Russia. As the date of the Normandy invasion drew nearer, there was an increasing amount of activity in the air and on the ground near to the school, which also provided much interest to the boys and concern to the masters.

I saw very little of my father during my time at Sandroyd. He never visited the school. My mother, however, managed to make a visit most terms. We sometimes were taken out to lunch and occasionally enjoyed a roast chicken, a great luxury in those days.

In 1941, my mother at last found a house outside London. It was in Boveney, a tiny hamlet with some dozen houses on the Thames by the first lock, upriver from Windsor and Eton. The house had been created by amalgamating three eighteenth-century cottages. Surprisingly, it, as well as the largest house in the hamlet, was owned by Eton College. Apparently, the school wanted to ensure that they did not get used for any dubious purposes. It remained my home until 1956, when I came down from Oxford.

It had been intended that John, the eldest of the three brothers, should go to Stowe, Simon, the middle one, to Eton and that I would go to Winchester in 1946. Allegedly the schools had been chosen, I am not sure by whom, to suit our personalities. However, in early 1945, my brother Simon's housemaster and my mother were at the same dinner party. Jack Upcott, the housemaster, asked my mother where she was proposing to send Timothy. She replied, 'Winchester, if he gets in next year.' Upcott then said, 'Well, why not send him to my House in the summer, I have a vacancy.' That offer was hard to resist, as having two sons at the same school at a time when travel was extremely difficult and petrol very restricted, and the school being only three miles down the road and within bicycling distance, would be very convenient. So my last school unexpectedly became Eton. I started at Eton only a very few days before the end of the war in Europe, VE Day. I enjoyed Eton from the start. I had my own room, albeit a very small one, rather than being in a dormitory. The food somehow seemed better and I got fewer chilblains. I was less cut off from home. There had been whole terms at Sandroyd when I did not see a parent or other visitor. Now I used to see my mother, and sometimes my grandmother, shopping in Eton, as well as having days at home several times a half, as terms were called at Eton.

If my academic career was not particularly brilliant, my athletic prowess did develop, so, by the time I left, I had won the school 100 yards and become twelfth man of the Field, which was the First XI of the curious game of football which all Etonians played, once described as combining aspects of rugger, soccer and hockey but leaving out the best points of each. I had also experienced my first taste of responsibility as Captain of House and Captain of games in the House.

My father did come to Eton on a few occasions; also he usually came to Boveney on one day during the holidays. While I was at Eton, as there were no longer the flying bombs known as V1s or doodlebugs or V2s, the long-range rockets, to worry about, I made a few visits to London which sometimes included a meeting with him. In 1947, to his and my surprise, I spent ten days staying at his house in Hanover Terrace, Regent's Park. It had been a very harsh winter with a lot of snow and a prolonged day and night frost. The thaw, when it came, was accompanied by heavy rain, and the result was catastrophic flooding in many areas, the worst from the Thames. Our house at Boveney, although only 200 metres or so from the river, was not flooded. However, the hamlet was cut off from the nearest traffic and main road by some half a mile of flood water and was inaccessible. When most of the lavatories stopped flushing, Eton had to be sent home. My brother Simon and I had to go to London, somewhat to the consternation of my fairly new stepmother, whom I had hardly met. After I left Oxford, several years later, I saw more and more of my father, particularly during my time as a director of the family business, J Sainsbury.

2

NATIONAL SERVICE

In 1951, on leaving Eton, I was required to do two years' National Service, as were all eighteen-year-old males, unless physically unfit. Stalin was ruling Russia and the Korean War had started. So few questioned the need for National Service. In the light of the perceived threat, the duration had recently been extended from eighteen months to two years. It could be in the Navy or Air Force, but most went into the Army. I made the easy choice of following my two brothers into The Life Guards. First, in order to qualify for officer training I had to pass the WOSBY – the War Office Selection Board. Most public school boys succeeded at that. So in January 1951, after a few days at the Regimental Headquarters, Combermere Barracks Windsor, which were very relaxed, including going home for dinner on two occasions, I went to the Guards Depot at Caterham which was the very opposite of 'relaxed'. All those joining the Foot Guards started their career there, but from the Household Cavalry only those hoping to become officers joined what was known as the 'Brigade Squad'.

The programme for those in that squad was famously rigorous. It started with four weeks at Caterham almost entirely devoted to drill – 'square-bashing' and cleaning boots and buttons, pressing uniforms and cleaning the hut in which we lived. Each recruit had a task; I had to clean a stove. My fellow Old Etonian recruit, later to be a fellow MP, Tam Dalyell 'of the Binns', was naturally tasked with emptying 'the Bins'. During those first four weeks, no one was allowed out of the barracks. Some years later, during a Party Conference at Blackpool, I was standing in the gallery beside Paul Channon and another colleague who had served in the Household Brigade, listening to the Home Secretary describing the harsh new regime which was to be imposed in prisons for juvenile offenders. We turned to each other and said, 'That's a soft option compared to Caterham.'

After four weeks we had the Adjutant's inspection, and if the Squad passed that, we were then allowed a couple of days home on leave. On returning we had another three weeks at Caterham, during which time we started to learn how to drill with a rifle, and indeed even to use it on

Part of Sergeant McMahon's Brigade Squad, February 1951.
Sergeant McMahon is in the front, second from the right,
I am in the back row on the right.

the ranges. At the end of that, there was the Commandant's inspection, and if we passed that, we could move on to the next stage of officer training. My squad was exceptionally lucky in being under the direction of a drill sergeant from the First Battalion of the Grenadier Guards who, remarkably, never swore, or almost never swore. However, on two occasions he was moved to swear at the same recruit, whose inability to master drill might be said to have justified the use of the 'F' word. On both occasions, Sergeant McMahon paused for half a minute or so, and then said *sotto voce*, 'You're enough to make a parson swear.' He succeeded in getting the unfortunate awkward recruit returned to Unit, so that when we came to the Commandant's inspection, his squad was once more the best that the Commandant had ever seen, as the Adjutant had said of us after four weeks.

The next step was at Pirbright, where we practised infantry manoeuvres, not exactly an important part of what was needed to become an officer in an armoured car regiment. And then it was on to the Officer Cadet School. There were two main ones: the Infantry went to Eaton Hall in Cheshire; the Cavalry, the Artillery and most of the other corps went to Mons Officer Cadet School in Aldershot. There, those heading towards cavalry regiments which had either tanks or armoured cars started learning useful things like map-reading and using radios.

Shortly after I arrived, there was the Aldershot District Unit Athletics Competition. Mons won quite easily, and I took part in the 4 × 110 yards and 4 × 220 yards relays, which were the sprinting part of the event. About halfway through my time at Mons, there was the Southern Command Unit Championships for the winners of the various district events. Again Mons were the victors. We also went up to Eaton Hall to compete against their Officer Cadet School and, on this occasion, won, which was not the normal result.

Every fortnight there was a passing-out parade for those who had completed their training satisfactorily. Two weeks before I was due to pass out and become an officer, I was told to my chagrin that I was being back-squadded two weeks. The reason given was that I had missed too much training because of the athletic activities in which I had taken part. I thought at the time that it was a rather strange excuse.

Some of the cadets agreed to take what were known as short-service commissions, and serve for three years instead of two. In order to give them seniority over those who were only doing the minimum National Service two years, they were gazetted to their new units the day of the passing-out parade. The rest of us had to wait another day; so I was still officially on the books of Mons Officer Cadet School the day after the passing-out parade. That for me happened to be the day for the final of the British Army Athletic Championships, in which Mons, having won Southern Command, were taking part.

So I was summoned back to Mons the day after I passed out to take part in the Army finals. It meant that I was not really able to celebrate becoming an officer on that first evening. The next day I drove back to Mons. The team assembled in front of the Guard Room and the officer in charge of sport asked who was the Senior Cadet present – after a pause, I suggested that I might be. So my first command became the Mons Officer Cadet School Athletics Team and I was able to call them to attention so that the Commandant could congratulate us for what the team had done and wish us good luck in the final. Mons finished third in that final. This was quite an achievement, because there were only a very few of the team who had taken part in all three stages. It did occur to me later that it was very likely that the reason for my being back-squadded was to make sure that I was available to compete in the Army finals.

There was one incident during my time at Mons that I found very revealing. Some of our training was done in one-tonne trucks which had a sort of hut on the back, containing the wireless equipment that would be found in a tank or armoured car. There were three trucks in a troop, and the exercise that day was taking turns at being in command of a troop of tanks which were actually one-tonne trucks. When it was my turn to act as the Troop Leader, I was told I had to give commands to my three tanks to attack and take a wood. The first thing I did was to get my truck to move to give me a better sight of the wood. I then gave my various commands and at the end of the exercise, the Instructing Officer said, 'Well done, an excellent start, you used your initiative to move to get a better view of the battle area. You gave clear and decisive instructions. Oh, incidentally, your battle plan was entirely wrong, all your tanks would have been destroyed and you wouldn't have taken the wood, but well done, you gave your instructions very clearly and decisively.' It seemed that good marks were given for being able to give your commands clearly and decisively, even if your plan was entirely wrong and your men were killed.

After a short period of leave, I arrived back at Combermere Barracks as Second Lieutenant Sainsbury. At that time, any officer leaving the barracks to go to London during the day was expected to wear a bowler hat, a stiff white collar, and carry a furled umbrella and gloves, regardless of the weather; the post-war world had yet to arrive.

In 1952, a large part of the British Army was based in Germany. Early in the year, the Life Guards were going to go to Germany to take over from their sister regiment, the Royal Horse Guards, known as the Blues. This required that we took over a great deal of equipment, including vehicles, and an advance party was sent out to sign all the necessary paperwork. The captain who was due to take over all the vehicles got appendicitis. I was chosen to go to Germany to join the advance party in his place, and given one week's embarkation leave. The day before I was due to start that leave, King George VI died. I was told that as we were the royal bodyguard, we were not allowed to appear in a place of public entertainment until after the funeral. That ruled out theatres, cinemas and obviously nightclubs, and apparently also restaurants. So my week's embarkation leave was spent at home twiddling my thumbs.

Although the war had ended seven years earlier, in 1952, the British Army of the Rhine (BAOR), was still an army of occupation. It is hard to comprehend now that at that time we were not allowed any fraternisation with Germans; so we had no social intercourse at all with those who were soon to become our NATO allies. The only Germans we met were in shops, restaurants and, in my case, our athletics coach. The armoured car regiments, of which there were three in BAOR, were a forward screen. Our barracks were the ones nearest to the inner German border which separated the British from the Russian zone, soon to become the German Democratic Republic; south of us there were American and French zones. One of our duties was to send out border patrols to show the flag along the border. However, it was interesting that the actual border guards were a German force called, I think, the Bundesgrenzpolizei, who were clearly former German Army troops. It was also interesting that all the exercises which we did involved retreating, it being assumed that in the event of a Russian attack we would retreat towards the River Weser, waiting for the arrival of more American and other reinforcements.

We were allowed one fortnight's leave during the ten months or so I was in Germany and this gave rise to another eccentric incident. This involved the 'Leave Train'. This was a train which started in Brunswick, not far from our barracks, and wound its way slowly through the British Zone, stopping frequently to pick up officers and men who were going on leave or ending their National Service. It so happened that the day I went on leave, I was the only officer getting on the train at Brunswick and so a major in the Transport Corps said, 'You have to sign for the train,' which I duly did. This meant that in theory as the train filled up with some quite senior officers, including at least one General, I was in command of the train. I had to sign more papers when we crossed the border into Holland and then finally, to my relief, sign off the train when we reached the Hook of Holland to board the ferry to go to Britain.

After completing two years' National Service, we were all required to serve three years in the Territorial Army. There were only five Territorial armoured car regiments. The three in England only accepted officers who were prepared to serve longer than the minimum three years. So those of us who were, reluctantly, doing the minimum ended up in either the North Irish Horse or, like me, the Fife and Forfar Yeomanry. Since the regimental HQ was in Cupar, Fife, not handy for Buckinghamshire or Oxford, I never got to any activity with the regiment other than for a fortnight a year. This was when the whole regiment gathered for manoeuvres away from the HQ.

The more senior officers, captains and above, were all Scots. They were joined for the fortnight of 'Camp' by a miscellaneous group of lieutenants, nearly all from England, many of whom were undergraduates. The mixture worked very well, although, to our disappointment, our average mess bill per head never reached that achieved by the North Irish Horse.

National Service completed, I was ready to go to university. I followed my elder brother John and my mother's two brothers in choosing Worcester College, Oxford.

3

OXFORD

Oxford University in 1953 was, like the rest of the country, only just beginning to move on from the war and immediate post-war years. Although there were no longer undergraduates returning after demobilisation to complete a degree or to do a short two-year degree after war service, nearly all male undergraduates had already completed two years' National Service and so arrived at Oxford aged twenty or twenty-one. All colleges were still single sex, and there were very few students from other countries except for the small number of Rhodes Scholars from South Africa and the United States. There was not yet a Middle Common Room, as there were hardly any postgraduate students.

The reforms of the 1960s were still to come. All undergraduates were expected to be back in their digs or college by midnight. Since everybody knew that this rule was unenforceable, every college had a more or less approved route for climbing in. For my own college, Worcester, it was relatively easy. After climbing over a gate from the road, you followed a route through the gardens into the playing fields and back to the college. The only hazard was being surprised by a wallaby jumping out of the bushes! At the time, the college had a small number of wallabies which roamed the grounds. Since our much-loved Dean, Harry Pitt, was of diminutive stature, not much taller than the wallaby, there was always the worry that the creature jumping out of the bushes might actually be Harry Pitt. He was in theory responsible for enforcing the rules.

Another surprising rule was that, in my college, attendance at Chapel on a Sunday was compulsory. A less surprising rule was that first year undergraduates were not allowed to have a car in Oxford. I had one – it was a twenty-first birthday present from my father – and the college knew I had one and kept it in Oxford. However, a blind eye was turned to this breach of regulations as long as I performed reasonably satisfactorily on the work front. In the second and third year, when a car was allowed, all students had to have a green light on their car, which was meant to be illuminated after dark to indicate that it was a car owned by an undergraduate. We all took the precaution of having a switch to enable us to turn off the green light when we were driving around after midnight.

Perhaps the biggest difference between the university then and now was the tiny proportion of the university age group who actually went to university. Small in the case of males, tiny in the case of females. Since possession of a degree was such a minority qualification, job prospects for those graduating were very good. A First would open the door to the most prestigious jobs in the public or private sector, but even a Fourth or a bad Third would qualify the graduate for a position as a prep school master. The consequence of this ease of getting a job, together with the older age of undergraduates, most of whom had already done their two years' National Service, led to a rather too relaxed approach to work among many of those at the university. I must admit that in my second year in particular I did a minimum of work. There were many good parties, and perhaps appropriately in view of my future careers, I became President of the Oxford University Wine and Food Society and a member of the Bullingdon Club.

The subject on which I should have been working was Politics, Philosophy and Economics (PPE), a course then only available at Oxford. In the mid-1950s, the study of economics was still heavily conditioned by the previous twenty-five years, the Great Depression followed by the Second World War, and with the need for total Government control of resources which that entailed. Recovery was slow and painful. Food rationing only came to an end in 1954, during my first year at Oxford. It was generally accepted that Government control of many aspects of the economy was necessary. The basic grounding in economics was something that I have found very helpful ever since. I was taught by Dick Sergeant, who I was told was a Fabian Socialist. However, what he taught about the merits of a market economy strongly reinforced my Tory views. Keynes was still the king of economic theory at the time; I don't think I had even heard of Hayek or Milton Friedman and the Chicago School. We all accepted as natural that there should be Government involvement in the economy to secure or maintain full employment. Nobody challenged the existence of nationalised industries. The Philosophy side of the course at least helped me to think logically, even if my full understanding of the works of Immanuel Kant fell well short of what would have been required for a First class degree. The Politics studied had nothing to do with contemporary political issues. As I recall, matters like the difference between a Federal and a Confederal constitution predominated.

Like most undergraduates, I dabbled in sport. I played tennis for the college; occasionally in inter-collegiate matches (cuppers), more often in league matches, and nearly always in the third pair. On 6 May 1954, I was playing against Christ Church in a cuppers match. As third pair, our last encounter was against the Christ Church first pair. We won the first game and lost the next twelve. This enabled me to run across the ground to the neighbouring Iffley Road running track. It had become known that during the match between the University and the Amateur Athletics Association, Roger Bannister was going to make an attempt to break the 4-minute mile. I reached the ground as the race was ending its first lap, so I was able to see the remainder of the race and hear the famous announcement which went something like this: 'Winner of event number 12, Roger Bannister of Merton and University Colleges in a time which, subject to confirmation, is a meeting record, a track record, an English national record, a British all-comers record, a European record, a world record,' and we still didn't know whether he had done it. Then came the magic words '3 minutes'. I don't think anybody heard the 59.4 seconds. Sixty years later, Susie and I were at Wimbledon to see Andy Murray win his first Wimbledon title. I have often wondered whether there is anybody else who was present at both these iconic sporting moments.

The other sport in which I had a fringe involvement was athletics. I have to admit that I never took this seriously enough; neither my training nor my lifestyle were very appropriate. Indeed, when I turned out the light in my room at five minutes to midnight one term, it was the only occasion during the term that that happened. It was because it was the eve of the University athletics trials. I was good enough to compete for Oxford in the relays on two occasions. When the match was at Oxford, the first event was the 4 × 110 yards, and I ran the second leg for Oxford, apparently rather well. I had been at an excellent party at Christ Church the night before, which had ended well after midnight. Oxford won the 4 × 110, and then lost the next five relays. The final event was the 4 × 220, and the Captain asked me to run the last leg in view of my success in the 4 × 110. It was a damp and rather cold afternoon, and my enthusiasm for running had by now considerably reduced. Luckily when I took over the baton, Oxford was already a long way behind and I think my poor performance was hardly noticed.

One very fringe activity with which I was also involved was the annual match between Oxford and Cambridge Old Etonians playing the Field Game. I captained Oxford and we managed to draw.

Among the less athletic competitive events, I took part in the relatively recently introduced annual wine-tasting match against Cambridge.

In my first year as a member of the team, Oxford did so badly that the sponsors of the event, Harveys of Bristol, threatened to stop sponsoring it unless we did better. The next year, when I was Captain, I am glad to say that we did do rather better but still lost by quite a margin.

I was rather more successful in the other non-athletic competitive event in which I became involved, and on which I spent rather too much time. This was bridge. I had only been at Worcester for two weeks or so, and I was having a cup of coffee in the room of a friend from Eton who I didn't know particularly well, although we had been near contemporaries. He was a Scholar and had been Captain of the School. I noticed on his table a book on bridge, and said, 'Simon, do you play bridge?' He jumped on my question, and I was invited to join him for a game that evening. It transpired that he was looking for a partner to join him, to make up the College team. The other pair in the team had spent their two years' National Service learning Russian and playing a great deal of bridge together, so they were an experienced and skilful pair. Simon was an excellent player and, as his partner, I learnt a great deal about bridge in general, and duplicate matches in particular. We formed a team of Freshmen to play for the College in 1953/54. It seemed that Balliol regarded bridge cuppers as their natural property. We came up against them in the second or third round and I can still remember the expression on their faces when, at half-time, the scores were added up and they found they were a long way behind this team of unknown Freshmen. We won bridge cuppers that year, lost to Balliol in the semi-final the following year and, I have to admit, won again in 1956 when, with our finals looming, our practice should have been fairly minimal.

After the war, Worcester College had an outstanding Provost in J. C. Masterman. He had succeeded in raising the profile of a small and poor college so that, if it did not rank with Christ Church, Merton, New College or Balliol in prestige, like Trinity it was hard on their heels. J. C., as he was known, not only knew all the undergraduates, but took a close interest in their studies and future careers. When I first met him before I went up, he asked what I intended to do. I replied that I expected to go into the family business but if I did not do that, then I would perhaps like to become a lawyer. His excellent advice was that if I might become a lawyer, I should not read Law but some other subject which would stand me in good stead during a legal career. So that was how I came to read PPE, probably the most useful subject for my second career.

As my Oxford career ended, I took the decision to join the family firm.

My choice was partly on the grounds of seeing no good reason not to. My brother John was already working there, and Simon, having finished at Cambridge and qualified as an accountant, was planning to join at the same time as I was. I must admit that my decision was slightly influenced by the fact that my father and his brother had in the early 1950s made complicated arrangements involving trusts and wills, aimed at ensuring that the business would remain in family hands for the next generation in spite of the very high levels of taxation then prevailing. These arrangements provided that the vast majority of the ordinary shares of the company would remain in the hands of members of the family working in the company. They included a provision whereby if I or either of my brothers did not become a Director of the company by the age of thirty-eight, then we would get far fewer shares under my father's will and trust arrangements. I was never able to discover the significance of the age of thirty-eight.

Shortly before leaving Oxford, having completed my Finals, I visited my grandfather, who was seriously ill in hospital. He still had a concern that education at Eton and Oxford might put off a grandson joining the family firm, not regarded as a particularly glamorous or exciting job. I was able to reassure him that it was my firm intention to do so. So after enjoying what I expected to be my last lengthy summer holiday for about forty years, I went to work.

PART II

John James and Mary Anne Sainsbury, 'The Founders', *c.* 1896
(Sainsbury Archive/Museum of London, Docklands)

4

J SAINSBURY:
MY FIRST CAREER

My first career was as a retailer. The first Sainsbury's shop had been opened by my great-grandparents in 1869 in Drury Lane, at the time a very busy market street. The ground floor and basement were the retail part of the property. The family lived on the first and second floors. My grandfather was born there in January 1871. My great-grandfather, John James (J. J.), had a humble background, his father having been a not very successful frame and ornament maker. He died, after a long illness, when my great-grandfather was only twenty years old. J. J. was then left to care for his mother and two sisters. He was clearly a man of great determination, with a good palate and a passion for orderliness, characteristics which contributed to his business success. When he was twenty-five, he married Mary Anne Staples, who was only nineteen at the time. The couple had met when they were both working in Strutton Ground, off Victoria Street. He was working for George Gillet, an oil and colour merchant. It was a business that sold a wide range of goods, including oils of all kinds, lamp and cooking, but not food. She was working in the dairy of Tom Hales, a friend of the Staples family. It was an unlikely union – Mary Anne's family had several shops in the area, while he was a near-penniless shop assistant. It must have been love that brought together two strong characters, both with ability and ambition. Mary Anne also had a reputation for having an exceptional palate and taste for butter, which contributed to the early success of the business.

There is an apocryphal story in the family that when my great-grandfather wanted to marry my great-grandmother, her parents said they could only marry when he had a shop of his own. After the birth of their first child, a girl who lived for only seven months, their doctor told her she would be wise to have no more children. In the next twenty years, the couple had six sons and five daughters, and all the sons played some part in the life of the firm. The story has it that after their marriage, and the birth of six sons, he thought he must have more shops so that each of his sons could have a shop of his own when he wanted to marry. So, for whatever reason, from early in its history JS started expanding, opening more shops, initially in market streets in central London, then throughout the capital and later in the suburbs, East Anglia, the South-East and the Midlands. By the outbreak of the Second World War there were 246 shops. Expansion was on hold for the next decade but then restarted, very slowly at first, at the same time as the change to self-service. So, by 1956, it was clear that the property and development side of the business was going to be of increasing importance and it was to that area that I, the third recruit from the fourth generation, was directed.

When I started in the business in October 1956, it had been run for twenty years by the third generation of the family. My father, Alan, and his brother, Robert, were respectively chairman and deputy chairman and were the joint general managers. Their cousin James was running the factory, and there were two non-family directors, Fred Salisbury and Norman Turner. Although the company had grown to be a leading food retailer in the south of England with a particularly strong market share in London and the South-East, the senior managers still expected family members joining the company to be on a very fast track to the boardroom. If they did not perform, they would be expected to leave.

Each arriving family member was therefore given an aspect of the business for which he was expected, in due course, to have board responsibility. My eldest brother John was already working in the trading side. This was the buying and selling, clearly the most important part of the business, for which my father was then the head. My elder brother Simon, who after Cambridge had qualified as an accountant, joined JS at the same time as I and was expected to succeed my uncle Robert as head of the accounting, personnel and administrative sides. It had originally been intended that I should work in the 'kitchens', as the factory was still known. It was then a very important part of the business, employing over 2,000 and turning pig carcases into the sausages, pies and ham for which the company was well known. My father's cousin, James, the third family member on the board, was the director responsible. It was the start of self-service, the supermarket revolution which had begun, very slowly, in 1950, that changed the direction my retailing career was to take.

One great advantage of a family business, run as Sainsbury had been for over eighty years by members of the family, is that ownership and management are in the same hands. One major disadvantage is that survival is too dependent on the family producing successive generations of successful managers. Since my father and uncle had between them only

87 Chalton Street, Somers Town, London, c. 1904, originally one of the Staples
family shops (Sainsbury Archive/Museum of London, Docklands)

four sons, it seems astonishing that it never seemed to have occurred to
either of them that one or more of their four daughters might have been
interested in and capable of working in the firm. My father had stood for
Parliament three times as a Liberal. My uncle had introduced progressive
personnel policies in the 1930s and all their daughters went to university,
but in the 1950s women in senior management, even in a family firm, was
something they did not foresee.

So it was the seven male family members, three from the third generation, four from the fourth, who would lead the company as it grew over
the next few decades, from being a regional food retailer, unquoted on
the Stock Exchange, little known outside London and the South-East, to
being a major public company and a national leader in food retailing.

In the mid-1950s few anticipated the sweeping changes that would
transform every aspect of food retailing in the next twenty years. In
1956, JS had some 250 shops, all but a handful being counter service. All
the shops sold butter, margarine and cheese and bacon, ham, pies and
sausages produced by the company's own factory. Nearly all sold the
limited range of canned and packaged items that was then available, and
many sold meat, including beef and lamb. However, before the arrival

J Sainsbury poster (Sainsbury Archive/Museum of London, Docklands)

of supermarkets, most meat was sold in butchers' shops, fruit and vegetables in greengrocers, bread and cakes in bakery shops, fish in fishmongers and household cleaning products in general stores. There were off-licences from which to buy beer, wine and spirits. So a full household shopping trip could involve five or six different shops.

In 1956, all JS shops were located within a day's return journey from the company's central London depots. The most distant were Norwich in East Anglia, Nottingham in the East Midlands and Bournemouth on the south coast. The gaps within that area were largely caused by an agreement made way back in the late nineteenth century between seven small retailers. They first co-operated in buying imported bacon and butter from Holland and Denmark to compete better against the much bigger rival business of Liptons, the grocers. The arrangement worked so well that they then agreed not to compete against each other. It was not until the Second World War that the surviving three of the original seven, JS, Greig and Coppens, decided to drop the agreement which would shortly have become illegal. JS did not have stores west of London in places like Slough, Bath and Salisbury, which was Greig territory, as were Bromley and Orpington in south-east London. Nor were JS in some south-west London suburbs like Richmond and Wimbledon, which were Coppens areas. Just before I joined the company, JS made a rare takeover of a competitor and bought Coppens, who had only about fifteen shops. At the time, Greig and Coppens shops were not dissimilar to JS shops. Most were small, between 16 and 20 feet wide, with a depth of 30–60 feet.

There were a few chains of butchers, greengrocers, off-licences, and fishmongers, but independents still had a very large share of the market for perishable food. Multiple retailers, chain stores, had a bigger share of the market in grocery. The biggest food retailer by turnover in every region of England except London was the Co-op. The company with the largest number of stores was Allied Suppliers, who had over 4,000 small shops trading under various names including Lipton, Home & Colonial and Maypole. Other leading chains included International Stores and various regional groups such as Greig.

The collapse of Co-op dominance in the 1950s and 1960s was symptomatic of some of the failings which were later to become more apparent in nationalised industries. The movement was slow to respond to the changing retail environment brought about by the advent of supermarkets. Reacting to competition and innovating was not something that the organisation as a whole, but particularly the smaller co-operative groups, were good at. Most co-operative groups were led by a board which was not particularly experienced in retailing and certainly lacked dynamism. They were often reluctant to close the small shops which so many of the members had used for most of their lives. Furthermore, they were short of capital to invest in the new larger stores which were needed for the change to self-service.

The collapse and later disappearance of Allied Suppliers had a different reason. The group was led by a very dominant chairman, Sir Lancelot Royle. It was his view that self-service did not suit the British. There was a boardroom battle going on between those members of the board who had a contrary view and Sir Lancelot. In 1955 Sainsburys had just opened Lewisham, their largest store; it was over 7,000 square feet, a giant by the standards of the time. It was proving difficult to fill all the space because many of the goods which were to become available later were not yet on the market. The store had cost a great deal to build, as it had a large basement which had to be tanked against the water pressure from the nearby river. The consequence was that it was far from profitable. On the morning of a day when there was to be a meeting of the Council of the Multiple Shops Federation, of which both Sir Lancelot and my father were members, my father paid a visit to the Lewisham store and found everything about it very unsatisfactory. When he arrived in the afternoon at the meeting, he fell into conversation with his old rival, Sir Lancelot, who enquired how he was, and was told by my father that he was in a bad mood because he had had this very unsatisfactory visit to Lewisham – the store was proving a great problem and was very far from profitable. Fortified by this information, Sir Lancelot returned to his business and told his board that he had it at first hand from Alan Sainsbury that supermarkets were not working, so Allied Suppliers was not going to be tempted down that path. It was a most effective bit of industrial sabotage, even if totally unintended. Within a decade, Allied Suppliers had ceased to exist.

In 1949 my father and Fred Salisbury, the assistant general manager, the number three in the business, who had been my grandfather's PA, went to America and saw the future – supermarkets. There were, however, a number of obstacles which would slow the arrival of the supermarket revolution in Britain. First, the post-war shortage of building materials and housing meant that until 1954 the former was rationed and a building licence, issued by Government, was required for any significant construction work. Permission to build new shops was only given for replacing war damage or providing small stores in new local authority housing developments. Secondly, self-service did not easily allow for dealing with food rationing rules and coupons. Thirdly, JS, as an unquoted family firm, had only a very limited amount of capital available to fund expansion. Finally, it was some time before the material and techniques necessary for packaging perishable foods for self-service display and sale were available in Britain. So by the mid-1950s, when I started at JS, the company had only five supermarkets and four small self-service stores; the food retailing revolution had hardly started.

In the early 1950s the company had started recruiting a few graduates each year as management trainees. The 1956 graduate intake was my elder brother Simon, already qualified as an accountant, myself and Derek Salisbury, son of Fred, the assistant general manager. The three of us had a general introduction to the company, going round all departments before spending two weeks in the training centre. This was where all recruits who were going to work in the shops learned various skills which are now no longer required in a supermarket. The most difficult skill was 'knocking up' butter. This was done using two wooden paddles, a butter beater and slice, and taking a piece which was hopefully near to ½ lb from a ½ cwt block of butter, which had been cut by wire into the near ½ lb segments. The piece of butter was put on greaseproof paper on the scales and, using the paddles, butter was added or taken away, until the weight was exactly ½lb, then the block of butter had to be wrapped in the greaseproof paper without being touched by a finger. Until the

Candling eggs at Wisbech, 1948
(Sainsbury Archive/Museum of London, Docklands)

early 1960s a customer buying butter in a counter-service shop had this procedure carried out in front of them. A rather labour-intensive activity, but perhaps the reason why a later history of the business was called *The Best Butter in the World*.

JS never produced their own chickens or eggs, but in the 1960s we had a chicken slaughterhouse near Bury St Edmunds and several small plants where eggs were 'candled'. Women were employed to hold two eggs in each hand (most eggs were smaller in those days) and inspect them against a strong light (hence candling) for defects. In those days, eggs largely came from small farms. Traditionally, this was the farmer's wife's role and it produced useful pocket money for her. Collecting vans went around the farms with tins of cash to pay the wives. When I wondered about security with all this money in the vans, I was assured that every farm in the area would react fiercely to any interference in this traditional method.

The second week at the training centre was a butchery course including how to prepare roasting joints for sale. The meat JS sold was either chilled from Argentina or Aberdeen Angus from Scotland. The company had a prize-winning pedigree herd by the River Spey and there was a commercial Aberdeen Angus cross herd near Peterhead, close to Aberdeen (where JS also had their own slaughterhouse). The reason JS kept their own cattle at this period is that they wanted to show suppliers the quality of the beef we wanted.

Sausages were one of the most popular of meat products produced by Sainsburys. Many of the pigs came from Great Uncle Frank's slaughterhouse in Haverhill in Suffolk; others came from Sainsbury's longest-established supplier near Tiverton. Another skill I learnt which was to prove useful during my Parliamentary career, was how to bone a side of bacon. A side of bacon was half a pig without the legs that had been smoked in a kiln. The ribs and various bones had to be removed before the side could be cut up into bacon joints and, most importantly, into back and streaky bacon rashers.

After our two weeks in the training centre, while Simon went off to start serious work in the accounting department, I joined a small group who for a few weeks formed the Christmas poultry office. It was then normal for virtually all customers who wanted a turkey or goose for Christmas to pre-order the bird, specifying the weight they wanted and when they would collect it. The big excitement of 1956 was that it was the first year that there were significant quantities of RTC (ready to cook) turkeys available. These birds required no work at the store, while the majority of Christmas poultry still arrived in boxes of half a dozen birds, plucked but still requiring attention to remove the innards. My job in the Christmas poultry office was to take the phone calls from shop managers. It was quite common for a harassed manager to find that the weight of the birds that had been delivered to his branch did not match the weights in the customer orders he was trying to fulfil. So I soon experienced a most important aspect of a family business: the family are different – very different.

A manager of one of the larger branches with perhaps thirty-five years or more service in the company might get quite angry about the problems he was facing with his Christmas poultry and express his anger on the phone, even demanding to know, 'Anyway, who am I talking to?' When he got the answer, the instant climb-down was embarrassing and I could understand why I was given the job of answering the phone. I was later told that the Christmas poultry office worked particularly well that year.

Two later incidents confirmed to me that family members were outside normal discipline or criticism. A little later, when I was on a programme of visiting stores in the company of an area superintendent, a very senior manager with oversight of one-fifth of the shops, I arrived over half an hour late at Tottenham, muttering feebly that I had under-estimated the duration of my tube journey. I had, but the main reason for my late arrival was the more usual excuse of oversleeping, which I didn't offer. There was no reprimand, just body language that expressed disappointment as much as disapproval, that the young lad was letting the family down.

Then, three years, later I committed a most grievous breach of company rules. Not to reappear for work after the short Christmas holiday was regarded as particularly reprehensible, not just in the shops, which faced a major challenge in getting stocked up and ready for reopening on 27 December, but also in Head Office. In December 1960 I was working as the unofficial deputy to Fred Parker, the manager of the Building and Engineering Division, of whom more later. He was, in theory, the most senior of senior managers, as other senior managers reported to him. I reappeared two days late after the Christmas break; the frost was palpable but nothing was said. I was not even asked for an explanation for my absence. Then at midday I announced that I would like to take Fred and the other senior managers I was working with over to the pub for a celebratory drink and explained the reason for my absence. When Fred Parker and the others heard that the reason for my late return was a trip to Paris to ask my future father-in-law for the hand of his daughter, then was 'the winter of discontent made glorious summer', for not only had my absence been sanctioned by my uncle, joint general manager and thus supreme head of personnel, but – better still – there was at last the prospect of a fifth generation of Sainsburys to carry the business forward.

All this was a consequence of the most important thing that happened to me during my career with JS: meeting and marrying Susie. Our first meeting was at a very surprising location, Eton College swimming pool. During my time at Eton, there had not been a swimming pool because, until 1947, swimming took place in a branch of the Thames known as Cuckoo Weir. However, as a result of contamination, there was an outbreak of polio caused by the water of Cuckoo Weir and that was the end of swimming in the Thames. When I had taken my swimming test, like everybody else I had to do it in the Slough public baths. After I left, the school built a large outdoor unheated swimming pool. Old Etonians living nearby were allowed to use this pool when the school was not in residence. In August 1959, I had some friends staying at my mother's house in Boveney, just up the river from Eton, and as the weather was unusually sunny and warm, we went over to Eton to use the swimming pool. There we met up with a very good friend, another Old Etonian, Ben Hanbury, whose family lived in Burnham Beeches. He had also come to the pool with a party of friends, which included Susie Mitchell. On their way back home, the Hanbury party stopped at my mother's house for a drink and at the end of the relatively brief encounter, I made a mental note that I was determined to see more of Susie Mitchell.

Initially this proved impossible, as Susie went off to live in Paris where her father was our military attaché. Luckily, when she returned to England in the spring of 1960, she moved in to share a flat with two other girls who were friends not just of myself, but also of Julian Benson and Mark Evans, with whom I was then sharing a flat in Chelsea. So, when the three bachelors decided to invite a few people round for drinks, almost top of the list of those we wished to invite were the two girls with whom Susie was sharing. Julian Benson said, 'There's another girl staying with them now called Susie Mitchell,' so without letting on that I had met her before, I said, 'We should ask her too.' Twenty minutes after she had arrived for a drink, I was bold enough to ask whether she would like to go out to dinner with me. Luckily she thought that was a better invitation than one she had already received from my brother, which was to give her a lift back to her flat in Eaton Terrace, where John also had his house.

'Dinner with Susie' first appears as an entry in my diary on Wednesday, 22 June 1960. Two weeks later we went to the theatre together, and on 11 July we paid our first visit to Covent Garden to see *La Bohème*. It was, however, late December before Susie finally accepted my repeated proposals of marriage. At that stage I had not met her parents, as they were still based in Paris. So on Boxing Day I flew out to Paris to meet my future parents-in-law, who made me feel very much at ease and arranged for a visit to the Marquis de Cuevas ballet that evening. On returning from the ballet, the rest of the family carefully left my future father-in-law, Alastair, and myself alone for what was expected to be a serious interview. When we were alone, he just looked at me and said, 'Well it's all right by me,' which was the second best news I'd ever heard. We announced our engagement in *The Times* on 31 December, and were married at St Michael's, Chester Square on 26 April 1961. We had a four-week honeymoon in Greece, my mother having said that she had had a four-week honeymoon and therefore it could be said to be a family tradition. The fifth generation arrived sooner than planned. We had a honeymoon baby, our first son, James, who was joined later by a sister, Camilla, a brother, Alex, and another sister, Jessica. They in turn have produced twelve wonderful grandchildren.

Before our wedding, there was a drinks party at the Savoy for many of the JS staff with whom I worked and their spouses. Only the directors were invited to the wedding. This was the first time that spouses were included in a company event. It wasn't just supermarkets that were a new idea in the 1950s.

When I had completed a programme of visits to stores, I was sent out to learn how the professional consultants, whom JS sometimes used for property and building activities, operated. I spent a month or so with a firm of architects and another month with a firm of quantity surveyors. A shorter time was spent with a consulting structural engineer and with a building contractor, but the most important, first and longest of these periods was with Healey & Baker, who were then a leading firm of commercial estate agents. This was a very interesting experience and gave me an insight into how the property world operated. It often seemed to involve sailing fairly close to the wind. Perhaps the least dubious of the many devices they used was pretending they had a client who wanted to buy or rent a particular property, when they hadn't. They hoped to persuade the owner to give them the task of getting a sale or finding a tenant. At the end of my time with Healey & Baker, the senior partner who had been overseeing my programme and who dealt with the little business which JS brought to Healey & Baker in those days took me out to a very good lunch at Claridge's. He was a substantially built man and at the end of the lunch, he said, 'Timothy, when you have looked at all the facts and figures and used the tables to help calculate values, what you need to remember is a good valuer feels it here,' at which he tapped his substantial stomach. It was good advice, as I have subsequently found that in property sometimes the best guide to value is your personal hunch.

After some eighteen months, I went back to work at JS, taking the post of PA and gradually becoming effectively deputy to Fred Parker, the manager of the Building and Engineering Division. I also started attending meetings between Fred Salisbury, the assistant general manager of the company, and the estates manager, Claude Aaron. Fred was the director responsible for Property, the Estates department and the Building and Engineering Division. He also had oversight of meat and poultry buying. I was reminded that Christian names were not used; it was Mr Parker and Miss Wilmer, his secretary. Everyone called the doorman Jack, but all others were addressed formally; only directors were expected to address each other by their first names. It was, however, necessary to distinguish between the six Sainsburys in the business. We were therefore known by our Christian names: I was Mr Timothy. However, when my Uncle Robert joined the business on the administrative side, the chief accountant was Mr Roberts, so Uncle Bob became Mr R. J. When my brother John joined, my grandfather was still alive and a very non-executive chairman. He was Mr John in the business, although Jack to his wife, and J. B. to his friends. So John became Mr J. D. Christian names only started to be used in the mid-1970s. I never even knew that my secretary for seven years, Miss Filby, was called Mavis until after she had married and left in 1974 to become a mother.

The seven family members of the board at the tills in 1969, the centenary year. *Left to right*: Mr Alan, Mr R. J., Mr J. D., Mr James, Mr Simon, Mr Timothy and Mr David (Sainsbury Archive/Museum of London, Docklands)

5

J SAINSBURY: THE SUPERMARKET REVOLUTION

I could scarcely have chosen a more exciting or challenging time to start my career on the property side of Sainsburys. Rationing had finally ended in July 1954, building licences had become much easier to obtain, and the earliest experimental years of developing self-service had been successfully completed. Now the company faced an existential challenge. Would JS be able to make the transition from a company with 250 counter-service stores, to a company operating supermarkets, and do so without losing its standards, particularly in the handling of perishable foods, bankrupting the company or failing to keep pace with the competition?

As always in the food retailing business, competition was fierce. If Allied Suppliers were slow off the mark with disastrous consequences for their business, others were more aware of the need for change. Leading the charge from existing UK businesses was Tesco, under the flamboyant leadership of Jack Cohen. There was also a major import from overseas in the shape of Fine Fare, owned by the Weston family. The statistics tell the story of the success JS had in meeting that challenge.

When I joined the company in October 1956, JS had 255 stores. I joined the board and took over full responsibility for the development programme in May 1962. The company still had only 255 stores, having opened sixteen self-service stores and supermarkets and closed sixteen of the older counter service stores. In the next twelve and a half years, from May 1962 to the end of 1974 when I finally relinquished all executive responsibilities, 150 supermarkets opened and 211 of the old counter service stores were closed.

Throughout the '60s and '70s, the number and average size of the store openings were steadily increasing. In 1962, the large double aisle counter service shop in Guildford was rebuilt to become a supermarket. As there was a council-owned multi-storey car park behind, but at a higher level than the store, I decided that a few checkouts should be at the back, connecting to a lift to the car park. This was, to general surprise, a great success.

From then on, providing car parking, or locating near a car park, became an ever-increasing factor in store location. Sometimes we were able to provide some car parking on site, in a basement as at Putney, or on the roof as at Harpenden. However, on most occasions, the new super-market was sited close to or alongside a local authority car park. When we did this in a development in the centre of Oxford, our new supermar-ket site was immediately alongside the main level of the local authority car park. To our consternation, Oxford City Council suddenly realised that the car park level could be used very profitably for more retail units. They changed their plans to allow for more retailing instead of car park-ing alongside our store. I thought this was outrageous and having failed to dissuade the Council from their plans, sued them for breach of con-tract. Oxford tried to get the case thrown out, but the judge held that although we might have a weak legal case, we had a strong moral case and therefore the matter should go to a full hearing. This of course meant that there would be a considerable delay before the development could proceed and, faced with that delay, Oxford City Council, led by the late Lady Janet Young, gave way. Janet later became a ministerial colleague, but she never held what I had done in Oxford against me.

By the end of the 1960s, car ownership was expanding rapidly and it seemed to be all too obvious that more and more families were using their cars for their main weekly food shop. It was also clear that the most con-venient, easily accessed, and most economical way of providing that car parking was at ground level. Most multi-storey car parks lacked sufficient lifts and indeed very often still required the use of some steps. However, it was proving difficult to persuade local authorities, and indeed central Government, to change their approach.

So, in an attempt to change what we regarded as outdated attitudes, Sainsburys held a two-day conference in Cambridge in September 1972. Among those attending was the senior official responsible for the over-sight of retail planning in the Department of the Environment. He was a charming fifty-something-year-old bachelor who lived in Chelsea. It seemed to me it would have been hard to find anybody less suitable to consider the shopping needs of a suburban car-owning two- or three-child family. Also present were seventy or so local authority planners. To ensure academic credibility, the conference was chaired by Professor Peter Hall of Reading University. As part of my presentation, I had a film made, designed to illustrate the difficulties customers experienced as a result of poor planning by local authorities. The most telling scene was one in which an elderly disabled woman was shown struggling on the staircase with her shopping at the Friars Centre in Aylesbury, where the local authority had saved money by installing lifts which only stopped at landings between the floors, so wherever you parked, you still had to go up or down a few steps. This part of the film was greeted with some laughter, after which Peter Hall reprimanded those who had laughed, saying that what they had witnessed was the failure of planners to understand the needs of the consumer.

By the early '70s, there were a few JS stores which were adjacent to large surface car parks and where the site was large enough for all the warehouse areas to be at the same level as the retail space. However, these few stores were in new towns or planned expansions to existing towns. Since the late 1960s, I had been pushing for permission to be given for what I called 'edge-of-town' rather than 'out-of-town' supermarket development. The argument for such stores that I advanced both at the conference in Cambridge and elsewhere was that the consumer shopping by car should no longer have to drive into the centre of town, thus increasing congestion, but should be able to shop nearer to where they actually lived. Edge-of-town stores could also be accessed by bus, and even, by those living closest, on foot. Food stores sell a larger physical volume of goods than those selling clothes or consumer durables. Locating such stores away from town centres meant thirty to fifty lorries every day would no longer have to drive into the centre to deliver food which would later be taken home in a customer's car.

Local authorities, and indeed central Government, were concerned that if out-of-town or edge-of-town stores were allowed, town centres would deteriorate and become abandoned by all forms of commercial activity other than the cheapest. This was a phenomenon which had already been seen in parts of the United States. I had therefore been developing the argument that there were significant differences between convenience stores selling everyday requirements, particularly food but also cleaning materials, which were purchased on a weekly basis or more frequently, and other goods such as clothes, white goods and brown goods such as furniture, which were infrequent purchases. Locating stores which sold convenience goods near to where people lived but certainly away from town centres had many advantages, as well as convenience for the customer. Most important was the reduction in traffic because of the sheer volume of those convenience goods which otherwise would have to be brought into the town centre only to be taken out in a customer's car.

It was appropriate, since our conference had been held in Cambridge, that our first edge-of-town store for which JS was able to obtain permission was in Cambridge, on the site of a disused factory. The store opened in December 1974, just as I finally gave up the last of my executive responsibilities in the company. It was an immediate success and is still trading, as are some thirty or so other stores which opened during my time as director responsible for development. The Cambridge Coldhams Lane store was also a prime example of one method JS used to finance the development programme. The site for the new store cost £130,000; the counter service shop in the centre of Cambridge, which we were then able to sell, fetched over £500,000.

The early 1970s also marked another major change for JS, a move to what I would call Phase 2 of the development of supermarkets. Second phase supermarkets were much larger, with an average sales area in excess of 20,000 square feet. They sold a wider range of goods, including fruit and vegetables as well as household cleaning materials, but perhaps most significantly they were the first generation of stores located and planned to cater for the customer coming by car rather than on foot or by bus.

Meanwhile, my elder brother, John, known in the company as Mr J. D., had taken over as chairman in 1969. Turnover and profitability were growing strongly in the years up to the flotation in 1973. In the decade after I gave up my executive responsibilities, between 1975 and 1985, both turnover and profits doubled in real terms. This reflects the brilliant leadership that my brother gave, building on the foundations laid by earlier generations.

Until 1960, all the goods sold in the Sainsbury stores were sent to the stores from central London depots grouped around the company's headquarters in Stamford Street. It was believed that it was necessary for the buyers to be able to inspect the goods that were being sent out before they were dispatched to the stores. This was particularly important for the perishables. In the second half of the 1950s, the growth of trade and the increase in the number of lines sold was putting such pressure on the available depot space that clearly a major increase was required. Two riverside buildings adjoining the Blackfriars headquarters were acquired, and some planning and costing was carried out on constructing a new multi-storey depot on the site. In 1959, I had made my first visit to the States to attend the course run by National Cash Register to persuade European retailers to adopt self-service. My visit included some time looking at developments in supermarkets in both the States and Canada, and I also visited one or two depots. At one of the depots, I recall the manager saying with pride, 'I run the most efficient multi-storey grocery depot in the States,' but, he added, 'What is efficient about a multi-storey grocery depot?'

Luckily, the board had realised that, and while I was away in the States, JS had acquired a disused Royal Army Ordnance Depot at Buntingford in Hertfordshire. The new depot opened in 1960, distributing non-perishable goods to north London stores. By then it had been realised that that move by itself would be insufficient to meet the rapidly increasing demand and to improve efficiency in distribution. The bold decision was taken to seek a site for a new depot which would handle perishable as well as non-perishable goods. I was given the task of finding a site of ten acres within twenty miles of London. I found a site of twenty acres fifty miles from London at Basingstoke. As the town had been designated for a major expansion scheme to accommodate London overspill, it was possible to get the necessary licences to construct the depot and also to obtain housing for staff wishing to move out from London. Construction began in the summer of 1962, and it is amusing to reflect that there was a short delay before the contractor was able to start, as he had to wait for the barley crop to be safely gathered in before building work could begin.

I had decided that since the main elements of the new depot were structural, a consulting structural engineer would be the lead consultant, supported by architects, rather than the other way around. That worked very well at Basingstoke, and subsequently for the rebuilding of Buntingford and for the new London depot in Charlton. When that opened in the late 1960s, the total area of new depots exceeded 1.5 million square feet.

The opening of the integrated distribution depots serving both perishables and non-perishables meant that the warehouse space adjoining the head office, together with the property on the waterfront which had been bought by the company when, astonishingly, consideration was being given to the construction of a new multi-storey warehouse, became surplus to requirements. Sainsbury's therefore became part of a consortium of property owners developing the large site adjoining the head office which became known as the King's Reach Development. The architect for the King's Reach Development, Richard Seifert, was best known as the architect of Centrepoint. He was particularly skilled at getting the most development possible allowed on a site, and consequently his work was often criticised. But he would respond to those architectural critics with, 'There will come a time when there will be tours of my work.' It is interesting to reflect that to some extent he was right, as Centrepoint is now a listed building.

There was a postscript to my involvement as a director of King's Reach. The main tenant on site was a publishing company. When it came to the first rent review, a dispute arose as to whether the lease as drafted reflected the intention of both the lessor and the lessee. This led to an unusual legal case for 'the rectification of the lease'. In order for King's Reach to win this case, they had to show that the lease did not reflect what had been agreed by both parties. Not surprisingly our tenant disputed this, as, if the lease variation we were seeking was agreed, they would have to pay rent for the space in front of the lifts.

When the issue eventually came to be tried, it became clear that I likely to have to give my evidence immediately before my fiftieth birthday. I was assured that I would be free to go to the party we had planned at our country house on the next day. Inevitably that did not happen. So I started my fiftieth birthday giving evidence in this interesting case. It hinged on what had or had not been agreed at board meetings of King's Reach Development some dozen years before. When cross-examined on this, my approach was to say that I do recall that these matters were discussed at the board meeting, though I could not remember the exact date or the detail of the discussion, but I did clearly remember what was agreed. I understand that the chairman of the publishing company, Sir Don Ryder, adopted an aggressive approach, saying that he was sure he would never have agreed to have the area in front of the lifts counted as office space. The judge seems to have preferred my rather more hesitant approach, and King's Reach Development won the case.

At the beginning of the 1970s, the family took the decision that J Sainsbury should become a public company. There were a number of reasons for this decision. One was a general feeling that it was no longer appropriate for a company of the scale and size of Sainsbury's to remain private, with the ownership of the company confined to members of the founder's family. A public offering of 10 million shares would enable all management and staff to participate in ownership if they so wished. This would make it easier to attract and retain in the company top-quality management. This was another major factor in deciding to go public. A third factor was that, while at that time the company had no urgent need for additional funds, it was recognised that going public made available an extra source of capital if required for further expansion.

By the end of 1972, with preparations getting under way for the public flotation, I had decided that my interest in and involvement in politics had reached a stage where I would like to try to become a Member of Parliament. If I were to succeed in this ambition, I would clearly no longer be able to be a full-time executive director of the business. So I discussed my idea with my brothers, who saw no reason to object, and they started thinking about how my executive responsibilities could be re-allocated.

Among the many papers that had to be signed in connection with the flotation was one saying that the executive directors were committed to continuing as full-time executives of the company, so I discussed with my solicitor whether I could sign that in view of my intention to try to become an MP. I had started the process by seeking to have my name included in the list of approved candidates. My solicitor said she could see no objection to my signing, as there were a large number of hurdles to be got over before I could become an MP and therefore no longer able to act as a full-time executive director of the company. The first was to get my name included on the list of candidates. That might not be too difficult. However, the next hurdle was normally a considerable difficulty, as some very distinguished Parliamentarians had taken a long time to find a seat, having been rejected by several selection committees. If chosen as a candidate, I would then have to get elected, and in the spring of 1973 the assumption was that the next election would not be for some two years. So I signed the document.

The share offer opened on 12 July 1973, and 14.5 million shares were made available. No less than £495 million was bid for those shares. This is perhaps the best evidence of the success which the company had had in making the challenging transition from a regional counter service retailer to a national supermarket retailer.

My career at JS did not come to an end in November 1973 when I became a Member of Parliament. I handed over responsibility for the Building and Engineering Division at the end of 1973. Gurth Hoyer Millar, who had been the director responsible for distribution and depots, took over. However, I did continue somehow or other to have responsibility for the Estates Department and property matters, working with Gurth throughout 1974 before I handed over to him my remaining executive responsibilities at the end of that year.

I remained a director of the company, the term non-executive director not then being very widely used. There was no formal structure or role for non-executive directors on the board of JS, and I was the only one for some time. Until the 1979 election, I remained a member of the Directors' Branch Committee, the DBC, which took most of the important decisions relating to retailing. I retained an office and a secretary at the company's headquarters in Stamford Street. Even after the 1979 election, when I became a parliamentary private secretary to Michael Heseltine as Secretary of State for the Environment, I continued as a non-executive director, an occasional attender at DBC meetings, and still kept an office and a secretary at Stamford Street. The Permanent Secretary at the Department of the Environment was not perturbed by this arrangement, commenting that with my name, there was no risk that I would be allowed to see any matters relating to Sainsbury's.

It was only after I was appointed a Government whip after the 1983 General Election that this rather unorthodox arrangement, or an arrangement which at least would be regarded as unorthodox now, came to an end. Even then, I was not required to have a formal blind trust for my Sainsbury shares or other investments. It was only understood that I would take no decisions relating to those investments. They would be taken by my solicitor until I was no longer in Government.

There was a postscript to my Sainsbury career, when, having retired from Government in 1994, it was again possible for me to become a non-executive director of the company. By then, there were a number of distinguished non-executive directors and a formal structure was in place for them to play their part in the management of the company. I rejoined the board as a non-executive director in 1995.

This was a troubled period. My cousin David had taken over from my brother John as chairman and chief executive at the end of 1992. In my opinion, this was a mistake. He had never served on any of the front-line retailing roles in the company. He was also by temperament not well suited to being chief executive of a business. There are many occasions when decisions have to be taken at very short notice and often without all the information and facts one might wish to have. This did not suit his deliberative style of management. He might have been an effective chairman, but he was not an effective chief executive.

The five non-executive directors of the company collectively and unanimously reached that conclusion. After some discussion, he resigned and subsequently had a distinguished and successful career as a minister in the Labour Government, serving in the House of Lords as Minister for Science, where he was not only successful but much respected. My retirement in 1999 meant that after 130 years, there was no longer a family member playing any role in J Sainsbury plc.

6

REFLECTIONS OF
A RETAILER

Food retailing must be one of the most competitive of businesses. Most customers shop weekly at two or more of the major food retailers and also buy items from specialists such as butchers, bakers and delicatessens. They are comparing prices, quality, range of products and service on every visit to a food store. Their experience could not be more different from that of customers of a nationalised industry. Those industries are monopolies giving their customers no choice. They often appear to be run more for the benefit of their employees than for their users. So my first reflection on my retailing career is that it was an excellent reminder that effective competition is the best safeguard of the interests of the consumer.

During my time at JS, from the mid-1950s to the early 1980s, food retailing had been revolutionised. Some of the largest retailers of the early 1950s had, by the end of the period, gone out of business. A number of newcomers had started up; some flourished for a while and then failed, others grew into successful national retailers such as Tesco, Morrisons and Asda. One factor decided which succeeded and which failed: the quality of their management.

It may seem all too obvious to emphasise the importance of management but it does explain one of the main reasons why Government, whether central or local, is usually bad at running anything. For any business to succeed, or indeed survive, in a rapidly changing and challenging environment, it is essential to attract and retain managers of quality. The best managers do not like being constrained by the committee structure and short-term financial planning which accompany local or central Government ownership; nor are they likely to get the remuneration they could obtain in the private sector, including participation in the profits, and possibly the ownership, of a business.

The most effective managers are constantly seeking to innovate and invest in their businesses. They will compare the performance of their companies with others in the same field, not just nationally but internationally. It is incidentally another problem with nationalised industries that, being monopolies, they cannot compare their performance with other similar businesses in their own country. So my second reflection is: never underestimate the importance of the quality of management to the success of a business.

My third reflection on my retailing career is that Government and its agencies do have important roles to play in the economy. The first is to regulate so as to protect competition. The second is to manage the economy in a way that keeps inflation under control. The third is to have labour laws that are sensible and balanced. During my time in the 1960s and 1970s as a director of JS, there were numerous reminders of the failure of Government on all three counts.

The first, and in some ways the most difficult, task for Government is ensuring competition. As Adam Smith pointed out, 'People of the same trade seldom meet together even for merriment and diversion, but the conversation ends in a conspiracy against the public or in some contrivance to raise prices.' In my view, since the 1950s, there has been a steady improvement in the mechanisms and agencies through which Government seeks to keep competition lively. One of the best arguments for free trade is that the wider the market, the more international it is, the better the competition and service to the consumer. In the 1970s, I recall several debates in Parliament which discussed the problems of textile manufacturing. For each debate, the Speaker would call Members who had textile factories in their constituencies and the emphasis would always be on the damage to employment in those businesses if duties or quotas were relaxed on textiles imported from the Far East. I suggested to the Speaker before one debate that discussion would be more balanced if some MPs were called to speak on behalf of the consumer and user of those textiles. It never happened. So poorer families with children, who spend a high proportion of their income on textile products, were being deprived of better value to protect a relatively small textile industry in the UK. Protection always damages competition.

By far the biggest problem the Government created for business in the 1960s and 1970s was the failure to control inflation. Food retailers, whose customers make weekly or even more frequent purchases, are the first to experience the difficulties which high inflation causes, especially to the elderly and the less well-off. A budget which is adequate one month is suddenly insufficient to provide what is needed the next month. The elderly find it difficult to understand why basic commodities can get more expensive month by month. If that was not bad enough, planning for investment, particularly for projects when expenditure is spread over several years, becomes exceptionally difficult.

Another side effect of high inflation was to exacerbate problems in industrial relations. If inflation is 2% or 3%, wage claims are usually for 3%, 4% or 5%. The difference being disputed is very small and it does not make much sense to either side to get involved in a lengthy strike over such a small difference. However, when inflation is 10% or 12%, or even more, and wage claims are 15% to 20%, the reverse applies. High inflation was certainly a significant contributor to the abysmal labour relations and the number of strikes which were characteristic of the 1970s.

JS, like every other business, experienced the damage to our business and to the economy in general because of unbalanced labour laws. The few but significant labour disputes in Sainsbury's mostly involved workers in the depots or the factory, rather than in the shops. However, strikes affecting our suppliers, the transport network, or vital services such as the telephone system, then mostly working through manual exchanges, caused endless problems to the business. Far too much management time was spent on dealing with the consequences of those strikes or planning actions that could be taken to minimise the disruption they caused. I would not pretend that keeping inflation under control is easy, but recent experience shows that it can be done. There are many contributory factors to success, one of which is certainly having sensible labour laws and another of which lies in the management of the macro-economy.

When I returned in 1995 to the board of J Sainsbury plc for a final four years as a non-executive director, I was appointed a member of the Remuneration Committee. After a year or so, it was suddenly decided that my shareholding in the company was such that I could not be regarded as an independent member, and so I was removed from that committee. I believe that decision was taken because I had started to express reservations about what was being put to the committee about increases to directors' salaries and bonuses. In principle, the idea of each company having a Remuneration Committee, the members of which are non-executive directors, is a good one. However, the committees nearly always seek guidance from remuneration consultants. They also have evidence given to them by the director of human resources of the company. Both those sources have an in-built interest in remuneration being agreed in the top quartile of pay in the industry with which they are concerned. It is impossible for everybody or even the majority of businesses to be in the top quartile. The result seems to me to be continuous pressure to increase rewards at a rate greatly in excess of inflation and unfortunately much faster than that being given to the majority of employees in the company.

In my view, the excessive remuneration packages too often given to chief executives and other senior management could have been revised or rejected if shareholders had played their part. The trouble is that up until now, far too many institutional investors have taken insufficient interest in this aspect of the companies in which they invest. Maybe they would get more involved if shareholders were given some legally binding power over remuneration. I suggest that any increase for directors more than twice that of the average employee should require positive approval from the shareholders. Also any bonuses for performance should require approval if more than 10% of basic remuneration.

Leaving school aged eighteen, spending two years doing my National Service and three years at university with a gap, meant that I started my retail career aged twenty-four. Because relatively few of my age group went to university at that time, although nearly everybody did National Service, most of my contemporaries had started work three or four years younger. Starting in a family business where members of the family were expected to take senior positions early in their careers, being that little bit older was helpful. Three years after starting at JS, I was chairing various committees dealing with the design and development of new stores where the other members would often be twice my age. That age gap also encouraged me never to forget to ensure that the other members of the committee were able to express their views.

After I became a director of the company in 1962, the range of decisions for which I was responsible greatly increased. They included the promotion and pay of the managers in the departments for which I was responsible, budgets for those departments and, perhaps most crucially, financial choices when seeking to acquire sites for new stores. I was frequently having to take decisions without all the information that I would have liked to have had available. Sometimes choices had to be made under time pressure and, on some occasions, when I was receiving contradictory advice. All this experience I found most useful later in my career.

Another side of a business career is the experience it provides of the consequences for business of the actions or inactions in local and central Government. JS, like every other business and the whole economy, suffered from the inefficiency of the nationalised industries. In general, a nationalised industry was slow to innovate, suffered from under-investment and provided a poor service to its customers. A classic example was new small businesses having to wait six weeks to get a telephone line. I found private customers in my constituency waiting for as long as six months for a service which is now provided in forty-eight hours.

My final reflection on my first career is how useful it was to prove in my second, and indeed third, careers. Management responsibility at a reasonably senior level in any business is a valuable experience for a Member of Parliament. At the very least, it provides a better insight into the workings of the economy, and how the activities of Government impinge on the success or otherwise of individual companies and the economy as a whole. It was also a constant reminder that success depended on satisfying the customer. That, in turn, required having a motivated and well-trained workforce. The modern emphasis on the importance of all the 'stakeholders' in a business, shareholders, employees, customer and society, was a *sine qua non* in food retailing.

The experience of chairing committees and having to seek compromises between the interests of different departments in a business was particularly valuable in the later stages of my second career when I held ministerial office. Inevitably, management responsibility involves expressing opinions which can be done more effectively and succinctly if one listens to all sides. Listening to some MPs' speeches, one wonders whether they had any awareness of the meaning of the word 'succinct'.

I completed my executive responsibilities at Sainsbury's in 1974 with a feeling that I had made a significant contribution to the success of the business, albeit in a supporting role. Massive progress had been made in replacing the old counter-service shops with supermarkets. The first edge-of-town stores with large surface car parks had opened, and JS had taken the first steps towards becoming a national retailer by opening stores in Yorkshire and Cheshire. The front line of a food retailer is the stores and supplying the customer. Finding sites for those stores, planning and developing them and maintaining them, was clearly a supporting role, but an essential one.

PART III

7
POLITICS – GETTING INVOLVED

Unlike many of my Parliamentary contemporaries, while at Oxford I took little or no interest in Party politics. Before I went up to Oxford, if asked I would have said I supported the Conservatives. My mother was an active member of our local Conservative Association and I had helped her deliver leaflets. My economics studies strongly reinforced my belief that a market economy provided a much better result for everybody, particularly the consumer, than any Socialist alternative. I had never discussed politics with my father on any of our infrequent meetings, so it was only much later that I became aware of the complex mix of political views in my family.

My father, born in 1902, became a Liberal, influenced by the social and political situation in the 1920s. He stood as the Liberal candidate for Woodbridge in Suffolk without success in 1929, 1931 and 1935. He joined the Labour Party shortly before the Second World War and was made a life peer by his friend Hugh Gaitskell in 1962. Later he was a founder member of the Social Democratic Party, the SDP. His three sons were all Conservatives but his brother, born two years later and trained as an accountant, was always a Conservative although not politically active. His son David supported the Labour Party before also being a founder member and major financial supporter of the SDP. When that Party was dissolved in 1990, he rejoined Labour rather than become a Liberal Democrat. The arrival of Jeremy Corbyn ended that allegiance.

I never spoke at the Union, and seldom attended. I hardly noticed the 1955 Election. It was, according to the *Annual Register*, a 'humdrum affair' and many observers regarded it as immensely dull. Sixteen months later, shortly after I had come down from Oxford, the world situation became anything but dull. On 22 October 1956, the Hungarian rebellion against the Russians started. They were demanding Imre Nagy's restitution to the premiership. The rebellion was subsequently crushed by a massive Russian military invasion of Hungary on 4 November. At the end of the month, the Israelis launched an attack against Egypt. This was shortly followed by British and French intervention which led to the Suez Crisis.

This unfortunate episode was eventually brought to an end under duress from the United States. It had, in the meanwhile, led to deep divisions in the Conservative Party and throughout the country. Politics had suddenly become very interesting indeed.

Shortly afterwards, a friend from Eton days, Colin Baillieu, persuaded me to join the Bow Group. This was an organisation founded at the beginning of 1951 by graduates who had become involved in Conservative politics at university, and who wanted to carry on their interest by conducting research. From its earliest days, the members were on the One Nation wing of the Conservative Party, Tories who were socially progressive, fiscally conservative and pro-European. Geoffrey Howe was an early leading member, and others who had already played a major role in the Bow Group before I joined the Council included David Howell, Tony Newton and John MacGregor, all later Cabinet ministers. Shortly after my time, Michael Howard, Norman Lamont and Peter Lilley were also active in the group. There was no doubt that many of those who played a part in the affairs of the Bow Group were seeking to promote their political career with a mind to becoming Members of Parliament. In the late 1950s, I can honestly say that I did not have this objective in view; it was not something which had occurred to me. As my wife, Susie, has often pointed out, when we got married she had no idea that she might become the wife of a Member of Parliament.

However, in the early 1960s I gradually became more involved in Bow Group affairs, and in 1964 I became the convenor of a research group discussing policies concerned with the location of population and employment. By no means every research group produced a publication, so, if a group did produce something, those concerned were likely to become prominent in the affairs of the group. Getting the writing done was the biggest challenge. A week's holiday in a wet Cornwall with our children provided me with the ideal opportunity to put down on paper the conclusions our group had reached. I was asked to take my draft to Central Office, where David Howell looked at it on behalf of the Conservative Political Centre. The first thing he did was point out that a political pamphlet is not like a university essay; there is no need to mention any arguments against the policies being proposed. The objective should be just to concentrate on the pluses, ignoring any minuses. He advised that my pamphlet should advocate a particular point of view or a policy and not draw attention to any weaknesses in the idea. So after suitably improving the draft, it was accepted for publication and came out in June 1966. The main recommendation was that we should establish a number of 'new growth centres' which should be designated as new cities for the second half of the twentieth century. At least some of the summary of the conclusions still reads reasonably well. Commenting on the then requirement for an industrial development certificate, the pamphlet said, 'but negative controls provide no stimulus to efficiency. Furthermore, as more and more industries become either international or plan on a European rather than national basis, negative controls could result in the loss of industrial growth to the country.'

On the strength of having produced a published pamphlet, I was asked to join the Council of the Bow Group. Then in 1967, I was persuaded, not very reluctantly, to stand for the office of political officer, a post which had been established some three years earlier and which was rapidly becoming a gateway to being chairman of the group. There were two candidates for the post. My opponent was Sir Christopher Bland, an old friend, and we sat next to each other awaiting the result of the ballot at the AGM. It seemed to take a very long time coming, and the tellers had come on to the platform and held whispered conversations with the chairman while we waited. Eventually Christopher and I realised that the election must have proved a dead heat. The complication was that the officers could not decide whether the chairman who had started the meeting would have the casting vote. He was Julian Critchley, who had proposed me. Or should it be the chairman who had just been elected unopposed for the coming year, Reg Watts, who had proposed Christopher Bland? Eventually, they decided in favour of the former and I became political officer. A year or two later, the rules were changed to make it clear that it would be the incoming chairman who had the casting vote.

A year later, I was being urged to stand for chairmanship by some members who regarded me as a less left-wing candidate than Christopher Brocklebank-Fowler. Much to the surprise of my colleagues, I decided not to stand. The demands of my job as an executive director of JS, together with a young family – our third child, Alexander, had just been born – seemed to me to make it impossible to provide as much time and attention to the role as it needed. Indeed, I felt I had probably underperformed as political officer. In addition, at the time I had still not developed an ambition or intention to try to become a Member of Parliament. Five years later, when I did seek to become a Conservative candidate, I was told that my Bow Group activities had strengthened my CV.

Shortly after the end of my Bow Group career, I found myself invited to start on a more mainstream political activity. The Conservatives had, somewhat surprisingly, won control of the Greater London Council in 1967. At the time, the GLC still had a system of additional members who were co-opted to committees, somewhat in the manner of the aldermen of the past, without having to be elected. I was asked to become an additional member of the Greater London Council Environmental Planning Committee. The Committee's main function was development control throughout the GLC area. Shortly after joining, I became deputy chairman of the Central Area Board of the Environmental Planning Committee. Additional members were debarred from becoming chairmen of sub-committees. The Central Area Board had oversight of the central areas of London with a population of about 3 million, which meant that they were in effect the most important development control committee in the country.

My time with the GLC was a most interesting experience, as it gave me an insight into how those sorts of committees operated, and how the interface between the officials and the committee members worked. There was a strong expectation that the recommendations of the officials would be accepted by the committee members. Only if the chairman of the main committee, or one of the sub-committees, themselves decided against the views of the officials was it likely that the committee as a whole would choose a different option to that recommended to them. There seemed to be a strong inertia factor at work.

I encountered an early example of this when at one of my first meetings of the Conservative members, a proposal was put to oppose a plan for a redevelopment on the corner of Hyde Park which is now occupied by the Intercontinental Hotel. The chairman put this to the meeting and when nobody said anything, I rather bravely spoke up to oppose the suggestion. It seemed that I was the only member who had taken the trouble of going to look at the site. I commented that it was occupied by buildings of no great distinction from a period which was very amply represented in London; whereas the proposal for the hotel was by an architect of some distinction, Sir Frederick Gibberd. Rather to my surprise, nobody spoke against my suggestion and indeed several supported it, as a result of which the committee decided not to oppose the redevelopment proposal. It was later called in by central Government. There was an inquiry, as a result of which the hotel proposal was approved and in due course built.

My role in the GLC was the first I had as a formal Conservative taking the Conservative Whip on the Environmental Planning Committee, although I was not actually an elected member.

My third major political activity prior to becoming a Conservative candidate was with the business team which was created by Ted Heath. The team was composed of people called in from business to advise Government on various aspects of Government operations which were felt to be closely related to normal business and commercial work. The task I was given was to advise the Government on the exercise of the property management function in Government. My involvement in the business team came about as a result of an invitation to join Christopher Bland for lunch. He was then working for a management consultant acting on behalf of the Government. At the lunch, we discussed how they might find somebody appropriate for the role which I was eventually asked to undertake. It seemed that the Government was experiencing a problem in finding a suitably qualified individual with experience of the property world who was prepared to give their time to the Government role and who would not come with too many embarrassing conflicts of interest or past allegations of dubious behaviour. The lunch ended with the old trick of the headhunters, saying, 'Then it looks like you would be the ideal person.'

I became a part-time temporary civil servant with an office in Whitehall and a Private Secretary to help me. I soon found that the Government had no system for assessing the value of the property it occupied and had apparently little or no interest in considering property values. If an office block was rented on a lease which might have reviews of the rent only every twenty-one or maybe even every forty-two years, only the rent currently being paid was charged to the department occupying the space and that rent might be only a fraction of the current market value. There was no system for updating the values of properties held freehold. There also seemed to be a reluctance to look into these matters, I suspect because departments were worried that some of their prime property might have to be forfeited when its true value was made apparent. I found that the Ministry of Defence and the Foreign Office were particularly guilty.

I wrote a report drawing attention to these shortcomings. At the same time that I was writing my report, another member of the business team, seconded from Bovis, H. J. Cruickshank, was studying maintenance costs of property. After our two reports were completed and the Government had given them proper consideration, it was announced that a new Property Services Agency, known as the PSA, was to be set up within the Department of the Environment to provide Government departments with property management services. The new agency, which was an accountable unit within the department, started operations in 1972, headed by a chief executive with Permanent Secretary status.

During the preparation of the report, I had only a limited opportunity to look at the overseas estate of the FCO. I went to Brussels where, because of our involvement with the European Union and membership of NATO, there was an unusually large amount of residential property owned by the Government. I stayed at the residence of the Ambassador to Belgium. It was a very large, early nineteenth-century property in a prime position opposite the entrance to the Royal Palace. I commented to the ambassador's wife, Lady Beith, that it seemed a very substantial residence and enquired how many rooms there were on the top floor. The answer I received was, 'I don't know, I've never been there.' It was not until the 1990s that the house became the home of our Ambassador to the European Union and the somewhat suburban house which he had previously occupied became that of our Ambassador to the Kingdom of Belgium.

I was, for a time, a member of a talking shop committee called something like the South East Economic Planning Advisory Council. It was quite rightly abolished when Margaret Thatcher came to power. However, I had, as much by chance as by design, accumulated some quite impressive-sounding entries on my CV for someone who had never fought a political election at any level nor held any Conservative Party office even as junior as a chairman of a Ward Committee. This certainly stood me in good stead when it came to moving towards becoming a Member of Parliament, starting with getting my name on the candidates' list.

8

HOVE BY-ELECTION

Most MPs would agree that luck plays a major part in a political career. It certainly did in mine. On 16 August 1973, I received a letter telling me that my name had been put on the list of potential candidates. On 22 August, Martin Maddan, the MP for Hove, died. Shortly afterwards, all those on the candidates' list received a circular asking whether they would like to put their names forward for consideration for the forthcoming by-election. Martin Maddan had had a majority of over 18,500 in the 1970 election, so it was a very attractive seat to go for. Since three years had gone by since the previous General Election, many of those who were looking for seats had already found them, including most of the strongest candidates. So a sudden vacancy in an apparently safe seat could certainly be regarded as a stroke of luck for somebody newly on the candidates' list. However, after thinking about it for a little while, I decided not to put my name forward, as I hoped to try for a seat nearer either to where we lived in the country, between Newbury and Basingstoke, or in London.

I then received a call from Bill Elliott, Conservative MP for Newcastle North, who was the Member responsible for candidates, asking me to call in to see him in Central Office. This I did on my way to Paddington to catch the train to join Susie and our children, who were holidaying in Cornwall. So I appeared at Central Office in rather more casual clothes than might have been expected. My discussion with Bill Elliott was also very unexpected. He asked me to put my name forward for Hove. He said that they could guarantee that if I did so, I would be selected to be interviewed and would get through the first round of interviews. He told me that there would only be two rounds of interviews, as it was a by-election, and that they wanted it to be held fairly soon. The reason they were asking me to do this was that they thought I was a strong candidate and that their surveys, after the recent defeats in Ripon, Sutton and Cheam, and Ely where Liberals had won previously safe Conservative seats, had shown that most of the electorate did not know the name of the Conservative candidate. It just seemed that the name Sainsbury might be easier to remember. The offer of guaranteed progress through the first round and, as Bill Elliott said, good experience in seeking a seat seemed too good to refuse; I should have said that I would discuss it with Susie, but instead I agreed to put my name forward and went on to Paddington and caught the 5.27 p.m. train to Bodmin Parkway to join my family in Cornwall. Susie was, initially, both surprised and not entirely happy about my sudden, unheralded, decision.

After a relaxing weekend, the selection procedure to choose the candidate to fight the by-election in Hove moved forward very swiftly. There were three stages. The first, a paper exercise, was choosing about thirty from the some 140 names which had been put forward, to be seen by members of the selection committee. I had been assured that I would be one of those and would progress to the third and final stage, when a lucky five would be asked to present themselves and their spouses to be interviewed and to make a ten-minute speech before some seventy selectors who would make the final choice.

After successfully getting through the first round of interviews, as promised, and becoming one of the lucky five, I had my next major stroke of good fortune. The widow of the late Member, Martin Maddan, was very keen to ensure that his successor was, like her late husband, a keen supporter of the European Union. Martin Maddan had been joint Honorary Treasurer of the Britain in Europe Campaign with my elder brother, John. This connection persuaded her that I was the best choice from the five and she therefore asked a very good friend of hers, a senior Conservative councillor, Bob Mitchell, to give me some help and guidance before and indeed during the selection process. Furthermore, she herself used her influence with the ladies on the selection committee to suggest that I was the best candidate to vote for. Meanwhile, Bob provided me with tips like not forgetting to mention Portslade in my speech because there would be several selectors from that area, which always felt rather neglected. I should also pay tribute to the work of the Young Conservatives, as there would be two or three from that group as well. In addition, he took me on tours round Hove, pointing out all the local landmarks and helping me to get more familiar with the geography.

Then just four weeks after my visit to Central Office, it was time for the selection meeting. The five candidates were each going to be asked to make a speech of some ten minutes or so before answering questions. However, before that, they would be spending three-quarters of an hour with their spouses socialising with the officers of the Association and the chairmen of the various wards. Our very good friend, Tim Rathbone, who had been selected more than a year earlier for the neighbouring seat of Lewes, had given Susie and me an excellent tip for that occasion. He said, 'Split up, you can talk to and possibly influence twice as many people if you are going round the room separately.' That proved to be a very effective bit of advice. Once more, good fortune favoured us. Two of the other candidates experienced problems: one was on a train which was seriously delayed and missed more than half of the time when he could have been socialising; the zip on the skirt of the wife of another got stuck and she and her husband both disappeared for some twenty minutes to rectify the problem, again losing very valuable time when they might have been influencing people.

The next major stroke of good fortune was my place in the sequence of speakers. The room in which we were to speak had a relatively low ceiling and was crowded and quite stuffy. Most of the selectors were rather elderly. It therefore seemed probable that, when it came to deciding, they would have the clearest memories of the first and last of the five candidates, indeed the first would probably be the best place to be and indeed that was where we were drawn.

Bob Mitchell had said he would seat himself at the back of the meeting and if he felt I was not speaking loudly enough, would raise his arm to indicate that I should speak up. This he did immediately after I started my speech, so I raised my voice and I am assured that I was heard reasonably clearly even by those, and they were numerous, who were slightly hard of hearing. After my contribution and answering questions, it had been agreed that one question only could be put to the spouse of the candidate. This was to ask the wife – we were all men – whether she would be prepared to play a part in the activities of the women's section. This is when the most remarkable stroke of good fortune occurred, because, when the question was put to Susie, she was able to say, truthfully, that on that very day she had hosted in our flat in London a lunch for the Chelsea Conservative women's lunch club.

There was one further bit of good fortune working in my favour, of which I was not aware until rather later. This was that both the president and the chairman of the Association had come to the conclusion that they wanted a candidate who was mature and preferably had experience and achievement in business or industry. The chairman had a son at Eton and I am told viewed Old Etonian candidates favourably. I got his vote in the second round after the other Old Etonian had been eliminated.

After we had done our bit, Susie and I went out and had a walk around the town. It was a very pleasant warm early-autumn evening. We returned to the hotel and joined the other prospective candidates and spouses, and waited for what seemed to be a very long time to know the result of the selection committee's deliberations. Then suddenly, without any forewarning, Patrick Hall-Smith, the chairman of the Hove Conservative Association, appeared, looked round the room, spotted me and said, 'We have chosen you.' The other candidates and their wives disappeared and a very astonished Susie and I were joined by the other officers of the Hove Conservative Association for brief congratulations before, for the first time, we had to face the local press. After a few questions to me, the journalist from the *Argus* turned to Susie and asked her what she would be doing during the campaign, to which she replied, 'I shall be fighting with my husband.' I suspect the word she had intended to use instead of 'with' was 'alongside'.

So, seven weeks to the day from the date of the letter announcing my inclusion in the candidates' list, I was adopted to fight a by-election.

Hove had chosen a candidate who had never fought an election. This in a way was advantageous. The by-election campaign was to be run by John, later Sir John, Lacey. He was a master of the art of campaigning and, lacking any previous experience, I was very happy to be guided throughout by him. Not only had I never fought an election, I had never been to a Party Conference. So the first move was to get me up to Blackpool and arrange for me to be called to speak in a debate. As a late arrival, I was found a room in a post-war – it scarcely justified the description 'modern' – hotel a long way along the front from the Winter Gardens. At least it was en suite, with a rather dirty plastic bath.

Those wishing to speak from the floor at a Party Conference had to fill in a form, which is then submitted to the Party machine for a lucky, and usually supportive, few to be chosen. John Lacey filled in my form, marking it prominently 'Candidate for the by-election to be called before 11.30'. The significance of the time was that that was when the proceedings were on TV. So when my Socialist half-sister turned on the TV to get *Watch with Mother* for her children, she was annoyed to find it showing the conference but astonished to see her brother was the speaker.

The debate during which I spoke was on the environment, and in my unexciting remarks I commended two proposed major projects: the Channel Tunnel, and Maplin on the Thames Estuary to be the site of the third London airport. Forty-four years later, the former is well established, but how to increase the capacity of London's airport is still being debated. After I was sent on my way back to London with the good wishes of the conference, the date for the by-election was announced and serious campaigning could start. But first a decision was needed as to where Susie and I would establish our living quarters. I thought that a suite at the Dudley, the best hotel in town, was the answer, but Jim Prior, the Party chairman, was concerned that it gave the wrong impression by being too upmarket. He eventually accepted that there was no reasonable alternative in Hove, so for four weeks the Dudley became our home.

Hove was one of the safest of Conservative seats and, in normal circumstances, the by-election should have been straightforward and an easy victory. There were however, three reasons for suspecting that it could prove to be a very hard fight. First, and most importantly, the by-election coincided with the Yom Kippur War. The United Nations imposed an embargo on any sale of arms to both sides. Israel had a number of British-made battle tanks, and the refusal of the Government to supply Israel with replacement gun sights for these tanks provoked a great deal of unhappiness among Jewish voters. Hove had a substantial Jewish population, maybe as many as 10% of all voters. I suspect that not many of them were happy to come out and vote Conservative on 8 November 1973.

Secondly, the economic situation was deteriorating, inflation was rising and the coal miners had started their go-slow, which led eventually to the three-day week.

Thirdly, Liberals had been winning apparently safe Conservative seats at by-elections for the last eighteen months or so. Ripon, Ely and Sutton and Cheam had all fallen. The Liberals had wasted no time in starting their campaign. Their candidate had been chosen even before the late Conservative MP's funeral had been held. This meant that they had been campaigning on the ground for nearly four weeks before I was able to start. Furthermore, they had chosen a strong candidate in Des Wilson. He had a PR background and was adept at getting himself and his cause publicity in the local, and indeed national, media. He had been involved with the campaigning charity Shelter in its early days, although he was not, as he claimed, its founder. This involvement with the private rented sector, which was substantial in Hove and which had many problems, gave him a good platform to attack both the local authority and the national Government. This meant that centrally and locally there was considerable anxiety about the outcome. Happily, because of my inexperience in these matters, I was much less aware of the worries than my team. So Susie and I were happy to get on with the day-to-day work of the campaign without concerning ourselves too much with the opinion polls and focus groups' opinions, which were being monitored by others.

The next four weeks were a crash course in electioneering, public speaking and getting to know Hove. After the adoption meeting, there were no less than seven further public meetings. When there wasn't an evening meeting, there was usually some other form of visit organised by my team. On one of these I was taken to a youth club in Portslade, not the most promising Conservative territory. It was there that the incident took place which has been much misreported since. I sat down next to a youth, perhaps of some eighteen years, who turned to me and said, 'I can't talk to you, you're rich.' It was late and I was tired, so I replied, 'I'm not rich, I'm very rich.' This very effectively broke the ice and I was able to have a short but reasonably amicable conversation with the youth. I don't think it produced a vote, as I was fairly sure that neither he nor probably anybody else in the youth club was likely to vote for me or any other candidate.

If meetings filled most of my evenings, campaigning took up most of the day. There was a press conference, after which Susie and I set off in what we called our circus. We would descend upon a part of Hove and while the helpers went down both sides of the streets knocking on doors and delivering leaflets, I would announce my presence over the loud-speaker and seek to meet people and answer any questions they might have. After two or three days, John Lacey realised that Susie was such an effective supporter that she would be better used by having her own cam-paign group, so we set off each morning with separate groups of helpers, Susie's including a junior minister or MP to help her with any difficult political questions.

For the national and local media, the story was the possibility of another Liberal victory in the eighteenth safest Conservative seat. With his PR experience, Des Wilson was doing a great job in getting himself publicity, particularly in the local media. Nearly always his press releases and most of his speeches were devoted to local issues such as street light-ing, the condition of the pavements and, of course, housing. He blamed all housing failures on the local Conservative council. The one national issue that featured strongly in the campaign was inflation. It was high and rising, reaching 10% at the beginning of November, and food prices featured in the list of goods most affected. Luckily, I was assumed by my opponents to be very knowledgeable on the subject, although as my main responsibilities had been in the development side of the business, I had

Brighton and Hove Albion's newest supporters, 1973
(*Brighton Evening Argus*)

not directly dealt with any food category. As a result, I wasn't bombarded with questions about the price of milk or six eggs. If I had been, I fear I would have been caught out.

The Yom Kippur War, which started on 6 October with the Egyptians launching a surprise attack across the Suez Canal and the Syrians attacking the Golan Heights, had ended with a ceasefire on 25 October. It was therefore a major news item for the first half of the by-election campaign.

An opinion poll published in the local paper the day before I was adopted gave the Conservatives a 1% lead, with 20% don't knows. For the next three weeks, we felt that we were not getting fair coverage in the local paper. Luckily, the president of our local Conservative Association was also legal adviser to the local paper and, as a result of his efforts, it was agreed that on the last Monday before the election, they would publish a photograph of Susie and me with our children on the front page. So Camilla, then aged ten, Alex, five, and Jessica, three, dressed in Brighton and Hove Albion colours, were photographed on the beach with Susie and me. James, our eldest, was away at boarding school. Afterwards, the only questions we were asked were about our 'lovely' children, how old were they, what were they doing, did they like Hove and things to that effect. We had found a secret weapon that Des Wilson could not employ.

The campaign involved a lot more serious and normal campaigning activity, including the surprisingly large number of seven meetings, during which I was assisted by a 'supporting speaker'. Four were Cabinet ministers, Keith Joseph, Jim Prior, Peter Walker and Robert Carr. As the campaign reached its climax, the number of canvassers deployed by the three main Parties steadily increased. The Liberals had always been efficient and enthusiastic about coming to help in other constituencies. Conservatives are normally not as good but, on this occasion, Lilian Silverstone, who was chairman of the South East area, sat on the telephone practically all day every day urging all other constituencies in her area to find volunteers to go and help in Hove to preserve the honour of the South East area at not losing by-elections. I am also glad to say that a number of friends from London came down to help, including Mark Evans, who was still driving to collect possible Tory voters on election day at about 8.30 p.m. It seemed to him there were no more possible Tories to get to the Polls when he thought maybe I should drive my car into a car load of Liberals in a kamikaze attack. I am glad to say that he didn't try that. The result of all this additional effort was that it was reckoned that on the last weekend of the campaign, no less than 500 canvassers were knocking on doors in Hove on behalf of one Party or another. There can have been very few doors which didn't get at least one knock over the weekend.

Thursday, 8 November 1973, the day of the by-election, was for Susie and me a quite relaxed affair. No more campaigning or speeches, just going round the town calling in on committee rooms and polling stations. One committee room was in the Association office next to the Baptist church. Rod Badhams, the *Argus* reporter allocated to follow my campaign, was a member of that church, which had a lectern outside with a Bible open at a different passage each day. I glanced at the Bible as I went past. It was open at First Timothy, the First Epistle of St Paul to Timothy. I like to think that Rod had chosen that passage.

The tradition in Hove was that, on election night, the candidate and his wife had dinner at the best restaurant in town, the Eaton, with the president and the chairman and their wives. This function started, flamboyantly disregarding any contribution those present might have been expected to make to getting the vote out or supporting those who were doing so, at 8.30. Shortly after 10.00, we were interrupted by a telephone call from John Lacey. He told me that the exit poll gave me a lead of only 1.5%, less than the margin of error. Suddenly my tournedos rossini tasted like cardboard. When we had finished our dinner, Susie and I went to the Vogue restaurant in Holland Road, where about ten Conservative agents who had been helping were dining with John Lacey. The atmosphere was funereal and my mood was not helped by being assured, 'Don't worry, you did everything you could.'

We went back to the hotel and then, after midnight, on to the count at Hove Town Hall. Hove was notorious for counting votes extremely slowly, so when we arrived there were only a few thousand votes already counted and worryingly it looked as if Des Wilson's row of votes was slightly longer than mine. I was greeted by the constituency chairman, looking deeply worried but trying to reassure me by saying that the best areas had yet to be counted. Indeed, very soon, my row of votes started stretching well ahead of Des Wilson's.

It still took a very long time to reach the point where the returning officer could announce the result on the platform set up outside the Town Hall. One reason for this was that, amazingly, the Labour candidate's votes were insufficient to save him losing his deposit, so his agent had demanded what is called a 'flip-through', when each pile of votes is looked at to make sure it contains fifty votes for the same candidate. This delayed the announcement of the result by a further half hour or so, and caused consternation when the rumour spread through the crowd outside that there was a recount going on. There were many of our friends among the crowd, including my sixty-nine-year-old mother. Her view was that having been the wife of an unsuccessful Liberal candidate on three occasions, she certainly did not want her son to be beaten by a Liberal. She had by then become a firm and active Conservative. Breaking all the rules, a policeman who had been inside the count came out to prepare for the announcement and went over to my mother and said, 'Don't worry, Madam, your boy is all right.'

We had 22,070 votes, 47.8% of the total and a majority of 4,846 over my next opponent, the Liberal Des Wilson. When it came to the announcement, which was made from a platform outside the Town Hall, there was a large crowd waiting, most of whom were Liberals expecting to greet a victory. They were so noisy after realising that Des Wilson had lost that I think my few remarks, and indeed the remarks of any other candidate, went unheard. To me, the most significant fact was that the only other candidate who declined to shake my hand was Des Wilson. Among the defeated candidates was one representing the National Front and another representing the Communist Party Marxist/Leninist of England, which needed to be distinguished very carefully from the Communist Party Marxist/Leninist of Great Britain, from whom I think they had split. Their lady candidate had attracted a certain amount of comment when she had started her campaign in the Brighton Pavilion constituency, mistakenly thinking it was part of Hove. Her main policy proposal seemed to be to urge people not to vote. They didn't for her: she got 128 votes.

It was just about 4 o'clock in the morning when Susie and I returned to the Dudley Hotel and for the first time in my life I had a police escort, one rather tired and disgruntled policeman who was delegated to escort me back to the hotel. The rowdy young Liberals had dispersed and we got back to the hotel safely without needing his help.

We were to fight six more elections. The first two were the February and October elections in 1974. The indecisive result in February which brought Harold Wilson to power with a tiny majority led to a second election during the year. The result of this was that I had fought three elections during less than a year. It seemed at times as if Susie and I spent the whole time knocking on doors in Hove. It did produce one reasonable joke in the *Sunday Express*, which suggested that by the October when I knocked on a door I might be met with the response, 'Not this week, thank you.'

Des Wilson was again my main opponent in the February election but his campaign was much less vigorous, lacking the outside help and the blaze of publicity from which he had benefited in the previous October. Susie and I campaigned in much the same way as we had before but without the outside help, so we went around together. Des Wilson's campaign faded away, leaving me with a greatly increased majority of over 11,500, 54.2% of the vote. This time, Des Wilson did manage to get around to shaking my hand and congratulating me.

After the blaze of national and local publicity that had surrounded the by-election, the others were dull affairs. My majority grew to over 19,000 in 1979 and then gradually slid back during the years of Tory Government. In 1992, it was 12,268, and I got 49% of the vote, the only time after the by-election when my share was below 50%. The number of meetings that we held diminished, so that during our last campaign in 1992 after the Adoption Meeting, we only held one. Attendance got lower, the Press got less and less interested in reporting the meetings or indeed anything else that I did as candidate, and fewer and fewer people attended the Count and subsequent declaration.

There were very few incidents of note. One, which occurred I think in 1983, was at one of the meetings, as always poorly attended. There were perhaps twenty people present, most of whom I knew because they were our supporters. Two large youths in their twenties arrived and sat down in the front row, right in front of the platform from which I was due to speak. I thought this looked ominous. As the meeting progressed, they did not take any hostile or indeed other action, they didn't heckle my speech, and afterwards they asked no questions and so, when the meeting petered out, I went up to them and asked if they had enjoyed the meeting. Their reply was, 'Oh yes, we are Swedish English language students and we wanted to see what an English election meeting was like'. I wished they could have come to something more interesting.

Another incident which should have been more widely reported occurred at the Declaration in 1979. I had received over 60% of the vote, Labour 21.5%, the Liberals only 17.4%. After I had made my few remarks thanking the usual suspects for the work they had done, the Labour candidate came to the microphone and said, 'Brothers, Labour is back in its rightful position in Hove, second'. The reason for this startling announcement was that Labour had at long last overtaken the Liberals and finally wiped away the ignominy of having lost their deposit both at the By-Election and at the first of the subsequent 1974 General Elections.

At every Election, as in the By-Election, on Saturdays Susie and I used to go to George Street, the main shopping street in Hove, and go down the Street from top to bottom and back up again, one of us on each side of the road, accompanied by two or three helpers handing out leaflets and pressing the flesh. In 1992, on the first Saturday of the campaign, when we got to the bottom of the street and met up, we looked at each other and said, 'that wasn't very good, it's not like it is usually, the reception was not that friendly or supportive'. Then, when we repeated the exercise on the last Saturday before the Election, after the famous Sheffield rally when we met up again at the bottom of George Street, we looked at each other and said, 'wasn't that entirely different, quite like old times'. The Sheffield rally, on 1 April 1992, which was eight days before Election Day, was an American-style event, attended by no less than 10,000 Labour supporters and the entire Shadow Cabinet introducing themselves as the next Home Secretary, etc., was regarded as 'triumphalist'. It was followed by a catastrophic 6% drop in Labour support. The result had been a noticeable change of mood, so I had no doubt about the outcome in Hove, but I remained uncertain as to the outcome of the Election nationally.

The Labour candidate only managed third place behind the Liberals again, in both 1983 and 1987. In 1992, Don Turner got back to second with 24.5% of the vote to my 49%. It is astonishing that Labour won the seat with a majority of nearly 5,000 in 1997 and have held it at every Election since, other than 2010.

The 1992 Election had been different from all the others in another way as, since I had become a Minister of State, and was Minister for Trade, I was given a tour to go round other seats, to speak at meetings, and hopefully help and encourage other candidates in their work. As a result, I spent much more time away from Hove and had the interesting experience of meeting half a dozen or so of my fellow candidates and seeing and hearing how things were going in their constituencies.

9

HOVE ACTUALLY – MY CONSTITUENCY

During the selection process, Susie and I had undertaken to have a 'home in Hove'. We had carefully avoided saying we would 'live in Hove'. After the by-election, I was able to borrow a flat just over the border in Brighton, owned by a friend of my mother's who did not use it in the winter. We were there for the first of the 1974 elections and then were able to rent a flat in Hove for six months while we found something more permanent. By the end of 1974, we had established our 'home in Hove'. We had bought a long lease on a flat in a converted house in Palmeira Avenue. It had three bedrooms, and a large living room with a balcony overlooking the county cricket ground. This remained our base in Hove for the next twenty-three years.

In his report on the by-election, John Lacey had written, 'He was ably supported throughout the campaign by his wife.' This support was continued for the next twenty-three years and was especially valuable because of the major role played in the affairs of the constituency by the women's committee, the ladies' lunch club and by the numerous ladies who were the majority of activists in nearly all the wards. Susie proved a hit with the ladies from the beginning. She usually accompanied me to any constituency function to which I went and herself attended meetings of the ladies, particularly the ladies' lunch club.

I had, more by chance than by careful consideration, become the Member of Parliament for a constituency that had many attractions to an MP. It was a compact and relatively small area, about 4 × 2 miles, with an adult population of about 66,000, which made it the standard size for a constituency and meant that throughout my time there, I was never affected by boundary changes. Furthermore, the boundaries to the constituency were the same as those of Hove Borough Council, which meant that I was one of rather less than 10% of MPs who represented one local authority and were the only Member of Parliament for that local authority. The Borough Council was always under the control of the Conservatives. Indeed, at one time, of the thirty-six councillors, thirty-four were Conservatives and two were Labour. Both the Labour councillors were called Leslie Hamilton, father and son. Father regarded himself as the Leader of the Opposition, his son was the Opposition Chief Whip. There came the moment, when by local tradition, it was Leslie Hamilton Snr's turn to become mayor. It was normal in Hove for the longest-serving councillor who hadn't yet been mayor to be given the role. There were unofficial soundings between the local councillors and myself as to whether having a Labour mayor was regarded as acceptable. I readily agreed, and am happy to say that our relations with the Hamiltons were always amicable, if non-political.

Hove had other interesting features, including being the home of the Sussex County Cricket Club, and for most of the time I was an MP, the home of Brighton & Hove Albion Football Club. By the time I was elected, the Sussex county cricket ground, which had always been in Hove, was rather less attractive than it used to be, as blocks of flats had appeared on the periphery, I suspect some of them on land which had been sold by the club. The presence of the ground in the heart of the constituency was popular, although not many of my constituents actually attended county cricket matches. The balcony of our flat provided a very good view of the ground, although sadly there were not many occasions when I was able to sit there and enjoy the cricket. One afternoon I do remember was when the Sussex captain, Tony Greig, was 100 not-out at lunch. As I had an afternoon of leisure before a further evening engagement, I was looking forward to enjoying some spectacular cricket. Sadly, the spectacular cricket lasted just one ball, as Greig hit the first ball he received very high into the air and was caught, whereupon the Sussex innings collapsed.

Hove was also the home of a 1st Division league football club, Brighton & Hove Albion, the Seagulls. When I was elected, they were only in the 2nd Division. However, large crowds were always attracted to the Goldstone Ground, which was in the middle of the constituency. The disruption caused by the football matches was not popular with the constituents who lived in the area. The complaints were most frequent when the visitors were one of the London clubs with a fairly noisy and occasionally disruptive following, Millwall supporters being the best known for causing trouble. In 1973, the famous football character Brian Clough was briefly the manager of Brighton & Hove Albion. Not long after I was elected, I was attending a dinner in one of the Brighton hotels. When I was waiting in the lobby, somebody pointed out to me that Brian Clough was also there attending another dinner. So as the Member of Parliament for the Club Ground, I thought I would go and introduce myself to the famous Mr Clough. He was not only quite a bit younger than me, but also a noted Labour supporter.

When I said 'Hello', Brian Clough made some remark about not expecting me to know much about football, so I responded by saying that having been born in Chelsea, I had been a lifelong Chelsea supporter and first went to Stamford Bridge in 1947, in the days when Tommy Lawton was briefly a Chelsea player. What I had not known was that Brian Clough, who as a player, had been an England striker, had wanted to emulate Lawton, a famously successful England centre-forward. So for ten or more minutes we discussed Tommy Lawton's career and his present, rather unhappy, circumstances. At the end of our conversation, Brian Clough patted me on the shoulder and said, 'You'll be all right, lad.'

I used to go to watch the Seagulls play maybe two or three times a season, usually at the invitation of the directors. The club seemed to do memorable things in election years. In 1979 they got promotion to the top division, under the management of Mullery. Driving past the Ground, standing up with my loudspeaker in my Range Rover, I was able to suggest, 'Let's make it a double for Maggie and Mullery!' Surprisingly the supporters going in who heard my injunction applauded. In 1983, another election year, much to general surprise, the club reached the Cup Final, where they had to play Manchester United. As the local MP, the Football Association invited me to attend the final at Wembley. However, before the date for the match arrived, the General Election had been called and I was no longer the Member of Parliament, just a candidate for the constituency. So after reflection, I decided like most of the population of Hove that I would watch the match on television. The match was a 2–2 draw after extra time, and in those days that meant a replay, which sadly the Seagulls lost, 4–0. Undaunted by the defeat, the club still had a celebratory ride through the town, which somewhat made up for the fact that, as well as reaching the Cup Final, they had achieved the unusual and unwelcome distinction of being relegated from the 1st Division in the same year. In 2017, another election year, Brighton & Hove Albion again achieved promotion to the premiership. To the relief of my former constituents, they no longer play at a ground in the middle of Hove, having moved to a much better-appointed ground on the outskirts of Brighton.

In political terms, perhaps the most important feature about Hove was that it was 'a safe seat' throughout my time as Member of Parliament.

My majority peaked at over 19,000 and in most of the elections I fought, I won over 50% of the vote. It is astonishing that it is now Labour that gets over 50% of the vote. Indeed, in 2019 Peter Kyle got nearly 33,000 votes, more than I ever achieved.

The constituency I first fought was Hove and Portslade. Portslade was a separate urban district which in 1974 was absorbed into Hove Borough Council. Just before I retired, Hove itself as a local authority was combined with Brighton to become the City of Brighton and Hove. The current Boundary Commission proposals for the Hove constituency are for the creation of a new and larger constituency to be called Brighton Central and Hove. It looks unlikely to have a Conservative Member of Parliament. It is becoming ever harder to maintain the identity of Hove, and the occasions when Hove residents accused of living in Brighton have to say, 'No Hove, actually,' have become more frequent. There are still those who claim to belong to a fantasy 'Hove, actually' club.

Throughout my Parliamentary career, I tried to visit the constituency every other weekend, usually accompanied by Susie. As, in those days, Parliamentary proceedings would usually continue until 10.00 p.m. on Thursdays, I would go down to the constituency on Friday morning, either by train or by car. I would then often have visits of some sort, to a school, hospital or business, followed by an advice session or surgery, as they are sometimes known. The advice session would normally continue on Saturday morning. When it was very busy, I might have seen perhaps twenty or so constituents, although the normal number would be more like a dozen. I rapidly discovered that most of the issues which were brought before me did not directly involve central Government. The constituent was more likely to be troubled by matters concerning housing (the responsibility of the district council) or education (the responsibility of the county council). However, few constituents knew that, and even fewer knew who their district or county councillor was or how to get in touch with them. So on those issues, I would be acting as a relay, referring the problem, if justified, to the relevant authority. The other main area of concern which constituents brought to me was about benefits and social services. Having discussions with constituents on these issues was a very useful way of keeping in touch with how policy impacted on people and families.

Many elderly people had small incomes from savings in addition to their pension. Very high rates of inflation created particular difficulties for them. Not surprisingly, they found superficial attraction if the interest rate they got on their savings was 12% or so, which offset the consequences of inflation at 15% or more. I was never able to explain satisfactorily that what really mattered was the difference between the interest rate they received and the rate of inflation. It was very hard to convince elderly ladies that they would be better off with 6% interest and 4% inflation than they were with 12% interest and 15% inflation.

Another difficulty which I, in common with most of my Parliamentary colleagues, experienced was the belief among my constituents, indeed even among some of my councillors, that my role was to represent Westminster in Hove rather than to represent Hove at Westminster. My ministerial career involved a great deal of overseas travel; being Minister of Trade made a significant difference to the number of times I could be in Hove. It was therefore not entirely surprising that, on occasions, there were adverse comments about my absence. I was however, amused to learn from one of my agents, who had been in Lewes as the agent for Tim Rathbone and who had then transferred to Hove to become my agent, that in Lewes there were complaints that their Member of Parliament had never become a minister. So when she transferred and found contrary complaints that their Member of Parliament was a minister and that meant that he wasn't in Hove as much as he might have been, she and I shared the view that constituents were sometimes hard to please.

Some Members of Parliament do make a particular point of giving most of their attention to their constituency. This is sometimes because they have a marginal seat. My two Brighton neighbours reflected the two extremes of Members of Parliaments' attitudes to their constituencies. Kemp Town was represented by Andrew Bowden. It was always a marginal and Andrew did an excellent job of keeping it Conservative until 1997; partly by being in the constituency as much as possible, and always seeking to be involved in any constituency issue. I did sometimes feel that he was over-enthusiastic in supporting populist causes. My other neighbour, in Brighton Pavilion, was Julian Amery, who regarded constituency duties with what I would almost call disdain. During the by-election, as far as I recall, he never made an appearance or made any attempt to help in the campaign.

Later, as my constituency neighbour, he was somewhat unexpectedly a help to me in maintaining good relations with my Conservative Association. In the 1970s, Conservative MPs often came under pressure from Association members and from other constituents, to support the re-introduction of capital punishment. Some MPs who opposed its re-introduction and voted against it when the matter came before the House found themselves in difficulty with their constituency Associations. In Hove, although a few of the leading members of the Association shared my view in opposing re-introduction, the majority of the officers and certainly a large majority of the members of the Association supported re-introduction. Julian Amery was quite rightly regarded as a leading and distinguished figure on the right of the Party. As he had consistently opposed the re-introduction of capital punishment, and indeed earlier supported its abolition, my views could not be regarded as dangerously left-wing and I was able to avoid what otherwise could have been a difficult problem.

There was an interesting change in the media during the course of my time as an MP. In 1973, the local newspaper, the *Brighton Evening Argus*, had high circulation locally and was clearly influential. Over the years, that circulation steadily diminished and local radio, then later local television, became more significant. In the period, national coverage in the press of what was going on in Parliament steadily diminished. When I was first an MP, even a modest contribution from the back-benches to a major debate would probably get two or three lines in the broadsheets. By the end of my Parliamentary career, not even a more serious contribution from the front bench would be covered in the newspapers. However, there was by then a Parliamentary television channel and radio coverage of proceedings.

Hove was sometimes, unkindly, referred to as 'God's waiting room'. The census provided evidence that the constituency did indeed have a well-above average number of voters of pensionable age. Hove also had a well-above average number of Jewish voters. However, there was no statistical evidence of this aspect of the constituency, although some estimates put the proportion of Jewish voters as high as 10%. Certainly canvassing and correspondence sent to me was a clear indication that there was a large number of voters with a close interest in matters relating to Israel and to the abiding problem of anti-Semitism. I had never been to Israel before becoming a Member of Parliament, but within a week or two of becoming a Member I was being urged by friends and colleagues to join the All-Party Parliamentary Group for the Release of Soviet Jewry. At the time, it was known that there were a large number of Jews in the Soviet Union who would like to emigrate to Israel or indeed, elsewhere, but were prevented from doing so by the Soviet authorities. Happily, while I was an MP, the need for such a group disappeared with the fall of the Berlin Wall in 1989 and the break-up of the Soviet Union. After the first election of 1974, the group sent a delegation to Israel, and Susie and I joined it for the first of the many visits we were to make to that remarkable country. My active involvement with that group maybe contributed to the very good relations I soon established with the Jewish community. When I was having a discussion with the chairman of the Jewish Representative Council, who knew my father and knew of his and my Uncle Bob's involvement with the Kindertransport, he remarked that he knew 'the apple never falls far from the tree'. I had never heard this saying before, but I understood it to refer to my support for Israel and matters of particular interest to the Jewish community, following what my father had done. My father never said anything to me about what he and his brother had done for some Kindertransport children in 1939. I only learnt about it gradually from what I read and heard from others. It seems the brothers provided accommodation, originally in Putney, later in Reading to get away from the Blitz, for some fifteen children for whom no foster-parents had been found. Stories suggest that they also provided what might be described as 'after care' in the form of pocket money and visits bringing sweets, and jobs at Sainsbury's.

In 1975, a Parliamentary group known as the Conservative Friends of Israel was established. There had for some time been a group of Labour Friends of Israel, and soon after the Conservative group was established, a Liberal Friends of Israel group was set up. All the time that I was not a minister, I was active in that group. Ministers are, by tradition, not allowed to take part in any back-bench committees, including all-Party groups. I was at various times treasurer, secretary, chairman and finally president of the Conservative Friends of Israel. Some of our visits were made with a delegation from CFI, others were private. As a Minister of Trade, I paid an official visit to Israel and set the target of doubling our trade, a target which I am happy to say was achieved only two or three years after my visit.

Every MP meets most frequently those constituents who are members of his Party and who are actively working in support of the Party. It is now a very serious problem that so few people seem to want to play an active role in Party politics. Shortly before the 1979 election, the Hove Conservative Association had the remarkable number of over 4,000 members. That number had very greatly decreased before I retired. When I last enquired, the Association had some 300 members. The Party is trying to persuade more of those interested in politics to join by reducing the cost of membership. What is needed is a greater recognition of the consequences of leaving membership to a few, often those with extreme or eccentric views.

10

FIRST IMPRESSIONS

On 13 November 1973, Susie and I had lunch in the House of Lords with my father, who had been created a Labour life peer in 1962 by his friend Hugh Gaitskell. He then went to the gallery of the Commons to watch proceedings while I got ready to take my seat for the first time. As I stood at the Bar of the House at the end of Question Time, I had to wait while a State of Emergency was declared by Robert Carr, the Home Secretary. This was because of the go-slow in the mining industry, an industrial dispute which was to change into a strike leading to the so-called three-day-week, the call of an early election and the surprising defeat of the Heath Government. However, having a State of Emergency declared before you took your seat was a splendid opportunity for an introductory joke on many subsequent occasions when I was asked to speak in other constituencies.

As I processed towards the Speaker with my sponsors on either side, a Labour Member sitting on the Opposition front bench below the gangway said, 'Where's your father?' to which I was able to reply quite truthfully, 'Up in the gallery.' After taking the oath and signing the book, shaking the Speaker by the hand, Ted Heath was there to shake my hand behind the Speaker's chair; I was a Member of Parliament.

There had been four by-elections on 8 November: Edinburgh North was a comfortable Conservative hold; Glasgow Govan saw the SNP overturn a Labour majority of 7,142 and achieve a sensational victory; the Conservatives lost Berwick-upon-Tweed by only 57 votes to the Liberals; and at Hove, Labour had lost their deposit. The *Economist* article on these results was headed, 'It's a State of Emergency for Labour too.' However, three and a half months later, Labour won the first of the 1974 General Elections.

I thought that I already knew quite a lot about Parliament but I learnt a great deal more in the first few weeks I was there, before once again I was off electioneering. One of the first things I learnt was the total inadequacy of the office provision for Members and their supporting staff. I was eventually found a desk in New Palace Yard in a room where six or seven other Members had their desks. A couple of weeks later there was a running Whip, which meant every MP was expected to be present all evening when there could be a Division at any time. Therefore, all the desks were occupied, and several secretaries were in attendance, one of whom had brought a baby and another a puppy, both of whom were active on the floor. My desk was back-to-back with that of Nicholas Fairbairn. He was busy on the telephone talking, I assume, to a constituent, a conversation which included a number of expletives which he did not delete. The office was overcrowded, over-heated and chaotic. My secretary had been allocated a desk in the attic space of the House of Commons in an area which was even more overcrowded, and fairly distant from my room. When not together, we had to use the not very efficient telephone service of the House of Commons to contact each other. It was not until I retired as a minister in 1994 that I was allocated a reasonable office together with adjoining space sufficient for a secretary and research assistant. I only got that by using my influence as a former Whip and because I knew in advance that I would need a new office after that summer's reshuffle.

In the 1970s there was no such thing as an induction course for new Members, even if you arrived after a General Election. Coming to the House after a by-election was rather like arriving at a new school after the term had started. I was entirely dependent on friends showing me where things were. I hoped to get guidance on procedures and on how things worked from my Whip, but the only piece of advice I remember receiving from him was that, in his view, the first three people who spoke at a meeting of the 1922 Committee were usually mad.

It took me a little time to learn my way around the large and complex building that is the Palace of Westminster and some of the outbuildings which were occupied by Members, their staff and other important parts of Parliament. On my second day as an MP, when I was being helpfully guided round by a colleague, as we walked through the No Lobby a burly figure came the other way and, as he passed us, stopped and turned. He said, 'You don't know me, I'm Eric Heffer on the other side. I did like what you said about the Liberals, I hate them.' I had been quoted as saying the Liberals had to do better than project the image of 'nice nothingness'. During my by-election, Conservative canvassers who were met by the response that a voter was wavering between Liberal and Labour would urge the voter to vote for Labour. In the same way, Labour canvassers finding someone wondering whether to vote Conservative or Liberal would urge them to vote Conservative. This surprising behaviour reflected the attitude of the local Councillors; Labour and Conservative worked quite happily together, but both were fiercely opposed to the Liberals, whom they regarded as interlopers into their cosy duopoly. Eric Heffer regarded them as class traitors. I believe that a more valid criticism is that too many Liberal Party supporters are happier with being a Party of protest than accepting the responsibilities and hard choices that come with Government.

If the office facilities were inadequate, the working hours of Parliament were extraordinary. On Monday to Thursday, proceedings in the Chamber started at 2.30 p.m. with prayers followed by Question Time. Other Business followed at 3.30 p.m., and the main vote would normally be at 10.00 p.m. There would often be business of a more limited nature afterwards with a debate lasting another hour and a half, which, with Divisions, would take one very near to or often past midnight. Select Committees usually sat in the morning, but much of the time I would not be involved in one of these. However, Standing Committees considering Bills would sometimes sit the most extraordinary hours. This occurred when the Opposition was doing something which was, strictly speaking, out of order: filibustering. The reason for the filibuster was often obscure but I suppose usually could best be described as showing the strengths of one's Party's opposition to the Bill being considered.

In 1976, I became a Member of the committee considering the detail of the Bill attractively entitled the Community Land Act. It was in fact a Bill enabling the Government and local authorities to take over, effectively nationalise, any land which they wished to acquire regardless of any objections by the owners or occupants. As was to be expected, this could not have been more strongly opposed by the Conservatives, now in opposition, and so we embarked upon a filibuster. One week the committee met on Tuesday and Thursday as normal at 10.30 a.m., adjourned at 1.00 p.m., and resumed again at 4.00 p.m., continuing right through the night until 1.00 p.m. the following day when the Rules required us to adjourn again. It was at the discretion of the chairman of the committee as to whether we took breaks, to enable us to take refreshment. The rest of the time, the Tory Members of the committee had to ensure both that there was a quorum present and that we kept proceedings going by making rambling, discursive but of course always relevant, speeches to as many amendments as we could dream up. If nothing else, it gave me an early experience of moving amendments and speaking in committee, at length. The Conservative Members of the committee were sustained during their marathon nights by Susie and one or two other London-based wives of committee members bringing in refreshments which we could enjoy in the corridor outside the committee room.

When the Bill returned to the floor of the House for the Report Stage, there was another filibuster. This kept the debate on a series of amendments going all night. By chance, I had been asked to move the final amendment chosen for debate. It was nearly 9 a.m. and the Whips asked me to be brief, as some of the lawyers present needed to get to their chambers. I am not sure that I would want my cause pleaded by a barrister who had been up all night.

The long hours and evening and night-time sittings did have one side benefit. They provided frequent opportunities for socialising, not just with friends and Members of your own Party but also with other Members in different Parties. Although in the dining rooms the Parties had separate areas and didn't sit together, in the bars, the tea room and the smoking room there was good friendly interaction. You got to know some Members from other Parties not just by looking at them across the floor of the House or across a committee room, but also by chatting with them while having a drink or tea.

Another way of getting to know colleagues from other Parties was through all-Party groups and all-Party sporting activities. Some back-benchers devote a great deal of time to all-Party committees. These exist for every subject that can be found to command enough attention, and include every country, however small, remote and apparently uninteresting. I joined the all-Party group on retailing, where I was sometimes viewed with suspicion by other Members more interested in supporting their small shopkeepers. I recall taking an interest in the activities of one or two of the committees concerned with the countries which I most frequently visited, including Italy and Turkey. Very shortly after I was first elected, Hugh Dykes, later to become a Liberal, persuaded me to take an interest in the affairs of the All-Party Committee for the Release of Soviet Jewry. That committee sought to publicise the problems of Jews seeking to emigrate to Israel. Few were able to do so, and many who tried were persecuted or even jailed, most famously Natan Anatoly Sharansky. Greville Janner, who was a moving spirit in this committee, always liked to ensure that non-Jewish Members were prominent among the officers. After 1989 and the fall of the Soviet Empire, it once again became possible for Jews to leave the Soviet Union and go to Israel or indeed to other parts of the world. The all-Party group was then dissolved, its work having been done.

As long as Parliamentary Parties have existed, there have been groups within those Parties where like-minded MPs come together to discuss or promote policies or particular projects. Some have a long life, others flourish for only one Parliament. In the Conservative Party, some of the groups form dining clubs, which usually meet in one of the smaller dining rooms in the House. It was because I knew Nick Scott well and had been involved with him in a small-scale business venture before I became an MP, that having only been a Member for a few weeks, I was invited to join Nick's Diner. Nick's Diner was not named after Nick, although he had been from its first days a prominent member, but was named after a restaurant in Highfield Road in Fulham run by Nick Clarke. It had been formed in 1971 by Members coming together to vent their concerns that Ted Heath was becoming too right-wing. Members of Nick's Diner have always been on the One Nation or some would say left wing of the Tory Party, with a strong pro-EU bias. Indeed I suspect that to some of my Conservative colleagues, members of Nick's Diner were scarcely Tories at all. We met usually fortnightly and sometimes had a guest to talk to us. It was to come and dine with Nick's Diner that Harold Macmillan made his first visit to the House of Commons for an event after his retirement as Prime Minister. In the late 1970s, not long before she became Prime Minister, Margaret Thatcher came to a dinner. As a result of the questions and comments which were put to her during and after the dinner, she was heard to say after leaving that she 'never wanted to have anything to do with that lot again'! But of course she did. Some like Tom King were in her Cabinet. A few, like Norman Lamont, moved from left to right across the range of views in the Party, with beneficial effect on their careers. Several others she made junior ministers. Ian Gow, when Margaret's PPS, created the description 'one of us' to identify the Prime Minister's strongest and most uncritical supporters. No members of Nick's Diner would qualify for that accolade. I was further contaminated by my close association with Michael Heseltine. However, my relative few discussions with Margaret were always cordial and she eventually promoted me to Minister for Trade, a senior, mid-ranking job.

The One Nation Dining Group was more long-established, mainstream, but still left-leaning and with a pro-EU bias. It was not long before I was invited to join that group, later succeeding Ken Clarke as Hon. Treasurer. The One Nation Group was always threatening to produce papers on various subjects but somehow never seemed to quite get round to doing the necessary work. It did, however, have very convivial dinners on a regular basis in the House.

Later I joined a more short-lived, but perhaps more distinguished, dining club, the Economic Dining Group. This had been formed by Nick Ridley and Jock Bruce-Gardyne and at one time had Enoch Powell as a member before he had to resign when he left the Tory Party. Membership was restricted to twelve and most members were strong believers in the control of the money supply being the key to the control of inflation. Unlike the other two clubs, the EDG met monthly to dine in a member's home. I therefore suspect it was my ability to provide a good venue, as well as a good dinner, which got me elected, because I was never a believer in the control of the money supply being the answer to inflation. It is fair to say that I wasn't the only one in that position, and certainly Ken Baker shared my views on that subject. The interesting point is that I was elected to the club at the same time as Margaret Thatcher. The group continued to meet after Margaret had become Prime Minister. She was no longer a member, but her PPS, John Stanley, became a member. Other members included Peter Rees, Cecil Parkinson, John Biffen and Peter Hordern. The discussions at our meetings focused on economic matters but we seldom reached a clear position, which is perhaps evidence of the truth of the old joke that if all the economists in the world were laid end to end, they wouldn't reach a conclusion.

Some of my constituents were surprised when I told them that there were several Christian groups and activities in the House. At various times, I took part in Bible study and through the All Party Christian Fellowship, a course on inspiring our prayer life. There was a monthly Anglican Communion Service at St Margaret's Church; I believe Roman Catholics and Methodists also had services and meetings. Every Parliamentary day starts with prayers led by the Speaker's chaplain. The format was the same every day and included the traditional prayer from the 1662 Prayer Book which starts 'Prevent us O Lord in all our doings'. This uses the archaic meaning of 'Prevent' meaning 'Guide'. I suspect there are many outside Parliament who would prefer the modern meaning. Some MPs were very keen on all-Party activities which happened away from Westminster.

The two organisations which send delegations overseas were very popular. Being chosen as a member of a delegation was a much sought-after position. It helped to be chosen to take part in a delegation if a Member had been active in receiving delegations which came to the UK. One of the organisations was the Commonwealth Parliamentary Association, the other was the Inter-Parliamentary Union. Sometimes the delegates on one of these overseas trips were even able to take their spouses. I was not tempted to become a member of any delegation until the last few months of my Parliamentary career, when I thought that as I had never been on one, I should perhaps ask to go to somewhere I would not otherwise be likely to visit. There was a delegation going to Iceland and I put my name down to join. I was invited to lead it; it proved to be a relaxing and enjoyable trip, the only problem being that my luggage failed to arrive with me and since our first engagement was to visit the President and have an official photograph taken, I was not looking my best in the casual clothes in which I had travelled.

I also went on one Commonwealth Parliamentary Association visit. It was to the AGM, which was always arranged in an attractive location. During my year in the Foreign Office, I was tasked with leading the United Kingdom delegation to the annual meeting which, that year, was taking place in Barbados. This was a relaxed and enjoyable trip except for the one session when apartheid and the situation in South Africa was debated. My role was to sit and be subjected to a series of verbal assaults from other delegates, all of whom would invariably be entirely friendly with me both before and after that particular session. After everybody had spoken, criticising the British attitude, I recall that I had to defend it, something which I did without any great enthusiasm but I hope covering up my reservations.

As well as all-Party activities, there were Party-based groups. I soon found myself a member of several of these. Another aspect of Parliamentary life in the late 1970s and 1980s was sporting activities conducted on an all-Party basis. The long-established Parliamentary cricket team had Nick Scott as a star batsman; the sporting group that I got involved in was the tennis team, which was drawn from both the Commons and the Lords. This had been in existence for some considerable time before I became an MP and had an annual match against the French Parliament as well as a number of matches against London clubs. I was told that the Parliamentary contest between Britain and France used to be sponsored by the Casino at Deauville until that unfortunately went bankrupt. By the time I became an MP, that match had to be funded by the players on the hosting side. I was also told that the French nearly always won. They had several special weapons to help them, the most obvious being the membership in their team of Bernard Destremau, who had been a member of the French Davis Cup team and I was told had even reached the semi-final of the doubles at Wimbledon. I was also told that he was the French equivalent of Ilie Nastase, being prepared to argue about a line call even when a set, 4–1 and 30 love up. The second secret weapon for the French was not so secret. It was that when we played in France, we played on clay, a surface with which most of us were unfamiliar. The third weapon they had was to insist that, when the match was played in France, a number of singles were included. The Parliamentary tennis team in Britain only ever played doubles. I played several times for the Parliamentary team against France, always unsuccessfully except on an occasion when the match was in England and I was in charge of the catering. Seeing that Monsieur Taittinger was a member of the French team – he was a senior senator at the time – I persuaded the agents for Taittinger in England to provide us with a suitable quantity of their excellent champagne. We were fortified by their wine and helped by the fact that Destremau, who arrived only just before the match was due to start and had not been present at the dinner the night before, found that he had been partnered with their weakest player. It was a logical combination. He, however, took umbrage and refused to take any ball that wasn't on his side of the court. He consequently lost two of his three matches and the British were victorious.

Another international sporting encounter which had a long history and continued for a long time after I had retired was the competition between the British Parliamentarians and the Swiss Parliamentarians on the ski slopes of Davos. A surprising aspect of this encounter had been that, at the time, it was usually won by the British. The reason advanced for this was that most Swiss Parliamentarians were elderly and came from lowland towns. When the Swiss started to elect not just younger males, but also females, possibly as a consequence of eventually allowing women the vote, the situation reversed. On one of the two occasions when I took part, one of the Swiss Parliamentarians was a lady who had been a ski guide. She was not unexpectedly a very great deal better and faster than our best competitors, who were the young Winston Churchill and John Hannam, who was also the captain of our tennis side. On the first occasion I went, we took our children and, on the second occasion, Susie's parents came with us. It was on the first occasion that I had my best result by going fairly slowly in the downhill slalom race to try to avoid falling. I was, I think, the second fastest to John Hannam of our team, because so many of the others had had a fall or missed a gate. Whereas in proper ski races the gap between competitors is counted in tens or hundredths of a second, in the Anglo-Swiss competition competitors were sometimes tens of seconds slower than others. But it was all great fun and carried out in the best of spirits, the British side being encouraged by the fact that they had a free ski pass and free ski guides for several days during the match.

The other activity with which I was involved throughout my Parliamentary career, and occasionally even afterwards, was bridge. There was an annual match on the bridge calendar when the House of Commons played the House of Lords, raising funds for charity. This was fiercely contested and continues to this day. In the 1970s, Harold Lever was the star player for the Commons before he was elevated to the Lords. He then became the best player for their Lordships' team. He claimed, I suspect accurately, that he was never on the losing side. On one occasion, most of the House of Commons team were invited by Harold Lever to use his office for a practice session before a 10.00 p.m. vote. His office was in the corridor with offices for Cabinet ministers, next to that of Tony Benn. When the Division Bell went, Tony Benn was astonished to see emerging from Harold Lever's office five or six Tories, followed by Harold Lever. It must have confirmed his worst suspicions about Harold Lever's political views.

The Conservative Party has always had a strong social side, ranging from numerous activities in constituencies to rather grand dinners and balls in London. Hove had plenty of the former, and soon after I was elected Susie was asked to chair one of the two major fund-raising dinner dances held in London every year. It was called the Blue Ball and raised funds for Conservative agents. Susie's major innovation was to hold it in central London at the newly opened InterContinental Hyde Park, where she got a particularly good rate as the hotel was so new. Some traditionalists thought that taking the event away from Hurlingham was very unfortunate. Most who had experienced Hurlingham food in those days welcomed the change.

The leader of the Party was always the president of the Blue Ball. So Ted Heath held that position. But by the date of the dinner, the situation had changed. Margaret Thatcher had started her long reign as leader of the Party, and Ted had started his long sulk. So on the night of the ball, Susie sat next to Ted Heath and I was seated next to Margaret Thatcher. Margaret's performance was very impressive. During the course of the evening, she spoke with every table and, as far as I could see, every waiter who came into the room. Ted Heath quietly sulked, and Susie didn't get to dance with him.

11

A BAD FIVE YEARS

On 1 March 1974, I was again elected Member of Parliament for Hove. The four months since the by-election had been an extraordinary period. It had started with the declaration of a State of Emergency because of the go-slow in the coal-mining industry, the 'three day week'. This in turn had led to endless discussions both within Parliament and in the media as to whether or not there should be a General Election. It had eventually been called and the unexpected result had been the emergence of a minority Labour Government.

The next six months was spent waiting for a second General Election to be called. That duly happened and Labour were again the largest Party, but with an overall majority of only three. As a new boy, I had not realised the extent to which Ted Heath was unpopular with various sections of the Party. There were some who were disappointed at not having been offered ministerial office and a few even more upset at having been deprived of it. The only surprise to many members of the Party was that the challenger who emerged was Margaret Thatcher. Some who might have stood did not do so in the first round because of loyalty to Ted Heath. However, when Ted was beaten in the first round, a few, such as Willie Whitelaw, did put their names forward for the second round when Ted had withdrawn. In the first round, I voted for Ted Heath and in the second round, for Willie Whitelaw, thus starting a series of votes in Tory leadership elections when I did not put my cross against the winning candidate.

1975 brought yet another election campaign. Harold Wilson as Prime Minister was leading a Party which was deeply divided on the issue of membership of the European Union. His solution was to put the issue to a referendum, a decision which has repercussions even as I write. I believe that referendums have no place in a genuine Parliamentary democracy. The main objection is that though the vote is meant to be on a single issue, it is impossible to ensure that the electorate vote on that issue rather than to show their general view of the Government of the day, or some other problem. A second set of objections relates to decisions as to what proportion of the electorate voting should be required to decide the issue, and what majority would be held to be enough. The third objection, which might be regarded by some as being anti-democratic, is that the issue being put to the electorate may be of some complexity and have implications and consequences which are hard to get over or explain. Be that as it may, Harold Wilson committed the country to the first referendum on whether to remain a member of the European Union.

The campaign that followed was fought on an all-Party basis; there was a Britain-in-Europe campaign which oversaw a local campaign in each area. I was working on behalf of the Brighton and Hove in-Europe campaign. The committee which headed our local campaign was not led by politicians, but by representatives of the local CBI, TUC, Vice-Chancellor of the University, chairman of the Football Club and other local luminaries. The campaign material was not issued by any political Party but rather by the Brighton and Hove in-Europe campaign. All the meetings were held on behalf of the campaign and had speakers from the Conservative, Labour and Liberal Parties.

There was a meeting in Brighton which drew an attendance of several hundred. The big attraction was Harold Macmillan, who came to his son-in-law, Julian Amery's, constituency to make one of his rare speeches after his retirement as Prime Minister. Afterwards there was a supper at which I was seated next to the great man. He passed on to me the advice on how to speak in the House of Commons which he had received from Lloyd George. The most important point was that a back-bencher should only make one point in his speeches in the House, repeating it in different ways. In his book *The Past Masters,* Macmillan records Lloyd George giving him the advice after his maiden speech in 1924.

The meeting in Hove attracted a brief mention in *The Times*, not because of its importance or bearing on the result, but because it was the only time that my father and I appeared on the same platform speaking for the same cause. My father represented the Labour-in-Europe campaign, and I the Conservative equivalent. I have no doubt that if the referendum campaign in 2016 had been fought on the same three-Party basis, the result would have been very different. The result in 1975 was more than 2 to 1 in favour of remaining in the EU: 67.23% voted Yes, against 32.77% who voted No.

The most interesting and politically significant activity in which I got involved in my first five years was as a member of the Select Committee on a Wealth Tax. This was a high-profile committee and, as a new boy, I was surprised to be chosen. I have little doubt that it was thought that

I was regarded as someone most likely to be impacted by the tax, and I did have contacts in the art world. In their first 1974 Manifesto, Labour had firmly committed themselves to such a tax: 'We shall introduce an annual Wealth Tax on the rich.' The second 1974 Manifesto was a little less positive; it included the statement, 'The Government has published plans for … beginning with the redistribution of wealth by new taxation on the better off.' This equivocation may have reflected the fact that, as is now shown by recently published documents, the Treasury were already beginning to have doubts. A key player in this was Harold Lever, who was Harold Wilson's adviser on financial matters. He had written to Harold Wilson as early as 7 June, between the two General Elections, raising the risk of a serious crisis of confidence in the business world if a Green Paper on the Wealth Tax made a crucial impact. Later he wrote to say that the Green Paper is 'political dynamite'.

As a result of Harold Lever's views and the doubts in the Treasury, it was decided to proceed by way of appointing a Select Committee. The committee would be charged with considering not whether there should be a Wealth Tax, but how best to construct such a tax. This was announced in the Queen's Speech on 29 October 1974, which included the statement, 'My Ministers will propose the establishment of a Select Committee to examine the form which a Wealth Tax should take.' The committee was duly appointed in December that year. The narrow Labour Parliamentary majority meant that the composition was eleven Labour members, nine Conservatives and one Liberal. The most revealing aspect of the membership is how many of the Labour members were on the moderate wing of the Party, several later defecting to the Tories or SDP. They included John Horam, later to become a Conservative MP, and Colin Phipps and John Roper, both later to become SDP members. Brian Walden, well known for his moderate and intelligent views, was also an initial member.

It seems to me that the hand of Harold Lever and the influence of the Whips' Office, with perhaps in the background the Treasury, had already decided that the committee's findings would not promote the introduction of a Wealth Tax, but might actually be an obstacle to the tax.

As the Treasury had feared, deliberations of the committee featured formidable attacks on the very idea. Academics who thought that a Wealth Tax was not the best way to tax wealth and a whole range of lobbyists who opposed it, either in principle, or as it would impact the assets they represented, dominated the discussion and the presentation of evidence. Even the committee's expert adviser, Professor Willis, had been one of the authors of a paper critical of the idea of an annual Wealth Tax. At the end of their deliberations, the committee produced five draft reports, each of which was put to a vote.

If you want to arrange for a member of a Select Committee to be unavailable on a critical occasion, one way to do so is for that member to be absent on an all-Party delegation. Colin Phipps went on a delegation to the Falkland Islands. You couldn't find a better place to make recall to take part in the voting on the draft reports less possible. In the absence of Colin Phipps, there was no longer a Labour majority on the committee. All five reports were voted down. The first to be put to the vote was from the far Left, the 'take it all away at once' report. I was sitting next to Neville Sandelson, by then a member of the committee and another who later defected to the SDP and, incidentally, Harold Lever's nephew. When the first and most extreme draft was put to the vote, Neville raised his arm in favour. I whispered to him, 'Neville, what are you doing?' He replied, 'Don't worry, Tim, it won't be approved and my vote will look good with my constituents.' He was right about the lack of approval, but I can't vouch for the reaction of his constituents. Since they later ejected him and replaced him with a Conservative, I have some doubts about his analysis.

The lack of an agreed report from the Select Committee was a major contribution to the whole idea being kicked far into the long grass in 1975. The idea of a Wealth Tax is still occasionally mentioned and it is worthwhile recording some of the objections which were raised during the course of the committee proceedings. One, which civil servants found particularly vexatious, was whether pension rights should be included in an assessment of an individual's wealth. At a time of high inflation, civil servants' pensions, which were inflation-proofed, were extremely valuable and in 1975, for a senior civil servant, they were worth over a million pounds, equivalent to over £7.5 million now.

The committee identified many problems for small businesses and farms, all of which tended to be under-capitalised and would find it extremely difficult to raise the money to pay an annual tax. Even if they were able to do so, it would reduce their ability to invest to improve productivity and output.

The arts lobby was very vocal and strong in its objections. It argued that a Wealth Tax would mean that much of Britain's precious arts heritage would be sold and end up driven overseas. After all, if a painting was going to be taxed every year, even at only 1% of its market value, when it produced no income, it became a very expensive asset to hold. At the end it seemed that in view of the difficulties of valuing and taxing personal possessions or racehorses, not to mention country houses, the only thing that could safely and easily be taxed was stocks and shares, including of course Government bonds. It was clear that they were a very unreliable indicator of someone's overall wealth.

I played a minor part in the deliberations of the committee and its sub-committees but I was able to see at first hand the brilliance of Peter Rees, using his skills as a QC to interrogate witnesses. There was also the early emergence of Nigel Lawson, nearly as skilful an examiner of witnesses. The final acknowledgement that the idea was no longer part of Labour's programme came in a written answer by Denis Healey, then Chancellor of the Exchequer, in November 1976 when he stated that 'the Government had decided that they should not introduce a Wealth Tax in the life of this Parliament'. He went on, rather optimistically, to say that the tax would continue to be an important part of their programme.

Committees of various sorts play an important part in the work of a back-bench Member. During the five opposition years, I was a member of Standing Committees considering various pieces of legislation. These included the Community Land Act, with the extraordinary hours to which I have already referred. There was also a Bill on rent controls which involved lengthy sittings and a degree of 'filibustering', which provided me with good practise in making lengthy speeches.

It is strange to reflect now that a lot of Parliamentary time was spent discussing primary and secondary legislation concerned with the control or regulation of prices and wages. Shirley Williams was Secretary of State for Prices and Consumer Protection, and I found myself on the back-benches of a committee debating the Prices Bill. There was a proposal to subsidise the price of bread. I tried, from my back-bench position, to explain to Shirley Williams that when there was a marginal tax of 98%, which is the rate that I was personally paying at the time, a subsidy of say 2p on the price of a loaf would save those who paid no tax 2p. However, if you were a higher rate taxpayer, you were saved £1. This therefore did not seem a very sensible use of the taxpayers' money, as the biggest beneficiaries would be the richest people. This idea seemed too complicated for Shirley to understand. Even with a marginal tax rate of only 45%, it is of course still true that subsidies on basic commodities or services which nearly everybody uses are of most value to those who pay the highest rate of tax.

On another occasion, we had reached the Report Stage of a Bill concerned, among other things, with price controls. It had been decided that in order to show the strength of our objection to the Bill, we would keep the Report Stage going all night. As it was a Report Stage on the floor of the House, unlike the Committee Stage of a Bill, all Members of the House were able to make a contribution to proceedings. Even so, the Whips often found it quite difficult by 5 o'clock in the morning to find enough Members who were awake and sober enough to make a speech to keep the debate going. I had been playing bridge but decided about 5 o'clock that it was time I did something more useful, and saw that there was an amendment down for debate in the name of a Scottish Nationalist relating to controls on the price of food, so I rose to make my contribution. One of my colleagues later told me that he thought, 'I will go and have my breakfast now,' and he went out and came back about forty minutes later to hear me say, 'And secondly.' Some of my colleagues would say that that hour's speech was the most useful speech I made in my entire Parliamentary career. I was able to take up quite a lot of time on the subject of the difference between back and streaky bacon! They vary greatly in price, but being adjacent to each other on the carcass, it is sometimes true, not of course in Sainsbury's, that something being sold as 'back' would have a little bit of streaky attached to it. This would clearly distort the price comparison. One of the incidental pleasures of a reasonably successful filibustering speech is the annoyance it causes to the Government. More time is taken up when the Government from the front bench or indeed anyone in the House tries to complain that the speech being made is out of order. I am glad to say that in spite of several efforts, my speech was found by the Deputy Speaker always to be entirely in order.

As well as the Standing and Select Committees, there is another type of committee with which a back-bencher can become involved. These are the Party committees covering each of the Government departments. When in opposition, these do have some input into the process of deciding on the Party's attitude to Government proposals and on policies that might be brought forward in a Manifesto. Each of the Committees is headed by the Shadow Secretary of State, but the rest of the officers are elected by all Conservative back-bench Members. I worked my way up from joint Secretary to joint Deputy Chairman of the Environment Back-bench Committee. In the process, I became aware for the first time of the extent to which different wings of the Party operated as pressure groups.

Basically, rather hidden figures prepared a list of preferred candidates for these positions on behalf of the right wing and the left wing of the Party. I became an accepted candidate on the left-wing list, and the only occasion I lost was when I had not yet joined the left-wing list and Michael Latham, who was on the list, was my opponent. Michael was one of a number of very able back-bench Members on the left of the Party who never got made a minister and, in due course, retired from Parliament and pursued a successful career elsewhere.

In the mid-1970s, a new organisation came into being, bringing together young Tories, mostly undergraduates or recently graduated, with progressive social views – the 'Tory Reform Group' or TRG. Peter Walker was the leading Parliamentary supporter, and I was involved from the beginning as a major financial backer. I continued my financial support for the TRG throughout my Parliamentary career, and indeed for some time afterwards. The group has had its ups and downs, but on the whole it has flourished, often as the only Conservative organisation that undergraduates regard as respectable to join. I am glad to say it continues to attract members and has branches in a number of universities.

One feature of the 'Bad Five Years' was the gradual increase in the number of Conservatives in prominent positions, including in the universities, where unusually it became quite acceptable to declare support for the Tory Party. This change from the norm in academia reflected the dismal performance of the British economy during the 1970s. It was a decade marked by high inflation and endless strikes which successive Governments tried to counter in part with controls on everything to do with prices and wages. These efforts were frequently frustrated by militant trade unions seeking to break whatever limit had been set. At one time, it was declared that differentials in pay had to be maintained; only anomalies could be corrected. Some wag came up with an answer to the question as to what was the difference between a differential and an anomaly. It was, he explained, 'If I am paid more than you, that is a differential. If you are paid more than me, that is an anomaly.'

The problems of the economy led at one moment for Britain to have to seek a loan from the IMF. Denis Healey, who was the Chancellor of the Exchequer throughout, introduced no less than ten budgets; two a year almost seemed to be the norm. Growing union militancy led to the winter of 1978/79 being blighted by massive and numerous strikes, many in the public services. It became known as the 'winter of discontent'. It was particularly appropriate that when the vote of confidence which brought down the Callaghan Government came on 28 March 1979, the catering staff at the House of Commons were on strike. On the rare occasion when every single Member of the Commons needed to be present, there was no food available to keep them going until the 10.00 p.m. vote.

The excitement of the occasion was greatly increased by uncertainty as to the outcome. There was a republican Member from Northern Ireland who was very seldom to be seen at the Palace of Westminster. It is said that Labour despatched a Whip to bring him over, as he was felt to be almost certain to support the Government. However, having come to the Chamber, and listened to some powerful speeches from other Northern Ireland Members complaining about what the Government had done, he abstained. When asked why he had come over to England and not voted, he said he had decided to 'abstain in person'. There were also doubts about the health of one or two other Members, one of whom sadly died only a few days after the vote and did not come although he had been expected to be able to take part. As a result, neither Party was sure as to the result. When a Labour teller appeared in the Chamber looking very cheerful, the Conservative side thought the vote was tied, which would mean that the Speaker would, by tradition, cast his vote for the Government, so that the issue could be considered again on another occasion. Then Tony Berry appeared carrying the piece of paper which the teller from the winning side has, to announce the result. The Conservative side had won by one vote; it was party time. Living in Great College Street, nearer to the House than any other Member, I had taken the precaution of putting several bottles of Pol Roger champagne in the fridge, Pol Roger being Winston Churchill's favourite champagne. After the vote, we gave an impromptu celebration party. It was reported, I think in the *Evening Standard* by a journalist who had been brought to the party by Norman Lamont on the understanding that the event was entirely off the record, as being the second best on the night, beaten only by that given by Margaret herself.

In 1979, as a senior member of the back-bench Environment Committee, I was shown a draft of the Manifesto covering the Environment Department. This covered very important areas like housing and local government. I commented that there was no mention at all about what we now call the environment, Green issues. I was asked to write something. With help from Tony Hutt from the Research Department, I produced a few sentences which formed the basis of what was eventually included. It was only ten lines, when even the arts got thirteen. It is interesting to

Meeting with President Reagan, 1982. The annual prayer breakfast
in Washington DC. I was one of the two British MPs invited
(photo © Rudolph Vetter, Alexandria, Virginia, USA)

compare those ten lines with the extensive coverage of the subject in more recent Manifestos.

In the 1970s, a major Christian event in Washington was the Annual National Prayer Breakfast. It had been started by Billy Graham and President Eisenhower. Normally two Members of the British Parliament were invited to attend, and one year Susie and I went with Bill Benyon and his wife, Elizabeth. It was a very impressive event, some 2,000 people enjoying an excellent breakfast and an inspiring address by Billy Graham. Beforehand, I was privileged to be in the line-up with some twenty-five others to be introduced to the President, Ronald Reagan, and the Vice President, George Bush, and their wives. The Vice President and his wife went along the line shaking hands with everyone, and then it was the turn of the President. He was brilliant, leaving each of us in the line believing that he was there simply to have a few words with whoever he was talking to. Nancy was equally impressive. I was also amused to hear the words as Mr President introduced the President of Vanuatu, who must have been the President of one of the smallest and least important countries in the world meeting his namesake at the opposite end of the spectrum.

12

A PARLIAMENTARY PRIVATE SECRETARY

I got a call from Michael Heseltine with an invitation to become his Parliamentary Private Secretary (PPS), only a day or two after the completion of the appointments to Margaret Thatcher's first Government. He had been made Secretary of State for the Environment. I jumped at the opportunity to join a politician I so much admired in the department with which I was most familiar, knowing that I was otherwise going to continue as a back-bencher. He invited me to come to a meeting of his ministerial team which was to take place in the Department of the Environment in Marsham Street the next day. When I arrived, I found myself going up in the lift with one of his junior ministers and his Permanent Secretary, Sir John Garlick, who was very puzzled as to what I was doing there. What he probably knew and Michael had either ignored or was not aware of, was that the appointment of a PPS was subject to the approval of the Whips' Office and, in theory, Number 10. I think Michael Jopling, the new Chief Whip, was not best pleased to hear that Michael had already appointed his PPS and it was nearly a week before approval, maybe even reluctant approval, came through from the Whips' Office. In the meanwhile, in the rush of activity in the first days of Government, I even found myself helping out on the drafting of Michael's first speech from the front bench when he was away at a Cabinet meeting.

During the next four years, I saw at first hand some of the qualities which enabled Michael Heseltine to be such a successful Secretary of State. First, he attracted the loyalty and support of his personal staff. Somebody once said if he asked them to jump out of a window, they probably would have done so. Secondly, not only was he particularly good at taking decisions but if something occurred, which was not what he would have wished, he would move on and not let the setback worry him. Thirdly, he had a very good technique with his red boxes: he did as many as he felt his weekend programme allowed. So it was not infrequent that if given four boxes, he would come back and tell his very competent and understanding Private Secretary, David Edmonds, that he had done two. David somehow managed to overcome any problems this created. Finally, he was always looking to get things done and was prepared to consider new and original ways of achieving an objective. A good example was his plan for Urban Development Corporations: independent bodies that could take over some of the urban land in very depressed areas and, using their own funds, get it developed, providing employment and a new impetus to activity and employment in the surrounding area. The first two UDCs, both very successful, were in East London and Merseyside. The legacy in East London includes London City Airport and the Canary Wharf Development. In Merseyside, there is the Albert Dock Development.

Parliamentary Private Secretaries are frequently referred to as 'bag carriers'. That was one task which I was not required to carry out, but there were routine activities which were expected to be done by a PPS as the eyes and ears of his or her Secretary of State. The first was attendance at meetings of back-bench committees which were relevant to his department. This was essential, particularly for the PPS of a Secretary of State. Throughout my four enjoyable years as Michael's PPS, there was one role which I have to admit that I did not fulfil very effectively. I was frequently urged by the Whips' Office and indeed others to try to get Michael to spend more time socialising in the House, in the Smoking Room or in the Tea Room. He did not find this an attractive activity, regarding it as somewhat of a waste of time. So there were only a very few occasions when I succeeded in persuading him to make an appearance for a meal or a drink.

The second main role is to sit on the second bench behind your Minister during Questions and debates so that you can fetch or take any messages to the civil servants who are in their place at the end of the Chamber. The third role is to assist in any Party activities that the Minister gets involved in. This aspect of the PPS's work can be very variable. On several occasions, I found myself involved with what might be called Special Operations.

In the summer of 1981, which was long and hot, there was rioting in some city centres. The troubles began in Brixton over Easter. By July the rioting was more widespread, and occurred in south London, in Manchester, Birmingham, Preston, Wolverhampton and Hull and, to a lesser extent, in other cities around the country. But among the very worst was that which took place over a week or more in Toxteth, an area of Liverpool. Michael had taken a particular interest in Liverpool and he asked Mrs Thatcher to allow him to spend some two or three weeks away from his day-to-day departmental duties while he went there, assessed the problem and produced some proposals to alleviate the situation. I was fortunate that Michael decided he wanted me, as his PPS, to be with him during his time in Liverpool. We were joined by Tim Raison, Minister of State at the Home Office, because of his responsibility for the police. So for two weeks I was not only able, I hope, to help Michael in his work, but also myself learnt an enormous amount about the nature of the problems in the poorer areas of a northern city.

Not the least of these problems was the appalling inefficiency in the management of the mass of local-authority-owned housing. The council house tenants mostly had an intense dislike for what they called the 'Corpi', the Liverpool Corporation, their landlord. They had good reason for this because of the total inadequacy which any repair, minor or major, was dealt with and the way in which unoccupied premises were allowed to deteriorate, very often causing further damage to neighbouring premises or, if a flat, to apartments adjoining or below.

The next and very worrying lesson I learnt was that there was no doubt that the police were deeply racist. A black lady whose shop had been burnt in the riots said that that incident had upset her less than what had happened to her son. He had got off the bus to walk a few hundred yards to his mother's home in a good suburb of Liverpool when a police car drove up alongside him. A policeman got out, shoved him up against the wall and said words to the effect, 'What are you doing here, you don't belong here, you should be back in Liverpool 8.' I recall sitting and chatting with policemen in the main police station over a snack when they more or less admitted, and were only slightly embarrassed, that, on the whole, yes, they were racist.

During his time in Liverpool, Michael Heseltine hit upon the idea of getting City dignitaries and captains of industry to come up to Liverpool to see at first hand the appalling conditions in the housing estates and the run-down appearance of the once great commercial heart of the city. The challenge was to persuade enough people of sufficient standing to join the tour. I was able to play a significant role in helping this because I personally knew some of the key players we wanted to attract. I was able to speak to Robin Leigh-Pemberton, later Baron Kingsdown of Pemberton, then chairman of the NatWest, to persuade him to come. One of his brothers had shared a flat with my eldest brother, and his younger brother was a friend and contemporary. His name proved particularly valuable in attracting other City people and indeed leaders of industry to join in, and I was able to help in getting several of those on board for the visit. It proved to be not just an outstanding public relations coup, but extraordinarily enlightening for those who came on the coaches, most of whom had never been to and had no idea of the conditions in a city like Liverpool.

The most important planning applications, and those which are particularly contentious, usually end up on the Secretary of State's desk. It would not be practical for the Secretary of State himself to go and look at the property or place where the issue had arisen; that would arouse too much interest and controversy. So on two occasions, Michael asked me to go and look at something and to tell him what the real situation was. My experience with construction at JS was useful in this role. The first involved the Grange, owned by the Baring family, a derelict William Wilkins designed house now used for opera. There was an application to demolish the badly damaged shell, which it was suggested was crumbling away and not capable of restoration. As the site was open and not far away from Basingstoke, I was able to go there and look around the building and see that it was structurally reasonably sound. Armed with that additional information, Michael was able to refuse the demolition, and many opera-goers have benefited since. Another similar case was the Billingsgate Fish Market Building, which was alleged to be bound to collapse if the refrigeration was turned off and the frozen foundations warmed up. Demolition was again being requested but, after a rather chilly inspection, the view I reported back to Michael was that the building was sound; I am happy to say that he refused demolition and it, too, has been in beneficial use ever since.

Politically the most interesting special operation in which I was involved also involved Keith Hampson and Tony Nelson, PPSs respectively to Tom King, Minister of Local Government, and John Stanley, Minister of Housing. The level of increase in rates and the allocation of the Rate Support Grant between local authorities was proving unusually controversial. The pressure was building to find a replacement system for the much disliked local rates. So, the three PPSs in the Department of the Environment were asked to take a survey of all Conservative Members of Parliament to obtain their views as to whether the present system should be replaced and, if so, by what. We carried out the survey and reached the not unsurprising conclusion that there was an overwhelming majority in favour of replacing the existing system of council taxes, and an equally large majority against any of the alternative systems that had been suggested, which included a local income tax, a Poll Tax and a Sales Tax. Not much later, Margaret Thatcher became convinced that the Poll Tax was the answer, with the well-known consequences.

There was a European Conference in Berlin of such little importance that no Environment Minister was prepared, or perhaps able because of other commitments, to attend. It was eventually decided that since the Government should have a representative present, I would be sent to make the brief and uninteresting contribution that was required of us. So under the label of Parliamentary Private Secretary to the Secretary of State for the Environment, I attended my first international meeting on behalf of the Government. I was told that some of those attending assumed that I must be particularly important because of the length of the description of my office.

I continued as Michael's PPS when he was made Secretary of State for Defence in January 1983. I was initially of very little use to him because I had broken my leg skiing over the Christmas recess. This meant that I experienced at first hand the strange ceremony of being 'nodded through'. This happens when an MP is within the area of the Palace of Westminster but is physically unable to get to and proceed through the Division Lobby. If the physical incapacity is accepted by the Opposition Whips, then the last Whip through the lobby, having given his name to the clerk, then gives the name of the Member to be 'nodded through', who is then duly recorded as having voted for whichever side was involved. There have even been occasions when a Member has been in an ambulance in New Palace Yard and, after either the Government or the Opposition Whip has opened the door to see that the Member is actually alive, if so he can then be 'nodded through'. There was a slight problem in my case. It wasn't doubted that on crutches I would not be able to reach the Division Lobby in time. What was unusual was that my Parliamentary office was in Dean's Yard, not really within the confines of the Palace of Westminster but making it even more impossible for me to get from my office to a Division Lobby within the statutory period of eight minutes after the Division Bell had been rung.

When I had recovered my mobility, I did do one thing which was of unusual interest. Michael suggested that I attend a NATO Conference in Belgium where various presentations were being made about the capabilities and equipment of Soviet Forces. One of the presentations concerned a new Russian warship – I think it was a 'Kiev' class cruiser – and the presentation was made to all the NATO representatives present in the auditorium. I was sitting behind two American Air Force generals and, when the lights went up after the presentation, I heard one turn to the other and say, 'Well, I don't know but they sure make dandy targets.' Luckily we have never had to find out whether he was accurate in his assessment. But I do worry that an enemy might take the same view about our new aircraft carriers.

13

INDECENT DISPLAYS
(CONTROL) ACT

At the beginning of every session of Parliament, there is a ballot which is of great interest to most back-bench Members. In 1981 I entered my name, as I had every year since 1974, and thought no more about it. So I was very surprised to learn a week or so later that not only was I one of the twenty lucky Members whose names had been selected as those who would be allowed to introduce a Private Member's Bill in the 1981 Session, but I was Number One, the first name to come out of the ballot box. Like nearly all other MPs, I had given no thought to what I might do if I was one of the lucky twenty, let alone number one.

If you come first in the ballot, you have two choices: either you can bring forward a Bill which does not have much chance, if any, of getting on to the Statute Book. But by bringing it forward, you can provide an opportunity for the subject to be fully debated and, hopefully, given publicity. The second alternative is to propose a Bill which is worthwhile, but which is not so controversial that it is likely to be opposed by a number of Members who could ensure that at one stage or other of the proceedings, it would run out of time.

After my success in the ballot, I was inundated with suggestions of all sorts and from all quarters as to Bills I might introduce. One that would definitely have fallen into the first category was very strongly recommended to me. This was to introduce a Bill to reduce the time limit for legal abortions. There was a very strong argument that the existing twenty-four-week limit was far too long. However, it was very clear to me that the subject was extremely controversial. Although I agreed strongly with the view that the twenty-four-week limit should be substantially reduced, it became apparent that any effort to do so would, at some stage or other, be frustrated by a dedicated band of opponents who would wish to ensure there was no change to the existing abortion law.

So my attention turned to opportunities in the second category, worthwhile Bills which did stand a chance of getting on to the statute book. The very first Bill that came before Parliament after I was elected was the

Cinematograph and Indecent Displays Bill, presented on 13 November 1973; it received an unopposed second reading but then ran out of time in committee when the General Election was called in February 1974. The second part of this Bill sought to bring under control the increasingly obscene material which was appearing on the covers of magazines and in posters and even advertisements in full public view. The Labour Government of 1974–79 did nothing to re-introduce the Bill, although there were five Bills on the subject introduced by back-bench MPs: three Private Members' Bills and two Ten Minute Rule Bills. All were unopposed but none made any progress towards legislation. In the meantime, public displays had become ever more lewd, something of which I was made particularly aware when, on one occasion, I walked through Soho with one of our younger children and had to try to distract their gaze away from what was visible in shopfronts. So after much deliberation, I decided to re-introduce part of what had originally been a Government Bill in 1973. However, there were many who were disappointed that I had not chosen to try to do something about shortening the legal date for abortions. Nevertheless, the Bill I chose was on the whole a popular choice among Christians in the House, of all Parties.

My choice attracted quite a lot of media attention and was clearly of interest to people living in London, especially in Soho. I was asked to do several pieces for the media. On one occasion, I went into Soho with a television crew and a journalist who was clearly pretty sceptical about the whole issue. She asked where we could see material of the type to which I objected. I was able to take her into a shop where I knew that at low level, and easily visible to a child, there were magazine covers featuring, among other things, bestiality. When the journalist saw what I was talking about, her attitude completely changed and she became clearly supportive. Even more remarkable was the behaviour of the television crew on another occasion when I was in Soho, when a rather drunken and very aggressive doorman or security guard for one of the shops physically attacked the man holding the camera. He kept filming. It was suggested to me that that not only showed professionalism but actually a belief that what he was doing was really worthwhile.

Drafting the Bill, which I was to bring before the House, was not too difficult, as there had been so many previous efforts, starting with the one which the Government itself had introduced on my first evening as an MP. It also did not prove too difficult to gather together an all-Party group of sponsors whose names would appear on the Bill and to recruit quite a large number of colleagues who were prepared to be available on the first Friday for Private Members' Bills, which was 30 January, to ensure that we succeeded in getting a second reading.

The sponsors who were prepared to put their name to the Bill included, on the Conservative side, Brian Mawhinney, Christopher Murphy, who was a very energetic supporter, Robert Rhodes James, who did the wind-up on the second reading, Ivan Lawrence, a lawyer whose professional qualities it was useful to have on board, and Peggy Fenner, who was one of a number of lady Members who were enthusiastic supporters. On the Labour side, Ernest Armstrong was a keen supporter, and Ron Lewis also added his name. From the Liberals, there was Alan Beith, who had been elected in a by-election on the same day as myself and, from the Scottish Nationalists, Donald Stewart.

There were sixteen speakers in the second reading debate, all of whom were supportive with a slight question mark over the views of Dr Shirley Summerskill, the Labour Member for Halifax. She expressed some doubt as to whether the Bill was necessary at all.

Paddy Mayhew, who was Minister of State at the Home Office, spoke on behalf of the Government. He called my opening speech 'delightful, wise and temperate'. However, he was quite guarded in his remarks, ending by saying that 'if the Bill is given a Second Reading, the Government's role will be that of a friendly or even affectionate neutral'. He said he was prepared to give me as much technical assistance as he could in an attempt to advance towards an objective with which most on the Government side warmly sympathised.

Nearly all the other speakers were much more enthusiastic supporters. They included Clement Freud and, with a late intervention, David Mellor. It soon became apparent that there was no risk that there would be an effort to talk the Bill out, and Robert Rhodes James was able to wind up well before 2.30 p.m. After allowing for David Mellor coming in rather late after the wind-up, we had concluded the debate with the Bill approved and read a second time and committed to Standing Committee C by 1.00 p.m.

The Standing Committee proceedings went quite well. We only required five mornings, and there were only two divisions, in both of which Sam Silkin and Dr Summerskill were the main votes against. On one occasion, they were joined by Ivan Lawrence from the Conservative side, who was otherwise a supporter of the Bill. The first sitting of the Committee was on 11 February and exactly one month later, on 11 March, we had the fifth sitting and the Bill was successfully sent back to the House for the Report Stage.

The Report Stage is a moment of high risk to a Private Member's Bill. As with the second reading, it is necessary to have a quorum present, but for Report Stage that is important at any time because a division might be called and could be lost if there were insufficient numbers voting. Once again, I had very good support from all sides of the House, from colleagues who said they would be available on Friday, 1 May for the Report Stage debate.

Having successfully navigated the Report Stage, the Bill proceeded to the House of Lords. Lord Nugent of Guildford very ably and successfully steered the Bill through its various stages, and it was referred back to the House of Commons on 2 July with hopefully non-controversial amendments. Lord Belstead, on behalf of the Government, 'expressed his appreciation for the skilful manner in which Lord Nugent had piloted the Bill through the House of Lords', and added that, 'I am sure that not only the sponsor of the Bill, Mr Sainsbury, in another place, but the House as a whole was greatly indebted to his noble friend.'

So on 10 July, the Bill reached its last stage in the Commons, dealing with the Lords' amendments. There were three Lords' amendments to be considered. I was going to propose that all three be accepted. The first amendment was a fine example of how easy it is to prolong the debate on a Private Member's Bill so that it runs out of time. The amendment was to change the wording from 'open to view' to 'exposed to view'. I spent less than three minutes proposing that the amendment be accepted. I was followed by three colleagues, all supporters of the Bill, who spent forty minutes discussing the merits of 'exposed' as opposed to 'open'. That much time was taken up by speakers not seeking to 'filibuster' the Bill. It would have been very easy to double the amount of time if obstruction had been the motive.

The other two amendments were dealt with much more speedily. In my final remarks, I was able to thank all those who had helped during the course of proceedings in both Houses, including Ernest Armstrong, who was a sponsor of the Bill but had in the meantime become a Deputy Speaker and was in the chair for the Lords' amendments proceedings. When I said I hoped that I would not be out of order in thanking the Deputy Speaker, he responded, 'I cannot possibly rule that out of order.' At the end of the proceedings, Patrick Mayhew, speaking from the front bench, said, 'Throughout the Standing Committee, the contributions from all quarters were unfailingly constructive. That demonstrates in itself the recognition in the House that the great body of opinion from constituents have wanted the tide to turn. That is the achievement with which my Hon. Friend, the Member for Hove, will always be associated. He has persuaded Parliament to turn the tide.'

Cartoon by Michael Heath,
October 1981 (*Evening Standard*)

14

WHIPS' OFFICE

Reshuffles – the comings and goings of ministers up, down or sideways seemed to be an annual event under Margaret Thatcher. After a General Election there is more movement, and the hopes of back-benchers, particularly the PPSs, that they will be given a ministerial post are that much stronger. So I must admit to having been very disappointed that the telephone call or summons to Number 10 did not come after the landslide victory of 1987. I felt that four years as PPS to a senior Cabinet minister had earned me the opportunity for a step up.

Back at Great College Street, before the House reassembled, I decided to walk to the Tate and enjoy a little culture. En route I met Alastair Goodlad by his house in Lord North Street. We chatted and he then asked me what I was doing. I said I was on my way to the Tate and anticipated more time in the future for museum visits. He gave me a quizzical look. The reason why became clear when I returned home, to be told by Susie that the new Chief Whip, John Wakeham, had telephoned and wanted me to phone back. I had said to Susie that I did not want to be a Whip. However, not being offered the job is one thing, turning it down another; rejecting an invitation to join the Whips' Office is not exactly a promising move in a Parliamentary career. So, somewhat reluctantly, I accepted John Wakeham's invitation and for the next four years served as a Whip.

One of the first things you learn in the Whips' Office is that the Whips are a team. They work together more closely than any other part of Government. The appointment of new Whips is approved by the PM, but all the Whips collectively decide who should be offered the post. When I had stopped to chat with Alastair Goodlad, he had just come from a Whips' meeting which had decided to fill the two vacancies in the office with myself and Michael Neubert.

I later came to realise that the system was not quite as democratic as it appeared. The office was given a very strong steer by the Chief Whip as to whom he, and the PM, would find most acceptable as new Whips. It would perhaps be best described as 'guided democracy'. I learned that Michael Neubert and I were regarded as 'a left and a right'. It was essential to the working of an efficient Whips' Office that the Whips reflected, as far as possible, all significant shades of opinion in the Parliamentary Party. So Michael and I were later described as reflecting the views of the Tebbit wing and the Heseltines.

The Chief Whip has a department and commands a team of twelve other Whips. He has two main roles. The first is to be the link between the office and the information they gather, and the Prime Minister and Cabinet. The second is to play the headmaster, seeking to discourage and discipline rebels and absentees with whatever weapons he has at his disposal. He has sticks and carrots. The sticks are first to tell somebody who is missing too many votes, or voting against his Party too often, that they are unlikely to get any promotion. This, however, is not a very effective threat to those who have had ministerial roles and returned to the backbenches; or to those others who are not interested in ministerial office but want to play a maverick role from the back-benches. The second stick is to threaten to report the Member to his local Party Association. However, often the Member has more credibility with his or her Association than with the Party. He does have carrots. There is the possibility of recommendation to ministerial office. But that has the same limitations as the stick and so, very often, he has to fall back on his powers of persuasion and personal authority.

The Deputy Chief Whip's main role is organising the activities of the twelve other members of the Whips' Office. This is the only part of Government where promotion is based solely on longevity in the department. The five more junior Whips are those who have been in the office for the shortest time and are officially Assistant Whips. The five most senior Whips are Lords Commissioner of the Treasury, a splendid and historic post. Apart from the title, it made no difference to the role or indeed the pay. The title had been given to members of the Whips' Office in the nineteenth century when the work of the Government Whips was developing and becoming more full-time. Being appointed Lords Commissioner of the Treasury enabled those five Whips to draw a salary, when MPs were unpaid.

The Deputy Chief Whip and the two most senior Whips had splendid and historic titles. The Deputy Chief Whip was Treasurer of HM Household. The next most senior was Comptroller of HM Household. The next in line was Vice-Chamberlain. These titles are of huge antiquity. The Treasurer and Vice-Chamberlain date back to the reign of Edward III, and the Comptroller to that of Edward IV. I never reached those elevated levels.

During the post-war period, the Whips had usually been former service officers who had not got ambitions for ministerial office and did not expect to be making many speeches. Under John Wakeham, this tradition changed and he wished the Whips to be mostly future ministers getting useful experience, not only of how the procedures of the House of Commons worked but also about the development and implementation of departmental policies. I found myself a member of a very talented group including one future Prime Minister, John Major, four future Cabinet ministers: John Wakeham himself, Ian Lang, David Hunt and Douglas Hogg; five future Ministers of State: John Cope, Alastair Goodlad, Archie Hamilton, Tristan Garel-Jones and myself; and two future Parliamentary Under Secretaries, Donald Thompson and Michael Neubert. The only two who did not hold office outside the Whips' Office were Carol Mather, a former Colonel, and Bob Boscawen, also a former Guards Officer, both of whom had been members of the Whips' Office for some time when I joined, having previously had distinguished military careers.

Each Whip was given a geographical area and was expected to keep in particularly close touch with the Conservative MPs for that area. On occasions, when there was a contentious issue or vote in the offing, we would be expected to contact all MPs on our list for their views. Before I became a Whip myself, my area Whip had been Carol Mather. Mather's army career had included being in Special Forces in Africa and later serving as an aide to Field Marshal Montgomery. He was an old school, right-wing Conservative and, not surprisingly, we did not get on, and our few discussions were short and usually revealed that we had diametrically opposed views on the issue under discussion. After I became a Whip, Carol could not have been more kind and helpful to the 'new boy' and he never held against me what must have seemed to him some dangerously left-wing views. This, I came to understand, was a classic example of the Whips' Office working as a team, always working together to fulfil whatever was the task in hand.

The day-to-day task for the office is to ensure the smooth passage of the Government's business. Whenever the House is sitting, there is always a Whip on the Government front bench. His task is not just to keep a note of who speaks and of anything interesting said. More importantly, sometimes in liaison with the Opposition Whip, it is his job to make sure that debates progress as planned, and that as many people as possible are given time to speak and also that any procedural motions which need

The Whips' Office, 1984. *Front, left to right*: Alastair Goodlad, Carol Mather, John Wakeham, Margaret Thatcher, John Cope, Bob Boscawen, Donald Thompson. *Back, left to right*: Douglas Hogg, Archie Hamilton, Tristan Garel-Jones, David Hunt, Ian Lang, John Major, myself, Michael Neubert

to be put are put at the right time. There is also a Government Whip as a member of all Standing Committees considering Bills, who also has the same task to ensure that the committee proceedings go smoothly. This often requires persuading back-bench Members on the Government side to say as little as possible. But most importantly his task is to ensure there is a quorum present at all times. Another function of the Whips is to be present at significant meetings of back-bench committees, ready to report on anything interesting or provocative that is said. This all means that when the House is sitting, the Whips are extremely busy, but when the House rises, particularly for the summer or other recesses, Whips have little, if anything, to do. So for the first time for a very long time, during the summer recess, I found myself practically unemployed, with only minor constituency duties to perform.

In addition to having a list of Conservative Members within a geographical area with whom each Whip is expected to keep in particular contact, every Whip is allocated a Government department and is expected to attend ministerial meetings of that department when political matters are being discussed. In my four years in the Whips' Office,

I was the Whip for the Department of Trade and Industry, the Department of the Environment, the Treasury and the Foreign Office, all of which were interesting and useful experiences.

One year, I was the Pairing Whip. The system of pairing allows two Members, one on the Government side, the other from the Opposition, to agree that they will both be absent for a vote. It had been in existence in one way or another since Parties came into being, but is no longer in use. In the 1980s, it was much used, even though many Conservatives did not have a regular pair because of the very large Conservative majorities. The Pairing Whip had to keep a record of who was paired. When it was a three-line whip, pairs were not normally allowed. Because we had such a large majority when I was Pairing Whip, we operated a system called bisques. This helped Members who did not have a pair to have an evening off when the business had a two-line whip, without imperilling the Government's majority. I suspect that I was not very popular in that role, as I was cautious in allowing bisques, or indeed other forms of absence.

There was, however, a well-established tradition that if somebody came to the Pairing Whip with a reason for absence that nobody else had thought of, they should be allowed to miss a vote. In my case, Toby Jessel asked to be allowed to be absent on a three-line whip so that he could attend the world première of his brother-in-law's Ninth Symphony. I reasoned that attending the world première of one's brother-in-law's Symphony might not be sufficient reason, but a Ninth Symphony certainly was, and I allowed Toby to be absent from the vote to hear brother-in-law Andrzej Panufnik's composition.

There was one occasion when my ministerial career nearly ended before it started. The cause was Sunday trading. For some time, there had been various efforts made to liberalise the laws which restricted trading on Sundays. Such restrictions were naturally anathema to the libertarian wing of the Conservative Party, but many others supported a relaxation of the restrictions on economic grounds which I personally believed were unfounded. I had always opposed unrestricted Sunday trading and my position on that was known to John Wakeham, the Chief Whip. However, when in April 1986 a Government Bill was brought forward to deregulate Sunday trading, it was initially made clear that this would, as usual, carry a whip, probably a three-line whip. As the day of the vote drew nearer, it seemed that there was not going to be a change of mind by the Government, although it was known that a number of Tories were unhappy about this. With two days to go, I was getting ready

Richard Willson's cartoon which appeared in *The Times* in November 1993 when Sunday trading was once more an issue (British Cartoon Archive, University of Kent)

to clear my desk and say goodbye to my fellow Whips when, at the last moment, the Government relented and it was agreed that there would be a free vote. This allowed me to abstain and remain a Whip. There was a rumour that if the Government had persisted with a three-line whip, there was a Minister of State, a Parliamentary Under Secretary of State, a Whip (which was me) and several PPSs who would have resigned and it was the collective opposition of those prepared to resign which led to the Government change of mind. The Government lost the vote on the second reading, the only time that happened under Margaret Thatcher. I much regret that on that occasion I was not able to contribute to the debate, as was still the situation in 1986 when the issue came up again, because by then I was a minister.

In my view, the economic arguments for relaxing laws on Sunday trading are very weak. The consumer is not going to spend more of their budget on either food or other goods because shops are open longer. Even if they did, it would mean that they had borrowed more, which is something the Government does not want to encourage. Stores having to be open longer to do the same volume of trade actually puts up their costs, not only because of the extended hours for heating and lighting, but because they are having to employ staff over a longer period. Retailing does not become more efficient, rather it becomes less efficient if the same amount of trade has to be done over a longer period. Even without Sunday opening, most shops today are open for at least sixty hours every week.

Another argument against relaxing the law on Sunday trading was that the law as it stood gave an opportunity to smaller, often family-run shops, to do some business which might otherwise be lost to them and damage their continued viability. Since the Conservative Party claims to be very much in favour of such small businesses, it seemed to me strange that so many colleagues were pressing for legislation which would seriously damage small retailers.

The third, and most substantial argument against a change, is making Sunday like any other day. I used to say that Sundays should be for God and the family, together with the small shopkeeper. Allowing normal trade on a Sunday means not only that a large number of people will then have to work on that day and not have the opportunity to relax with other members of their family, but also many people living in and around shopping centres would find that Sunday was no longer quiet and peaceful but had become just like any other busy working day.

Every year, before the summer recess, the Whips entertained the Prime Minister to dinner. The dinner was usually at Number 10 and we were all assembled around a long table. I made it my practice to sit on the same side as Margaret Thatcher and as far away from her as possible, believing, rightly, that keeping a low profile was wise on these occasions. The 1985 dinner was remarkable for the acrimonious discussion that developed about the Government's economic policies. I was sitting next to John Major, on the other side of him from the Prime Minister. He was the Treasury Whip and had been asked to report on what backbench views were on the Government's economic policies. He reported correctly and honestly that there were considerable worries and a degree of discontent. This message was not well received by the Prime Minister, who proceeded, as she sometimes did, to attack the messenger in what I thought was a very unreasonable way. As the attacks on him got stronger and more unreasonable, he turned to me and said, 'I can't take this any more, I'm going to walk out.' I managed to persuade him not to leave, and let the affair as far as possible blow over. John recalls the consequences of this dinner in his autobiography. They led not long afterwards to Margaret promoting him to his first ministerial role. Maybe in that intervention I made my most substantial contribution to British politics and to the Conservative Party!

In 1984, the Party Conference was once again in Brighton. Susie and I were staying in our flat in Hove. At 7 a.m. on the morning of 12 October 1984, we were woken by a call from our daughter enquiring if we were all right. When we asked, 'Why shouldn't we be?' she asked if we had heard about the bomb. Shortly afterwards I got a call asking me to go down to the Conference Centre, as it was essential that Conference proceed as planned, not allowing the IRA bomb to disrupt proceedings. When I arrived at the Conference Centre, I was asked to go to the Royal Sussex County Hospital and establish a communications centre there. I was asked to keep Number 10 and Conservative Central Office informed about the condition of the most serious casualties, one of whom was our Chief Whip, John Wakeham. One of the lessons learnt was the importance of having a good communications network between the hospitals to which casualties were taken and the centre of Government. It was a very difficult and emotional day. Happily, as it progressed, the prognosis for John Wakeham's very serious injuries improved. When Colin Ingleby-Mackenzie arrived, I was relieved of the sad duty of having to tell his sister-in-law, Sarah Berry, that her husband, Tony, had been killed.

In the 1980s, it was normal for a senior Whip to be sent off during the summer recess on what we called 'Whips' Trips'. These visits were to smaller countries which did not often get visited by Foreign Office or other departmental ministers. Occasionally, they would be to an event like the inauguration of a new Head of State or Government in such a country. Whips are full members of the Government but not, of course, ministers. When on these trips, they get treated as, and called, 'ministers'. Foreign governments often find it hard to understand the role of a Whip in a fully democratic Parliament. The misunderstanding often arises because of the absence of such a role in their own country. On one occasion, when Tristan Garel-Jones was in a Spanish-speaking country for the inauguration of their new President, he tried to explain the role of a Whip, including the word 'discipline'. This excited his hosts, who assumed it was a key role in Government.

My 'Whips' trip' was to West Africa, and started in the Gambia. That gave me a first experience of the high quality of Foreign Office briefs. The first sentence of my brief on the Gambia was 'The Gambia is an unlikely country'. Geographically that is true, as it stretches several hundred miles inland from the estuary of the River Gambia. This former British colony got its strange shape from nineteenth-century efforts to stop the slave trade, which started with a fort at the mouth of the river and then required activity further and further upstream. When the areas of influence for that part of Africa were being divided between France and Britain, the French colony of Senegal was created, which entirely surrounded the Gambia, a British colony.

On the first evening of my visit, there was a reception at the High Commission after which I went out to dinner with the High Commissioner and other guests, including some doctors working at the medical research establishment there. I had, of course, been warned to be very careful about the drinking water, so I was somewhat astonished to see everyone happily drinking from jugs of water. The doctors said that the quality of the water was excellent, it was only in the dry season that you had to be a bit careful! While I survived that evening, the following evening was more difficult. We went up river to look at an aid project and I spent the night in what I was told was the only air-conditioned round thatched hut, known as a rondoval. That was fine when I went to bed, only to wake up at about 1 a.m. sweating heavily. I had not been warned that the generator which ran the air-conditioning would be switched off at midnight. So the next morning I was greatly in need of a shower, which I was able to take in another small hut – the problem was that when I opened the door, the shower was already inhabited by a dozen large frogs! I missed my shower. When I left, I was thanked for having stayed so long. I expressed surprise, as my visit had only lasted for forty-nine hours, and was told that the previous ministerial visit (also by a Whip) had only lasted forty-seven hours!

I went on to Senegal, where I was privileged to have a meeting with the President. He was an alarming sight as he emerged from his office with television lights behind him, being well over two metres tall. My third visit was to what is now Guinea-Bissau, formerly the Republic of Guinea, and from there I went on to Liberia, not long before the country dissolved into chaos and civil war. My brief required me to protest about a recent incident when a number of students had been shot for demonstrating. The Government line seemed to be that nothing had happened, or maybe a few people had fallen over a cliff when running away. This excuse sat uneasily with the presence of signs to the prayer room in every Government office I visited.

My first two years in the office were of interest in getting to know the proceedings and routines of the House, and of committees and working with the departments, in my case Environment and the DTI; most of all getting to know better many of my colleagues. During the next two years I was constantly hoping that every time a reshuffle came round, I would be moved upwards out of the office. It didn't happen. I became a Lord Commissioner of the Treasury and worked with the more important departments of the Treasury and the Foreign Office. I still felt frustrated at the absence of more responsibility and the opportunity to speak in the House or in Committee. I was particularly upset after the 1987 election, when all the Government appointments had been made and I was still without the offer of a ministerial office. The new Chief Whip, David Waddington, rang me and asked if I would carry on in the Whips' Office. When I said that I was reluctant to do so, he persuaded me that it would be very helpful if I would carry on for perhaps six months or so while he settled into his new role. After some hesitation, I agreed to do so.

15

TWO YEARS IN THE MINISTRY OF DEFENCE

So it was as a reluctant Whip that I went to Number 12 for my first Whips' meeting of the 1987 Parliament. When I arrived, David Hunt, the new Deputy Chief Whip, asked if I could stay behind at the end of the meeting as he wanted a word. I assumed that as I was now a fairly senior Whip, he wanted to talk to me about something to do with the office. During the meeting, we were all told that Archie Hamilton, who had been a junior minister at the Ministry of Defence, had been appointed Margaret Thatcher's new PPS. This appointment was greeted with much enthusiasm, as we all agreed that he would be very good at the job, as indeed it proved.

At the end of the meeting, when David Hunt came up to me and said that the Prime Minister would like to see me and would I go through to Number 10, it only took me about a second to realise that the only reason for the call must be that I had been chosen to replace Archie at the Ministry of Defence. So, unusually for a very junior appointment – indeed the last ministerial appointment of the new Government – I enjoyed a twenty-minute chat and a cup of coffee with the Prime Minister and her new PPS. When I rang my new office, I got another pleasant surprise. Not only was I addressed for the first time as 'Minister', but when I asked the office what they wanted me to do that afternoon, they asked what was I planning to do and I said I had intended to go to Wimbledon. 'Well, you should go, Minister, we haven't got anything for you here,' was the encouraging reply I received on the start of my ministerial life. When I returned from Wimbledon, another good surprise was to find that already a driver and the car allocated to me at the MoD had been transferred from Archie to myself and was available to drive Susie and me to Number 10 for a Reception for the new Government that evening. An early indication of the way the MoD differed from other departments was the fact that I had been allocated a Ford Granada – a car distinctly bigger than that normally allocated to an Under Secretary of State – the reason being that the department felt that ministers could not have smaller cars than generals and admirals, for whom they were in a sense responsible.

So it was on 25 June 1987, a fortnight after the General Election, that I took up my role as one of the five ministers in the MoD. The Cold War was still pretty cold, and the department's budget was huge, 3.9% of GDP. The excellent Secretary of State, George Younger, was assisted by Ian Stewart, Minister of State for the Armed Forces, and David Trefgarne, Minister of State for Defence Procurement, both assisted by an Under Secretary of State, Roger Freeman, for the Armed Forces and myself for Procurement. It was only six years since there had been ministers for each of the Armed Forces. During the war and in the early post-war period, there had even been Cabinet ministers for each of the Services. It was only since the 1960s that the MoD and its procurement activities covered all the Armed Forces.

I was in a department where everybody and everything seemed to be given initials. Mine were US of SDP in the MoD, Under Secretary of State for Defence Procurement in the Ministry of Defence. My particular responsibilities were for procurement for the Royal Navy. However, as David Trefgarne, the Minister of State for Defence Procurement, was in the Lords, I had to answer most questions on procurement in the Commons. I soon realised that an Under Secretary of State in the Ministry of Defence had a great deal to be said for it compared with the many other posts that Under Secretaries of State occupied. First, there was very little, if any, legislation and therefore you were not tied up for long hours in Standing Committees considering Bills. Secondly, the civil servants in the department were not only above average in efficiency but also nearly all shared an enthusiasm for the department for which they were working. Thirdly, George Younger was very happy to delegate. He was a good team leader, and was supported by an outstanding Permanent Secretary, Sir Michael Quinlan.

However, some colleagues regarded a post in the Ministry of Defence as unattractive. This was because it was a low-profile department for an Under Secretary of State. There were very few debates and therefore the Under Secretary had only a handful of opportunities during the year to speak from the front bench. Defence Questions attracted a relatively small number of participants, most of whom would be called 'defence buffs'. A lot of the time both Defence Questions and the few debates were relatively non-confrontational and therefore attracted little, if any, attention in the media. On the other hand, the job had some interesting aspects for those who liked overseas visits and, even more, for those who enjoyed activities with the Armed Forces. Ministers in the MoD had plenty of opportunities for what might be called 'boys' own adventures'. The serious point behind these expeditions was to enable ministers to see at first hand what the various Services were doing and to get a better understanding of the challenges they faced.

I had only been a minister in the department for a few weeks when I made my first expedition. I flew to Scotland and then took a helicopter to make a night, active service, landing on a Commando carrier. This involved landing on the carrier's deck with only verbal instructions and a very small infra-red light to guide us down. Safely on board, I was then subjected to an informal lecture from an admiral lasting over an hour, on the history of amphibious warfare. The Navy were very efficient at conveying the importance of the work of the Navy to new ministers.

That was a minor adventure compared with some that were to follow. There were several opportunities to fire weapons. When on a visit to Northern Ireland I went to an indoor range and fired the latest model rifle, even I found it almost impossible to miss the target. More interestingly, later on, I went with George Younger to Germany when we were faced with the decision as to which new battle tank to choose. There were three possibilities. So George and I went out on to the ranges and had the opportunity to fire a few rounds from the American tank, the Abrams, the German tank, the Leopard, and the British model, the Chieftain. Firing from a stationary tank with modern sights and range-finding equipment it was almost impossible to miss, although I believe that George did miss one of his shots. On that expedition I was accompanied by my excellent Assistant Private Secretary, Debbie Brothers. She was only about 5ft 2in and looked much younger than her thirty-odd years. However, she was able to persuade those in charge of the tanks that she should be allowed to fire a few shells herself. Apparently the rules required that live ammunition which had been issued could not be taken back off the range. Firing the latest tank guns was definitely one of the high points of her career and an enjoyable one in mine.

I paid a visit to the Hereford headquarters of the SAS. During the visit, I went to what I believe is called the 'Killing House' and took part in an exercise on rescuing kidnapped hostages. I was put in a room with a number of life-size cardboard cut-outs to represent my terrorist captors. I was blindfolded and told under no circumstances to move from where I was. After a short pause, low-intensity stun grenades were thrown into the room and in rushed members of the SAS, firing live ammunition. I was grabbed by two and hustled from the room. Afterwards, I was able to look at what had happened to my cardboard cut-out captors; each one had a small round hole in their forehead where the live ammunition had gone. It was an impressive demonstration of the capability of our special forces.

The coldest thing I have ever done in my life was to go to northern Norway, inside the Arctic Circle, to join 45 Commando Group on an annual exercise. It was February 1988 and, as was to be expected inside the Arctic Circle, night-time temperatures were down to about minus 25 degrees Celsius and the day-time temperatures lower than minus 10 degrees.

The annual exercise, which involved Norwegian Armed Forces and British and Dutch Marine Commandos, was based on the Allies confronting a Russian force which was assumed to have invaded from round the top of Scandinavia, where Norway has a small frontier with Russia. Once again, I was based on a Commando carrier and very early in the morning of the second day of my visit, the Colonel commanding the Marine Commandos and I, with a few others, embarked on several fast-moving outboard powered boats called Rigid Raiders and made a very fast, cold and windy journey to go ashore where Dutch Commandos had already arrived and posted barely visible green signal lights to show where we were to land. There was some mist, which reduced visibility, and as the shore party waited for the main body of Commandos to make their landing, we could hear the engines of their craft and then realised to the acute embarrassment of the Colonel that they had missed the shore markers and carried on further up the estuary, leaving us alone on the shore. It transpired that having missed the markers, when they went ashore they found themselves in a boatyard which had a secure perimeter, which was a further source of embarrassment. To my regret, I was not a party to the post-mortem. I would dearly like to have heard what the Colonel had to say.

The next day included a helicopter trip over some fjords which enabled one to see the extraordinary topography and understand better why it was so hard during the Second World War to bomb the giant German battleship the *Tirpitz*, when it was anchored in a fjord. It was almost impossible to hit the target flying across the fjord because it was so narrow and the sides were so steep. In order to bomb a ship, or any other target in the fjord, it was necessary for the aircraft to fly along

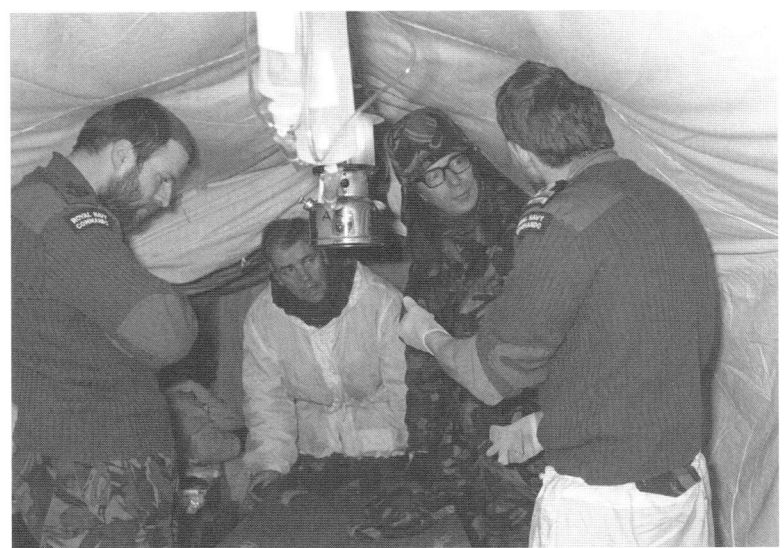

The advanced casualty station, Arctic Circle, Norway (Crown Copyright)

the fjord, making themselves extremely vulnerable to any ground defences. After many attempts, they managed the almost impossible in November 1944.

At the end of the day, I had an evening meal in a tent on the ice followed by an attempt to get some sleep. I was reminded that the most important thing was to put my boots inside my sleeping bag, otherwise they would be frozen so hard in the morning that I would not be able to put them on. The next stage of the exercise involved the British Commandos setting an ambush on one side of the frozen lake to attack the Norwegians, who were playing the role of the Russians advancing along the far side of the lake.

After the ambush and the exchange of a great deal of blank ammunition, I was shown how casualties were evacuated. A sledge was made out of two skis which were joined by metal bars. Metal supports from the skis supported two ski poles, between which there was a groundsheet on top of which I lay in not one but two sleeping bags. I was then dragged across the lake to the far side, where there was an advanced casualty station. Not long before, I had cracked the bone on the point of my shoulder while skiing and I was still suffering slightly from the after-effects. When I was pulled forcibly from my double sleeping bag, I felt that I was quite ready to be received into the tent where the doctor was awaiting casualties. He explained there was not really very much he could do to help anybody who was genuinely injured, pointing out that the drip which was hanging from the roof of the tent was frozen. I was then able to return to the Commando carrier for an extremely welcome hot bath and breakfast. When I asked why a bath was part of the equipment of the boat, I was told it was very useful for reviving people suffering from hypothermia, as they could be put into a warm bath. After breakfast, I flew down to Oslo for bilateral discussions with the Norwegian Defence Minister. I like to think that I made sense, but I am not entirely sure, as I had the feeling that I was still defrosting.

Although my main responsibilities were for the procurement of naval equipment, I was constantly answering questions in the House on equipment for the RAF and the Army on behalf of David Trefgarne, who was in the Lords. Because of that, the RAF suggested that I should take a flight in a Tornado fighter. My predecessor, Archie Hamilton, had not been able to do so because he was too tall to fit into the cockpit of the observer gunner who sits behind the pilot. So off I went to an RAF base in Lincolnshire, where I was first given a lengthy, more than one hour, briefing on all safety aspects of my forthcoming flight and had the special overalls that I had to wear explained to me. They had pressure bands in the legs to stop all my blood going down there during manoeuvres. At the beginning of the briefing, I was told the only thing I had to do during the flight was to turn on the main radar after we had taken off. This was not turned on when on the ground, as it could be dangerous for anybody walking near the front of the aircraft. There was one thing which I very much hoped I would not have to do, and that was to operate the ejector seat. While on the ground this was under the control of the pilot, but after take-off I would be responsible, if required, to press the button. As I recall, I was told that even if I was no longer conscious, my parachute would deploy so as to bring me safely down to earth, or more likely into the sea.

I got on board the plane, and we took off quite safely and smoothly and I was asked to turn on the main radar. I was sitting in a very confined space entirely surrounded by switches and dials, and by then, I had totally forgotten where to find the right switch to turn on the radar. There was a fear that the flight would have to be aborted unless I could find the switch. Eventually, with the help and guidance of the pilot up front, I was able to do so and we continued on the flight; it was a fascinating experience. The RAF produced what was called a target of opportunity for me to lock on an air-to-air missile and go through the motions of discharging it. After that, we didn't exactly do a victory roll but the pilot waggled the wings from side to side, which had a decidedly unpleasant effect on my stomach. I didn't mind so much when we climbed rapidly and did the loop-the-loop, but nearly came to grief by being sick when he made a sudden drop from 20,000 feet down to 12,000 feet, leaving my stomach some way behind. I must admit I was glad to be back on the ground without being sick and still just about able to walk away from the plane.

An expedition more directly related to my responsibilities took place in November 1988 when I flew to Glasgow and went on to the Gare Loch base of our nuclear submarines. From there I embarked on HMS *Swiftsure* and in the evening set off down the Clyde towards the sea. I was accompanied on the trip by the FOSM [Flag Officer Submarines], Vice Admiral Sir John Coward. Also on board were several officers near the end of what was known as the Perisher course. This was the final hurdle they had to surmount before being appointed captain of a nuclear-powered submarine. I had been rather nervous as to whether I would feel claustrophobic. In the event, I was kept so busy during my waking hours and found the submarine so spacious that I had no worries in that regard. Interestingly, the cabin I had for my two nights on board I shared with FOSM. The Captain retained his cabin and it was his second-in-command and the Chief Engineer who were replaced by FOSM and myself. The space in the cabin was extremely limited, indeed it was really only practical for one of us to stand up at a time. FOSM kindly allocated me the lower berth, which seemed to have marginally more room than the upper berth and was certainly easier to access.

When we reached the mouth of the Clyde, *Swiftsure* submerged and for the next thirty or so hours I was under water. During the next morning, I watched the Perisher course in action. One of the candidates for promotion was put in charge of the boat and he was tasked with avoiding detection by a destroyer and aircraft. When we heard the ping which indicated that the submarine had been detected by sonar, the Perisher candidate had to give instructions to try and keep the submarine out of theoretical harm's way. It seemed to me that he was keeping very calm and giving clear instructions and I asked FOSM, who was standing next to me, whether he was doing all right. I was reassured on that point and told it had been a little unfair for the candidate, as the destroyer had been told where we would be located.

Later in the day I saw round the entire boat, discovering to my surprise and slight concern that because there were so many extra people on board, my Private Secretary had had to sleep in a sleeping bag on one of the empty torpedo racks. That evening, after supper, I watched a film with FOSM and the other officers on board. It was an innocuous romantic comedy. I was told that that was not normally the sort of film that was shown but it had been included especially for my benefit. On the second morning, FOSM and I became part of another exercise, as we were to be put ashore on a launch in the Clyde as if we were spies. After getting ashore, I was driven to Glasgow airport, took a plane down to London and from there a train bound for Hove. Five different forms of transport in the same day. I rather wished I had found a bicycle at some moment.

Although I was able to enjoy these various activities, there was serious work to do. Most of naval procurement was concerned with submarine warfare. The naval budget was largely spent on submarines and frigates and destroyers designed for anti-submarine warfare, and their equipment. My first question to my Private Secretary was, how do I begin to understand what is involved in anti-submarine warfare? I got a rather surprising reply: 'Minister, you should read Tom Clancy's *The Hunt for Red October*.' This I duly did, and I have to admit that two years later when I moved on from the department, I didn't feel I had learned much more about submarine warfare than the knowledge I had gained from my enjoyable read of that book.

There were basically two aspects to my work. The first was concerned with the procurement function; the second with supporting British arms exports. It was this work that led my children to describe their father's job while I was in the MoD as being an international arms dealer. A more truthful description would have been that I was helping the export of arms of various types which were British-made. The Government itself does not manufacture much by way of arms of any type. So most of what was being exported was made by a variety of companies, some very large, like the company which is now British Aerospace; others were quite small. In total, arms manufacturing employed some 300,000 people in the UK. Exports, as well as providing good jobs and foreign currency, normally would lower the cost to the British Armed Forces of whatever was being exported. This is because research and development costs would be spread over a greater volume of production. In addition, longer production runs allowed lower unit cost. Supporting arms exports is, however, inevitably very controversial. There are some who argue that they shouldn't happen at all; others are concerned about the use of the arms we export by what they regard as dubious regimes.

However, it is my opinion that careful consideration of the issue shows that the international trade and transfer of arms is both necessary and justified. My starting point is to accept that countries have a right to self-defence, involving the use of force if necessary. It follows that every nation is likely to need at least some weapons. For small, particularly Third World, countries, to have to manufacture even limited quantities of those weapons would require a quite disproportionate amount of their available manufacturing and engineering resources. Importing the arms would be much less expensive, as well as leaving their indigenous skills for more important work.

I accept that much of the international trade in arms is between developed countries and different considerations apply. But efficiency and the sensible use of resources are again relevant. It would be extremely wasteful for every member country of NATO to design and develop their own battle tank or anti-aircraft system. Sharing development costs or buying another ally's products makes sense. There is a long history of this happening, going back to before the Second World War when the celebrated Bren gun was developed by Czechoslovakia at Brno and by Britain at Enfield, hence the word Bren. A more recent example is the Eurofighter, later called the Typhoon, which was developed and manufactured jointly by Britain, Germany, Italy and Spain.

When an arms trade or transfer is between allies, there should be no reason to object. The issue becomes more complicated when the supply of arms is to a friendly nation, but one with whom there is no direct defence treaty. This is when it is essential that careful consideration is given to any proposed arms exports. Clearly there will be instances when it would not be sensible to give approval. First, there are proposed transfers to those countries which pose a threat to our own national security or to that of a dependent territory for whose defence we are responsible, or to an ally or close friend. Secondly, and this is sometimes less straightforward, there may be occasions when the recipient country might be under the control of a regime whose general character and activities are regarded as so intolerable that we would not wish to do business with it. Then there are occasions when a proposed transfer of arms might be to a country where the arrival of additional weapons might exacerbate or unbalance an ongoing political confrontation, and threaten peace in the area. There are also cases when it might appear that the recipient country is seeking arms of a type or quantity which are disproportionate to its genuine security needs.

The United Kingdom has a system of licensing the export of any arms or armaments, or the transfer of such equipment. Before any sale of arms, an application has to be made for an export licence. The application is considered against published guidelines. It involves consideration by the Foreign and Commonwealth Office, the Ministry of Defence and the department responsible for International Trade. Clearly in some instances, the decision to give or to withhold approval would be a matter of fine judgement. It must be recognised that there are few, if any, governments whose domestic and international behaviour is beyond all criticism. There may be occasions when a transfer which might seem entirely justified at the time looks dubious in the light of changed political and international circumstances ten years later. But in general, I felt my role in supporting the export of arms and armaments by British manufacturers was entirely justified.

Looking at the issue solely from the interest of the British Government, the manufacture of a particular item in greater quantity to that required by the British Government would usually reduce the cost to the British Government and therefore to the taxpayer. This is a significant additional factor in the approval of the manufacture and international trade in arms, and that is without introducing two other arguments: the first, that the arms manufacturer provides a great deal of employment. Secondly, that a refusal to supply will not mean that the country who is seeking to purchase does not get the arms. It will, in all probability, obtain what it is seeking from another source. That will reduce any influence the British Government might have had on the behaviour and use of the arms concerned and possibly increase that of a less attractive regime.

So I had no inhibitions in supporting British arms manufacturers in their efforts to sell their products to NATO allies like Turkey, or friendly and peaceful countries like Malaysia and Singapore. I did, however, have some doubts about how Indonesia might use Hawker Hunter jets; would it only be for pilot training? Luckily, I was never involved in the sale of arms to Saudi Arabia, as these were dealt with at a high level and sometimes by David Trefgarne. I do not deny that the UK may not always have made the right decision, but I am confident that before any export licences were given, the application had been carefully considered.

Later, when I was Minister for Trade, I got involved in the after-effects of two cases when the system failed. The first, the so-called 'Arms to Iraq' affair, followed an export licence application which gave incorrect information about the end use of some machine tools. The second was the 'Super Gun', when there was general uncertainty about whether the large diameter steel tubes were for the oil industry or were intended for a military use. As the Scott Report found, 'Muddle undoubtedly had a part to play.' The result was that there was no application for an export licence.

Ministers in every department inevitably get involved in matters which are confidential and have papers put before them carrying various classifications of confidentiality. In most departments for most of the time, matters which are confidential are only so classified because they have not yet been publicly announced. In the Ministry of Defence, some of the classified material involves national security and was likely to remain classified for some considerable time. In the first few months of my time in the Ministry, I had two experiences of the problems associated with keeping matters confidential. The first was very surprising; the Permanent Secretary said he needed to come to see me. This was almost unprecedented, as Permanent Secretaries do not normally come to the office of a Parliamentary Under Secretary. Not only did Michael Quinlan come to my office but he required my Private Secretary to leave so that we had a discussion à deux. It transpired that he felt that I should not be asked to give an untruthful written answer to a mundane Parliamentary question without being told why. The question involved the work of GCHQ Cheltenham and, at the time, hardly anything about it was in the public domain. To keep it that way, the answer I was asked to give to an innocent question was not accurate. However, the degree of security attached to the issue was such that nobody in my private office could be allowed access to it, and so Michael Quinlan himself came to brief me on the background and asked me to accept that I would give the answer to maintain the secrecy surrounding Cheltenham. I had no hesitation in doing so.

My next experience involving classified material was the first time I saw anything top secret, indeed it was the first time that anything had come across my desk with that classification. It did not involve the security of the United Kingdom or the capability of our Armed Forces. It concerned the Royal Yacht *Britannia*. The political sensitivity around the future of the Royal Yacht was such that any papers relating to the difficulty of maintaining her in service over the next few years were classified as top secret. Eventually the age of the boat and its high running costs led to it going out of service, to almost universal regret. *Britannia* had been designed at a time when it was expected that she would be used to take the Queen and other members of the Royal Family on official visits to the Dominions or dependent territories. By the time she came into service, the Queen was not going to spend seven or eight days crossing the Atlantic to get to the Caribbean, so inevitably she travelled by air. The second function of *Britannia* was to act as a hospital ship in times of conflict. When the Falklands affair came along, she was neither suitable nor available and so never served in that role. Her third function was to act as a floating hotel or temporary royal residence in which the Queen could entertain during an overseas visit. The Royal Yacht could also be used to promote British exports. In order to be suitable for royal entertaining or trade promotion, she needed to have large spaces for accommodating several hundred guests, together with back-up catering facilities. It is interesting that when the Royal Yacht Squadron had its 200th anniversary celebration in 2015, the Royal Yachts of Denmark and Norway were present but they, like the Royal Yacht of Spain, are yachts for the personal use of the Head of State and are not of a size to accommodate entertainment other than on a very small scale. When the issue of whether *Britannia* could be replaced was discussed, one idea that featured prominently was that the replacement boat could be a training ship, like the sail-training ships that several countries possess. However, when the idea was explored more fully, it became clear that the uses were basically incompatible. So *Britannia* went out of service without replacement.

There were other parts of the MoD for which I had responsibility; some surprising, others frightening. The surprising included the Meteorological Office, which, at the time, was part of the MoD. The reason was rooted in the nineteenth century, when weather forecasting first got going, because the forecasts then were primarily for the benefit of the Navy. In the peacetime 1980s, the work done by the office using its computers, which were then located in Bracknell, was mainly for the BBC. I even had to answer questions about the accuracy of the weather forecasts given by the BBC. They must be one of Britain's most popular subjects of conversation. I recall that I answered to the effect that on an average of over five years, they were more than 80% accurate. I think that was for Wales. I have a suspicion that most people would think that that was not a truthful answer.

Another surprising aspect of my responsibilities was the work of the MoD Police, Britain's only fully armed police force. They were responsible for guarding a number of MoD installations, including the Aldermaston

Atomic Weapons Establishment. I discovered in my relatively few dealings with them that they had a very strong trade union and secondly, that most of the constables and other police seemed to be quite elderly. I suspect that this was because many of them were ex-servicemen.

Turning to the frightening, I did have to answer questions about the Aldermaston Atomic Weapons Establishment because that came under the responsibility of David Trefgarne. To help me understand what was involved, I paid a visit to Aldermaston and was able to put my hands in what are called the glove boxes which protect those processing the material from radiation. The piece of plutonium I picked up was extraordinarily heavy. If how to make an atom bomb was frightening, Porton Down, the chemical warfare establishment, was terrifying. It was included in my responsibilities and when I visited the base, the chief scientist held up a relatively small phial of liquid and claimed it was enough to kill most of the people in the world. I should, however, stress that the work of the Establishment was concerned not with using such weapons, but with saving people from being killed or injured as the result of the use of chemical weapons by others. Sadly, as we have been reminded recently, that still remains a threat against which we need to be on guard.

My responsibilities for the procurement of naval equipment took up nearly half of my time. Trying to get 'value for money' (VFM, everything and everybody in the MoD had initials), was the biggest challenge. In 1636, Charles I's mighty flagship, *Sovereign of the Seas*, cost more than three times the original estimate. The King had insisted on putting more guns on to *Sovereign of the Seas* than had originally been planned, to get the number up to 101. In addition, he wanted a lot more gilding. I am afraid that the Ministry still gets accused of gilding the lily. There is a long history of cost overruns and delays in naval procurement. Those cost overruns and delays have been criticised more often by the Public Accounts Committee than the spending programmes of any other Government department. The introduction of more competition and the reduction in the number of cost-plus contracts under the direction of Peter Levene, who was the very effective Chief of Defence Procurement (CDP), reduced rather than eliminated the problem. Information technology and computers are at the root of it. Developments in IT proceed at such a pace that while a ship is being built, taking perhaps three years, the capabilities of some of the systems which will be carried on the ship can be revolutionised. In order to accommodate the improved radar, sonars or weapons systems, variations may be required to the original design of the ship, which is just a platform for carrying that equipment. It is understandable that the Navy does not want to launch a ship which is already outdated, any more than the RAF would like to have a new aircraft that was not carrying the latest and most effective equipment. Compromise is required between the need to keep within the budget, maintain the programme and ensure that the completed ship, plane or vehicle is fit for purpose. Not surprisingly, the compromise is not easy to reach and even when a reasonable arrangement is concluded, there is likely to be some increase in cost and some delay to the programme. Thirty years after I started at the MoD, and nearly four centuries after the launch of *Sovereign of the Seas*, the MoD is still wrestling with this intractable issue.

There were numerous meetings, many visits to defence contractors and a great deal of paper which came across my desk. The theory is that civil servants propose, and ministers decide. I do not recall taking any decision of significance during the two years when I was Under Secretary of State for Defence Procurement. This is perhaps not as surprising as it might seem. The first and most important decision involving defence is how much money can be spent by the department. That decision is taken by the Prime Minister and the Cabinet. The next critical decision is how the available money will be divided between the various forces and responsibilities. That decision must be taken by the Secretary of State for Defence, advised by the Chief of the Defence Staff, the Permanent Secretary and their team of assistants, civilian and military. When the Navy have got their allocation, the decisions as to how it will be used are either guided by directions from the Secretary of State and the Chief of the Defence Staff, or will be decided by the Admiral who is Chief of the Naval Staff and his support team. Responsibility for implementing their decisions lay with the Chief of Defence Procurement. This post had been created in March 1985 specifically for Peter Levene, who was effectively a poacher-turned-gamekeeper who had been recruited as a Special Adviser six months earlier by Michael Heseltine. Peter had been a very success-ful chairman of a company that manufactured and bought defence equipment for sale not only to the Ministry of Defence, but worldwide. When you have the benefit of advice and support from such experts, it is not advisable to second-guess or override their recommendations. I very much doubt if I would have been able to do so even if I had wanted to change any recommendation on a procurement issue coming from the CDP.

Richard Willson's cartoon in *The Times*, 1988

Probably the most significant defence procurement issue which fell in my area of responsibility during the two years I held the job was the decision to place an order for three Type 23 frigates with the same shipyard. The previous policy had been to spread the orders for naval ships around three or four of the shipyards which were capable of building a frigate or destroyer so as to keep them all in business. Although, under the guidance of Peter Levene, the Ministry of Defence was seeking to ensure as much competition as possible in defence procurement contracts and to eliminate the old-fashioned cost-plus contract where all the burden of overruns and delays fell to the Ministry of Defence, the MoD had realised that placing an order for three similar vessels with three different yards was a very inefficient method of procurement.

The recommendation to place the contract for the three ships with Yarrow Shipbuilders Ltd on the Clyde clearly would save at least £10 million per ship when compared with placing the orders with different shipyards. The most surprising thing about the announcement of the order was that, although it was being placed with a Scottish yard, by a Scottish Secretary of State for Defence, I was allowed, the most junior minister, to make the announcement to the House. It was the most high profile Parliamentary thing I did during my two years in the Ministry of Defence. The Statement and the Supplementary Questions lasted some forty minutes. For several days afterwards, I was occasionally stopped in the House by a Scottish Member who wished to thank me for the order having been placed in Clydeside. Sometimes they did so in an accent from the Glasgow area that I found very hard to understand. But I did appreciate the thanks.

All the MoD Ministers were *ex officio* members of the Admiralty Board, along with the most senior Admirals and Civil Servants. In the nineteenth century, this body commanded the British Navy; in the 1980s, it met occasionally to be photographed in the historic Admiralty Board Room in Whitehall. I was amused in 1989, when I was present, to see that as soon as the photographer had finished his work, three of the four Admirals put on the spectacles they had not wanted to be recorded as needing.

The department had five ministers when I moved on in July 1989. At that time, the Army personnel numbered 170,000 compared to 78,407 in April 2017. The department still has five ministers. Comparing the work-load I subsequently had in the FCO or the DTI, I felt that I had been under-employed in the MoD. When I arrived, I was greeted with the words, 'We have nothing for you here.' If 'not much' is substituted for 'nothing', I think that might have been an accurate description of the work of the US of SDP in the MoD.

16

FOREIGN &
COMMONWEALTH OFFICE

In the summer of 1989, it was expected that there would once again be a reshuffle of the ministerial team and that this time there would be many changes. I began to wonder what my ministerial future, if any, was likely to be; up, down or sideways. I took the perhaps somewhat rash step of writing to the Chief Whip to point out the very long-term nature of the issues with which I was concerned in the Ministry of Defence and suggesting that perhaps remaining in my post to continue to deal with those problems would be a good idea. It was not to be. The big reshuffle started on 24 July.

The headlines were Geoffrey Howe leaving the Foreign and Commonwealth Office to become Leader of the House and Deputy Prime Minister, and John Major becoming Foreign Secretary. Further announcements were of other Cabinet appointments. Then came news about a number of Ministers of State, and finally changes among the Parliamentary Under Secretaries of State. I had heard nothing until the early afternoon of 25 July 1989, when my Private Secretary said, 'You're going to the Foreign Office.' This opinion was reinforced by a well-informed source, namely my driver, who was of the same opinion. I said, 'Well, I know nothing about that, and so I am going to carry on as US of SDP in the MoD until somebody tells me not to.' My first appointment the next morning was in Crawley, visiting a defence contractor; so having heard nothing, I set off in my ministerial car on the morning of 26 July 1989 to go to Crawley. It is interesting to reflect that in those days before mobile phones, it was not until I reached the premises of the defence contractor that I could be given a message, 'Please ring Number 10 immediately.' I did so, and was put through to the Prime Minister, Margaret Thatcher, who said, 'Tim, I gather you're in the country,' slightly implying that I was away in some rural retreat. So I hastily explained that I was on MoD business visiting a defence contractor, and was told by the Prime Minister that she would like me to go to the Foreign Office, which, in the circumstances, was not a great surprise. I was then told that I should return immediately to the FCO to take up my new responsibilities; so the unfortunate defence contractor, who had prepared for a ministerial visit, had my presence for some twenty minutes, most of which time I spent on the telephone.

John Major, the new Foreign Secretary, had been promoted from Chief Secretary at the Treasury, one of the most junior Cabinet appointments, to one of the most senior, much to general astonishment, including his own. His ministerial team included four Ministers of State. One, Lynda Chalker, was responsible for Overseas Development, in those days still part of the Foreign and Commonwealth Office. She had been in that post since 1986 and was to continue there until the end of the Conservative administration in 1997. The other three Ministers of State were, like myself, all newly appointed in the July 1989 reshuffle. They were William Waldegrave, Francis Maude and Ivon Brabazon, our man in the House of Lords. The sole Parliamentary Under Secretary of State in the FCO, me, completed the team.

I was greeted by my excellent Private Secretary, Martin Hatfull. He later became our Ambassador in Indonesia, having served as Number 2 in Japan. He told me what my responsibilities were going to be. Each of the ministers in the department had a geographical area in which they took a particular interest and for which they were generally responsible. I was amazed to be told that my area was the Americas. At first sight, this seemed astonishing. There was, however, a logical reason. In 1982, when Malcolm Rifkind had been appointed as Parliamentary Under Secretary at the Foreign Office, he had been told that he had no geographical area for which he would be responsible. He said that he thought this was absurd and surely every Foreign Office minister should have part of the world in his care. The explanation he got was that since the other three ministers in the department were all of Minister of State rank, appointing a Parliamentary Under Secretary with responsibility for any area could be regarded by the countries in that area as somewhat demeaning. The solution to that problem was to make Malcolm Rifkind responsible for the Soviet Union and its empire. This was on the entirely logical grounds that it didn't matter if they felt insulted.

By the time I arrived, the junior minister was given responsibility for the Americas. This was on the grounds that matters concerning the United States or Canada would be dealt with at 'a high level'. South and Central America were areas which were not regarded as having particular importance for the United Kingdom, either in diplomatic or trade circles.

Then there were all those Caribbean territories, five of which were still dependent territories, which we formerly called colonies. They were all small, and it was felt they could not complain if they had a Parliamentary Under Secretary as their Foreign Office Minister. There were other islands included in my brief: St Helena, remote, difficult to access and I never got there; Ascension, largely run by the Americans as an airbase and with no permanent indigenous inhabitants; and the Falkland Islands, which were the most important part of my area of responsibility in diplomatic terms.

I had responsibility for a number of other departments and issues. I can only assume that they were regarded as of lesser importance, and that is why they were allocated to the Parliamentary Under Secretary.

Significantly, one of those was the United Nations Department. My subsequent experience with some of its agencies, both in the FCO and later as Minister for Trade, convinced me that there is unfortunately a lot of waste and unnecessary work carried out under the United Nations umbrella. This should not detract from the extremely important work done by the Security Council and sometimes by other parts of the United Nations. There is perhaps a parallel with the European Union in the sense that the fact that there is waste and useless activity should not mean that you regard the whole organisation as useless when there is very important and useful work being done by parts of the organisation.

Consular Affairs was another department which the FCO was beginning to recognise had more importance than had traditionally been attributed to it. To the general public, the Consular Department is the public face of the FCO. Those who get into trouble overseas, lose their passports, or unfortunately get caught up in crime, disasters, fires or accidents, can become very dependent on help and advice from consuls. And of course, there is the very important matter of issuing or refusing visas. One politically sensitive area which fell within my responsibility was the funding of the BBC World Service. In the days before what seems like almost worldwide availability of wi-fi and world news through the internet, the short-wave service of the BBC World Service was a vital service for Britons living overseas; it was often the only way to keep in touch with world news. Members of Parliament on overseas visits or abroad on holiday also found it of great value. The grant to the World Service and the availability of the service in different countries was a sensitive issue in Parliament. Finally, there were other bits and pieces of less political or international significance. These included our relations with the International Committee of the Red Cross, based in Geneva, and the

Treaty Department, which looked after the texts of the 800 or so Treaties to which Britain was a party. Altogether it was an interesting and diverse workload.

Appointments to the most senior ambassadorial positions, Washington, Paris, Bonn and the European Union, are made by the Foreign Secretary after discussion with the Prime Minister. Appointments to the next level of ambassadors are made by a small committee called the Number One Board. The membership is headed by the Permanent Secretary and the Second Permanent Secretary, and includes one minister. I was surprised to find that I was the minister. Clearly the decisions of the board were significant not only for relations between the UK and the country concerned, but also for the career of the diplomats involved. It didn't take me very long to discover that, while my contribution was always asked for and listened to politely, it was clear that the decision had been taken in advance by the officials. I do not recall any occasion when what had been already decided was influenced by my input. The meetings did, however, provide me with an opportunity to emphasise the importance in the twentieth-century world of trade and investment relations, something which had until quite recently been regarded as rather below the Ambassador's level.

After my appointment was announced, I was amused to be approached by my Parliamentary neighbour, Julian Amery, and assured that in his view, the Foreign Office was the only department of which it was really worthwhile being a member. Julian had taken a lifelong interest in international affairs and believed in the importance of diplomacy. For some of my colleagues, foreign travel, which was an inevitable accompaniment of being a minister in the FCO, was the main attraction of the department.

I had been a Foreign Office minister for less than three months when the penultimate drama of Margaret Thatcher's premiership occurred. Nigel Lawson, the long-standing Chancellor of the Exchequer, resigned in October. John Major's rapid ascent towards becoming Prime Minister continued with him being appointed as Nigel's successor; it was the job he had always wanted. Douglas Hurd was appointed Foreign Secretary in his place, also getting the job which he had always wanted and for which he was extremely well qualified. He proved to be as good a Secretary of State for a junior minister to have as had George Younger. The only time he asked me to come and explain to him what I was proposing to do on a particular issue was the annual agreement with the BBC for the funding of the World Service. With the collapse of the Soviet Empire, there was a new priority to increase services to the countries of Eastern Europe which were now independent of their previous Soviet oversight. After some discussion, I agreed with John Tusa some changes in priorities, including dropping broadcasting to France. In addition, I rejected any suggestion that Government might fund an idea which was being discussed of a BBC Television World Service. That, of course, is now very well established and successful without needing Government funding, relying instead on a previously forbidden income source, advertising. When I discussed the proposals with Douglas, he was happy to agree with them and I am glad to say that they did not prove to be controversial in the House.

If the Government has a small majority, the Whips' Office will have to limit the travelling of junior ministers. Happily, in 1989, the Government had a very large majority and being told that I must be in the Division Lobby was seldom an obstacle to the numerous overseas trips that I was expected to make. The lesser departments for which I had responsibility required some interesting travel. Consular Affairs took me to Turkey, where I found Timothy Daunt still the Ambassador. Much to the annoyance of the Turkish Government, we introduced a visa requirement for Turkish citizens travelling to the UK. This had become necessary because of the number arriving ostensibly as tourists but, in reality, seeking to find work and settle. In retaliation, a visa requirement was imposed on British visitors to Turkey. This was, however, a fairly farcical procedure because it merely required a visitor to pay a modest amount and have a stamp put in his passport. This meant queuing up on arrival at the airport to get the stamp in your passport, before joining a second queue for immigration. I never heard of anybody being refused a visa.

Another trip caused by my consular responsibilities was to Spain, when early in the year I found myself in Benidorm. Some British summer visitors to that resort had been behaving very badly, leading to arrests and sometimes imprisonment. We wanted to find some way of reducing the publicity and work for the consular department which all this trouble caused. Arriving out of season, the main risk to my safety in the resort was tripping over a zimmer frame. My day in Benidorm ended with a dinner given by the mayor in a restaurant pretending to be a British pub. The pretence was heightened by having a television showing the conclusion of a particularly exciting Test Match between England and the West Indies, taking place in the West Indies. Unfortunately my place at the dinner was with my back to the screen, which made it very difficult to follow the final exciting overs. As I recall, the match ended in a draw. I departed from Benidorm not having thought of any obvious way to reduce the amount of drunken and disorderly behaviour by British tourists that summer.

Visiting the peaceful, tranquil city of Geneva to see the International Committee of the Red Cross and other UN agencies based there could not have been a bigger contrast. My United Nations role also took me to Paris, to visit UNESCO. The British Government had become so upset at the extravagance, incompetence and possible corruption in that organisation that we had ceased paying a subscription, as also had the United States. During my visit, we were promised reform and an efficiency drive. Very shortly after my return to the UK, UNESCO announced a yet further appointment of highly paid officials with no obvious function, so, at the time, we did not rejoin. Having been a founding member state when the UN came into being on 4 November 1946, we had then ceased our membership of UNESCO on 31 December 1985. Twelve years later, the Blair Government announced that Britain would rejoin, at the start of the first Parliament after I had retired.

I also went to New York for the annual debate on the Report of the Human Rights Committee. I was given an anodyne draft speech which I was allowed to strengthen slightly. The fact that it was to be delivered by the Under Secretary of State, and that I was allowed to say in the mildest terms that it would be a good idea if governments paid more attention to the United Nations Convention on Human Rights, only goes to show how unimportant the occasion was. It was clearly not expected that my speech would be reported, or even listened to, even in the UK.

The installation of a new Head of Government is an occasion when a British Government representative, other than the Ambassador or High Commissioner, is sometimes expected to be present. There were two occasions when I found myself fulfilling that role. The first took me to Brasilia for the installation of a new President who, at the time, was regarded as a great white hope to improve the governance of Brazil. He was young, and regarded as honest and capable.

Fernando Collor de Mello, representing the National Reconstruction Party, had won the second round of voting by a margin of 6%. He was appointed President on 15 November 1989. Such was the importance attached to the occasion that I was playing a supporting role to Geoffrey Howe. I was intrigued to see that he treated the whole affair in an appropriately relaxed way, even taking out his camera to take a few snaps while we were queuing up to meet the new President. I have to report that, sadly, that President ended up being jailed for corruption.

In 1989, because of the number of overseas visits that ministers had to make, the FCO paid for ministers to take their spouses on two occasions each year. In addition, the minister was able to take his spouse if he paid the air fare and any additional accommodation costs if the presence of a spouse would not cause any inconvenience to the ministerial activities during their time overseas. One of the trips on which Susie accompanied me was my visit to Brazil. We had read in a book by Quentin Crewe about his travels around South America in a wheelchair, and how helpful all the British diplomatic staff had been during his trip, other than our then Ambassador in Venezuela. We were therefore to some extent warned about the, perhaps I should be generous and call it the old-fashioned, behaviour of our Ambassador in Brasilia, who had been the Ambassador to Venezuela who had been unhelpful to Quentin Crewe. He met me on arrival at the airport in Brasilia and totally ignored the presence of Susie, neither speaking to her nor shaking her hand. His wife could not have been more friendly and helpful. But to the Ambassador, it seemed that a junior minister's wife did not exist in his domain.

The Ambassador's residence in Brasilia was a modern house with modern furniture. Shortly after arriving, we sat down in the living room for a briefing session, sitting around a glass-topped occasional table. While we held our discussion two pugs appeared to be enjoying sexual congress under the glass table. Whether they actually enjoyed it or not, it was hard to tell because of the extent of the grunts and other noises which emerged, and they were totally ignored by the Ambassador. I found it very hard to keep a straight face and follow his example, behaving as if the pugs were not present, although both audible and visible to all of us.

On every other visit when Susie accompanied me, she was welcomed and often had a programme of her own. Indeed, some ambassadors said it was a real help to have a minister's wife present, because if there was to be a dinner, it made it easier to invite the spouses of officials who might be attending, it being quite likely that the ladies had never received an invitation to the Ambassador's residence before.

I made one Caribbean visit at very short notice, following Hurricane Hugo. The hurricane, which was one of the strongest in the Caribbean in the twentieth century, was also very slow-moving, which gave it more time to cause devastation on any island over which it passed. It had struck the small island of Montserrat, a British dependent territory, with devastating effect. I went there about a fortnight after the hurricane to see at first hand the effect and to discuss our aid programme with the Governor. At the time of my first visit, there was effectively nothing green left on the island. They said every leaf and every blade of grass had been blown away. Even the Governor's residence, which was quite a solidly built house, was damaged, albeit not badly enough to prevent us staying there and having a final lunch there. The Governor had invited the First Minister and four or five of his Cabinet colleagues, together with the Leader of the Opposition and two or three of his shadow ministers. One minister failed to turn up; he was Minister of Housing. At the end of the lunch, we discovered that he had been busy down at the docks, where a consignment of corrugated-iron roofing had arrived as relief material. He was supervising the distribution of the material to make sure it went to his friends. This led to the early departure from the lunch of the Chief Minister and the Leader of the Opposition, who went off together down to the docks muttering that they were 'going to fix him', referring to their Housing colleague. I never discovered the outcome of their encounter.

I returned to the island some months later to see how it was recovering and how effective our aid programme had been. I was astonished on the second visit to see how much and how fast the vegetation had recovered. The island was green again, and even trees seemed to have made some rapid growth. Most homes had been repaired and were at least watertight. Sadly, the hummingbirds, for which the island had been quite well known, had not recovered; they had all been swept away by the hurricane or died of starvation in its immediate aftermath.

On another of my Caribbean visits, the last island we visited was the delightful but not particularly tourist-orientated island of Dominica. The island is distinctive in many ways, having one of the most rugged landscapes in the Caribbean. It is largely covered by a multi-layered rain forest, and its few beaches have black sand. At the time, the Prime Minister was Dame Eugenia Charles, an elderly and formidable lady much respected in the Caribbean and who I understood enjoyed good relations with Margaret Thatcher. I think it was mutual admiration between two powerful ladies who were uncompromising leaders of their countries.

I was therefore quite apprehensive about how our meeting would go. Dame Eugenia received Susie and me on the balcony of her residence sitting in her chaise longue, as she had recently broken her leg. Susie's presence was very helpful for our quite lengthy discussion. I understand the report back was that the young lad was all right!

Susie with me on my visit to Dominica, 1990

The other occasion when I represented the Government at the installation of a new Head of State was perhaps the most extraordinary event I ever attended. Margaret had wanted to send a Cabinet minister, but those asked had found good reasons to remain in England. So it was the junior FCO Minister who found himself in Managua, representing Great Britain at the inauguration of Doña Violeta Chamorro as President of Nicaragua.

It was her unexpected victory over the Sandinistas that gave the occasion its importance. Daniel Ortega, the Sandinista leader and incumbent President, thought he had the election in the bag. He controlled all aspects of Government and all the press. The opposition only had access to one TV station and that with such limited range that it could not be watched even in all the areas of the capital. But on election day, Doña Violeta had won so clearly that her victory could not be denied with so many international observers looking on. This was the background to the most bizarre event I have ever attended.

The setting for the ceremony was the first surprise: a baseball stadium. With its association with the Sandinistas' great enemy, the USA,

Passing the Presidential sash, Nicaragua, April 1990

it was a strange choice. The covered stand at one end accommodated all the official guests. The open stands housed the Ortega supporters on one side and the Chamorro supporters opposite. A platform had been erected in front of the covered stand. Ortega with his 'commandantes' in their fatigues lined up on it to await the arrival of the President Elect. She was to enter the stadium in a car from the far end and drive around in front of the stand that held the Sandinistas. The official stand was packed with heads of State and heads of Governments from all of South and Central America – all of whom had entered on foot. Only one Government's representative was allowed to enter the stadium in a car and, like the President Elect, drive past the open stands to the platform. Vice President Dan Quayle, representing Ortega's enemy, and neither a Head of State nor of Government, arrived that way and took his place in the stand only some five metres from where I was sitting. As he arrived, a heavily built man with a bulge under his armpit and a microphone in his ear took his place beside me. I was not reassured, as it seemed to me that an assassin spraying the area would probably spread his fire wide enough to include me as well as the Vice President.

All was ready for the arrival of the President Elect. She was driven past the stands, not of her supporters, but of the Sandinistas. They predictably greeted her with boos and catcalls, plus the occasional water bomb. She arrived safely at the foot of the platform, climbed the steps and then greeted Daniel Ortega with a kiss on both cheeks and repeated this greeting all the way down the line of waiting 'commandantes'.

I was told I should not have been surprised. Nicaragua is a small country. Violeta was the fifth Chamorro President, Daniel, the fourth Ortega in the office. The families had intermarried and both had close relatives on the other side in the campaign. Next, the presidential sash was passed from one to the other and the ceremony was completed without any problem. As we left, I shook hands with the guest who seemed to attract both the most attention and the greatest respect: President Castro. It was a brief, friendly encounter!

In the evening there was an official celebration party. The location was again somewhat surprising. It was held at a golf club. Before the official event there was a more select event, held in a private house. This was for the representatives of those governments regarded as supportive of Doña Violeta, together with a few of her other friends and supporters. We all formed a queue to be received by the President and to congratulate her. I saw that etiquette required not just a handshake, but also a kiss on both cheeks. So when it came to my turn, I followed the procedure, only to receive a further kiss from the President to take back to Margaret – I didn't dare. On my return, I waited until we were in the most crowded place, in the House of Commons, the Division Lobby. There I told the PM of the singular mark of appreciation of her support that I had received and hurried away without any physical contact!

During my few days in Nicaragua I was based, as were many of the delegations, in the InterContinental hotel in the capital, Managua. The city had apparently never fully recovered from a devastating earthquake some years earlier. Some blocks in the city centre had no surviving buildings and the cathedral still lacked a roof. The InterContinental hotel, both inside and out, would not have been out of place in any city in North America. In Managua, it was an incongruous sight. It was there that I had another unexpected brief encounter. Coming down in the lift I was with a lady in a white linen suit. When I emerged into the lobby, our Ambassador greeted me, saying, 'You were lucky.' Enquiring why, he pointed out that my companion in the lift had been Bianca Jagger. A missed opportunity for at least a handshake.

I made several visits to the West Indies. My predecessor in my post, Tim Eggar, had warned me that there was no point in trying to persuade

Parliamentary colleagues that any trip to the West Indies was anything more than a holiday jaunt, however hard the work; and it was sometimes surprisingly hard work. On one occasion, I managed to visit four different islands on the same day, starting in one, fitting in another two, and ending at a fourth. Admittedly, there were many fairly relaxed times, including as I recall one alfresco lunch attended by the Prime Minister and all his Government when the only subject discussed was cricket. The subject which was nearly always on the agenda was drugs. These created increasing problems due to the illegal trade through the West Indies, usually on the way to the United States, though sometimes heading for Europe, of drugs grown in South America. I attended a major conference in Jamaica, bringing together representatives from both North and South America, on the drug trade. My schedule included a breakfast meeting with the representatives of the five Dependent Territories who were attending the conference. The Chief Minister of the Turks and Caicos Islands failed to appear. I was later told the reason was because he was too busy dealing with his drugs business in the docks! He later ended up in jail and, for quite a considerable time, the British Government had to take over direct rule of the Turks and Caicos Islands, which, sadly, I never got to visit.

During the conference I had a bilateral meeting with Michael Manley, the Prime Minister of Jamaica, a senior and much respected Caribbean politician. During the discussions focusing mainly on the problems caused by the drug trade, the question arose of alternative crops which might be grown by the farmers instead of marijuana. Coffee was the obvious best prospect. However, the coffee price was somewhat depressed. I advanced the theory that if the Americans could be persuaded to drink stronger coffee, of which they drank a lot but mostly very weak, then the world price of coffee would go up, which would benefit the efforts to persuade farmers to grow alternative crops to marijuana. Michael Manley commented, 'You're quite right, Tim, even in the White House, you can't get a decent cup of coffee.'

One unexpected problem, and one which I never met on any other occasion, was when I was in Grenada. I was accompanied by two officials, and the Prime Minister of Grenada had nobody with him at all. We subsequently decided to solve the problem of him not apparently taking a note of what we discussed and agreed that I send him a letter telling him how much I had enjoyed the meeting, during which we had discussed and agreed, etc. It was an example of the normally quite laid-back

William Fullerton, the Governor, and I meet other inhabitants of the
Falkland Islands, 1990 (photo © Martin Hatfull)

approach to government in the West Indies, which is admirable in some
respects but leads to problems in others.

My visit to the Falklands in February 1990 was probably the most
important overseas visit that I made. I was there for eight days, the
intention being that I should seek to reassure the Falkland Islanders that
although we had restored diplomatic relations with Argentina, we had
no intention of entering into any negotiation concerning the sovereignty
of the islands. By the end of my eight-day visit, I felt that at least I had
been in the same room, if not actually shaken hands, with every adult
Falkland Islander. My programme did not allow any time for enjoying
the salmon fishing, which is apparently very good. I did, however, take a
flight in the fisheries protection aircraft, and flew over an island where
I was told that half a million albatross were nesting. It was the most
amazing sight. On my return to the UK, we stopped at Ascension Island.
I was privileged to be allowed to leave the airbase during our relatively
short time on the island and was taken by our resident agent to the beach
to see where, at that time, the great green turtles were coming up out of
the sea to lay their eggs. Apparently the turtles swim some 1,100 miles
from their habitat off the shores of Brazil to the tiny dot that is Ascension
Island, where they mate, go ashore and lay their eggs before returning to
Brazil. When the baby turtles hatch out, each mother having laid about

100 eggs, they make a dash for the sea, many being caught and eaten en route by predator birds. Those which make it to the sea then set off to swim, unguided and unaided by any parent or adult turtle, back to Brazil, where perhaps one or two in 100 make it. After that excitement, I was glad to get back safely into my RAF Trident aircraft to Brize Norton. It was a lengthy and not particularly comfortable flight at the end of a fascinating visit.

Moving from the MoD to the FCO greatly increased the amount of overseas travel I did, but it did not increase the amount of House of Commons work which a junior minister was expected to do. Neither department produces much, if any, legislation. Therefore, the normal main activity of a junior minister helping to deal with Committee and later stages of a Bill, and supporting a Minister of State on the floor of the House, does not happen. The opportunities for a Parliamentary Under Secretary to shine, or otherwise, in the FCO and MoD, are few and far between.

There was, however, one unusual occasion when I did have to handle a piece of legislation. Pakistan had been expelled from the Commonwealth for its failure to adhere to democratic government. After democracy had been restored, a one clause Bill was required to re-admit Pakistan to the Commonwealth. This was uncontroversial and was scheduled to be discussed after the 10 p.m. vote in a debate limited to one and a half hours. I was expecting proceedings to take a maximum of half an hour, and had advised Susie that I hoped to be back at our home in Great College Street by 11 o'clock. Much to my surprise, as I came back into the Chamber after the 10 o'clock vote, I saw that I was opposed on the Opposition Front Bench by no less a person than the Shadow Foreign Secretary, Gerald Kaufman. In addition, behind him on the Opposition back-benches were perhaps as many as a dozen Labour MPs looking as if they might want to contribute. This made me very apprehensive, fearful that we were about to be faced with some sort of ambush. However, after my initial remarks and relatively short speech, Gerald Kaufman rose to his feet, welcomed the Bill, stated his support and went on to praise the Pakistani residents in his constituency. I then realised that these various Labour MPs wanted to make something equivalent to a maiden speech enabling them to draw attention to the Pakistani-run restaurants and other businesses which flourished in their constituencies. So the debate ran for the full one and a half hours without at any stage becoming controversial, but it was a rather weird occasion.

By far the most important event that occurred during my year at the Foreign Office was the fall of the Berlin Wall and the crumbling of the Soviet Empire. I, in common with everybody else, was astonished at these events, perhaps more astonished than most because it was less than six months since I had been in the Ministry of Defence concerned with the number of frigates and destroyers we had in place in order to hunt the predatory nuclear-powered Soviet submarines. In my time in the MoD, we still confronted Soviet forces in central Europe and were prepared to engage in a high-intensity conflict. My very modest contribution to the collapse of the Soviet Empire was to summon the Bulgarian Ambassador to register a complaint about the manhandling of a British journalist who had been observing a demonstration in Sofia. I can hardly claim that the decision the following day by the Bulgarian Government to stand down was the consequence of my strongly worded complaint.

I only spent one year as a Foreign Office minister. In the summer reshuffle of 1990, I and the three Ministers of State who had been appointed the year before at the same time as myself were all given new positions in other departments. This was an outstanding example of Margaret Thatcher's tendency to tinker with the composition of her Government far too often. In the Foreign Office, you are dealing with people and places rather than a piece of legislation which has a Parliamentary cycle that lasts less than a year. It could be said that after a year, a Foreign Office minister is really only beginning to get to know the places and people with whom he or she deals. One thing I think that all four of us would have agreed on was that in that year we had been experiencing excellent advice from the high calibre Foreign Office staff.

I am often asked whether I enjoyed my time as a minister. There were many occasions when I would have found it hard to say 'Yes'. However, because of the wide variety of interesting people I met and the fascinating places I visited during my time at the FCO, the answer would usually have been 'Yes'.

17

MINISTER OF TRADE

Having only been an FCO minister for a year, I was not expecting to be involved in the summer reshuffle of 1990 and was somewhat apprehensive when I received a telephone call to go over to Number 10 in an hour and a half's time. I was brave and asked whether I would be pleased with what I would hear. I was reassured by being told the answer was affirmative. My interview with the Prime Minister was brief and friendly. It included no special comments about the work I had been doing in the Foreign Office, nor any particular comments about the work I was to do as Minister of Trade, although I was left in no doubt that the job was thought to be of some importance. I have never regarded Alan Clark's *Diaries* as an entirely reliable source of information, but I was amused to read later his diary entry for Friday, 31 January 1986. According to the diary, Margaret Thatcher told him how important the job of Minister of Trade is. It was, she said, 'the second most important job outside the Cabinet after the Financial Secretary', but she went on to say, 'Don't shout that around.' She also said, according to Alan Clark, it needs someone with 'a brilliant brain'. I can only conclude that she had decided four years later that such brilliance was no longer essential.

My third Government department was another of the major departments of state, albeit not as prestigious and grand a one as the FCO or the MoD. Like the other two, it had five ministers. The Secretary of State was Peter Lilley, so for the first time after serving under George Younger, John Major and Douglas Hurd, I found myself working for a Secretary of State whose position was very much on the right of the Party. Peter was a libertarian and a Europhobe. My fellow ministers were initially Douglas Hogg, as Minister for Industry, and John Redwood as the Under Secretary of State, definitely a left and a right. Alexander Hesketh was the Department's man in the Lords.

I had been in the department less than four months when the situation changed. At the beginning of November, Margaret Thatcher was forced into a further reshuffle following the dramatic resignation of Geoffrey Howe as Leader of the House and Deputy Prime Minister. Douglas Hogg moved, John Redwood was promoted to Minister of State, and Edward

Leigh arrived as Under Secretary of State. Tim Renton, who was Chief Whip at the time, described in his memoir how Margaret Thatcher declared, 'The DTI will be a really right-wing Department.' She said this apparently with evident satisfaction, adding that, 'Tim Sainsbury is the only left-winger there, and a left-winger who has far more money than all the right-wingers put together.' Tim Renton seems to have protested that I wasn't a left-winger, commenting about my family not having made all that money by being left-wingers. He must have known that my father was still an active peer, formerly Labour then SDP, and that my left-wing credentials included membership of Nick's Diner.

Parliamentary Under Secretaries of State and Ministers of State are both referred to by the media as junior ministers. However, I soon realised that there is more difference in the two levels of minister than is at first apparent. Ministers of State frequently represent their department at meetings of Cabinet sub-committees. It is in those meetings that real decisions are taken and issues fully debated; something that seldom happens in Cabinet. The Committee Stage of Bills will often be run by the Minister of State, supported by the Parliamentary Under Secretary. It was also soon clear to me that the civil servants treat a Minister of State with that extra bit of respect, recognizing that he or she has more authority. Then there are the peripherals: Ministers of State often acquire their own Parliamentary Private Secretary. This I did after a while. My first was Dudley Fishburn. He would have made an outstanding minister, having great ability. However, he was one of the few who found Parliamentary life does not suit them. So, not having played a sufficient role in debates and Questions to get promoted, he retired and worked for the *Economist*. My later Parliamentary Private Secretaries included Eric Pickles, who later became a Cabinet minister and Chairman of the Party, and Angela Knight, who was outstanding in that role, as she was when she became a Treasury Minister. I was also amused to find that I was allocated a much better room during the Party Conference that October. Indeed my room was so good that after I had had it for two days, it was passed on to Douglas Hurd.

The job description for the Minister for Trade is quite straightforward: first, promote British exports and encourage inward investment. This requires close co-operation with the Foreign and Commonwealth Office and with numerous industry organisations. The second role is responsibility for trade policy. This I was to have for four years. I became a frequent visitor to Brussels for trade councils, leading up to the meeting in Morocco to agree what was known as the 'Uruguay round' of tariff reductions under the GATT and the establishment of the World Trade Organisation (WTO). A lot of travel was involved. In 1991, as well as a number of visits to Brussels, I went to seventeen other countries.

The third part of my job description was to stop exports which we did not wish to happen because of international obligations or our national interest. I was to spend nearly as much time over the next two years dealing with such issues as I was promoting exports. When I arrived at the department, there had already been three incidents when exports to Iraq had given rise to considerable media interest. The first related to chemical precursors which could be used to make forbidden chemical weapons. These chemicals also had a variety of other uses. This complicated topic did not take up too much of my time.

That could not be said in respect of the second illegal export, which was of steel tubes, described as being part of a petrochemical complex but which it subsequently emerged were intended as components of the so-called Supergun. The Supergun project, known as Project Babylon, began in 1988. It appeared that Saddam Hussein was seeking to build a series of 'Superguns' based on research dating back to the 1960s by a Canadian artillery expert, Gerald Bull. It seems likely that he believed that, using Dr Bull's research, he could construct an artillery piece with a long enough range to reach Israel from Iraq. It seemed a very bizarre idea. Components for what would have been an enormous gun were sourced from various places, including Walter Somers Ltd, a steel company in the north-east. It is clear that if employees at Walter Somers had known that the tubes they had been asked to provide were intended for a gun rather than a petrochemical plant, they would have known that they needed to apply for an export licence. Shortly after I became Minister of Trade, we were effectively at war with Iraq. The idea that we had supplied that country with components for fantastic lethal weapons was a very exciting issue for the media. Luckily, as it had all happened before I was in post, my main involvement was to explain what action had been taken by the department since the matter had come to light, to try and make sure that something like that never happened again.

By the time I first became a departmental minister, our children had all left school. We did not need to take our holiday during the school holidays so I usually volunteered to be Duty Minister during August. This was not normally an arduous job, since once Parliament rose, Cabinet ministers, Permanent Secretaries and political correspondents all tended to disappear and Westminster life became quite laid back. Those still around kept normal office hours. I looked forward to devoting most of August 1990 to finding out what my new job involved, particularly as I had very little previous knowledge of trade and its many national and international aspects. It was not to be. In the early hours of 2 August, Iraq under Saddam Hussein invaded the small Gulf State of Kuwait. This act of aggression opened a new chapter in the unhappy history of the Middle East. Saddam Hussein was after the massive oil reserves of Kuwait, which he claimed should be part of Iraq.

The United Nations responded to this act of aggression speedily and unanimously imposed a total trade embargo on exports to Iraq. As a consequence, an emergency Cabinet meeting was held at Number 10 to which I was summoned, as Peter Lilley, my Secretary of State, was on holiday in France. The discussion focused on the importance of the UK observing the embargo.

Not long afterwards, a senior civil servant came to see me to say the dreaded words, 'Minister, we have a problem.' It was a very bizarre problem which had its origins in the Second World War and also involved bananas. Anticipating the outbreak of hostilities on 1 September 1939, the House of Commons passed through all stages in some twenty minutes the 'Import/Export and Custom Powers (Defence) Bill'. This Act gave the Government powers to control any exports or imports by regulations which did not require debate in the House of Commons. Section 9(3) of the Act provided that 'This Act shall continue in force until such date as His Majesty may, by Order in Council, declare to be the date on which the emergency that was the occasion of the passing of this Act came to an end and shall then expire.' This seemed quite straightforward and carried the assumption that at the end of the Second World War, the Act would cease to apply. The reasons why this did not happen were examined at great, some would say excessive, length by Sir Richard Scott in his Report of the Inquiry into the Export of Defence Equipment and Dual-Use Goods to Iraq and Related Prosecutions.

In 1983, a company called Chris International Foods Ltd had been refused a licence to import 220 tonnes of bananas from dollar-area countries. There was a quota for what was known as 'dollar bananas'. This quota was intended to protect banana imports from our dependent territories and former colonies in the West Indies from competition from bananas from Central America. The latter were usually more competitively priced, being produced on large plantations on flat land as opposed to production by smallholders, often on very sloping land. Surprisingly, both parties in the judicial review of the Chris International Foods case seemed to accept that the Act remained in force and that the emergency had not come to an end because no Order in Council had ever been made. One factor in this surprising decision was that, at that time, Germany was still divided into West Germany and the GDR, and there was no Peace Treaty with East Germany.

I had had an early example of Peter Lilley's approach to trade matters, which also showed his ability to listen to his junior ministers. When he learnt about the quota for the import of bananas other than those from our former colonies and dependent territories in the Caribbean, he immediately thought it should be abolished. The result would be lower-cost bananas in the shops. Having spent much of the previous year dealing with the countries and dependent territories which produced those bananas, I was able to point out to Peter the disastrous consequences this would have on their economies. If they were deprived of much of their earnings by the loss of the banana trade, it would greatly increase the burden on the UK to provide support by other means. Somewhat to my surprise, I was able to persuade Peter to maintain the quota system, and to continue to protect our banana imports from the Caribbean.

In August 1990, after the Iraq invasion of Kuwait, the situation had changed. It was no longer possible to argue that the emergency which had caused the 1939 Act still existed. Officials in the DTI therefore came to the conclusion that the Act, which had probably been vulnerable for some time to determined and rigorous legal challenge, was now even more vulnerable. Hence my hearing from one of my senior officials those dread words, 'Minister, we have a problem.' There was a total trade embargo for Iraq, sanctioned by the United Nations. With our past record of arms and other exports to Iraq, it was vital that our enforcement of the embargo was not left vulnerable to any legal challenge.

The obvious solution was to introduce a very short Bill to clear up the possibility of a challenge by giving the 1939 Act permanence. This could be done with a one-clause Bill, which would remove the provision for the expiry of the Act. Achieving this objective speedily and without undue publicity clearly required the co-operation of the Opposition.

The Shadow Secretary of State was no less a figure than Dr Gordon Brown. Peter Lilley was the Secretary of State and, as Minister for Trade, my opposite number was Joyce Quin. The first step in the process of obtaining the necessary co-operation was a brief meeting between myself and Gordon Brown behind the Speaker's chair, the most convenient neutral ground. This was followed at the end of October by a more formal meeting at which Peter Lilley and I were present and there were officials to make a note of what happened. This led to a further meeting which was just between myself and Joyce Quin, again with officials present. The outcome of these meetings was that after the Opposition had recovered from their shock at discovering that it was the 1939 Emergency Powers Act which controlled all our imports and exports, they agreed to co-operate in the process of making the Act permanent.

So, on the evening of Thursday, 29 November, in a debate lasting barely twenty minutes in which only I and Joyce Quin spoke, a Bill to make the 1939 Act permanent received Second Reading, was committed to a Committee of the whole House, immediately considered reported without amendment, read a Third Time and passed. There was, however, an elephant in the room. Regulations made under powers provided in primary legislation, that is to say an Act of Parliament, are normally subject either to positive or negative Resolution procedure. Positive Resolution requires that the regulations be debated; negative Resolution requires that they can be debated if there is a motion put forward to have a debate and time is found for that motion to be debated. It was therefore rather extraordinary that all the numerous Regulations made under the Import and Export Control Act 1939 had been made subject only to the negative Resolution procedure and only a very few debated.

During discussions at the DTI about the 'problem', it had been decided that if necessary, in order to obtain the co-operation of the Opposition, we could offer to include in the proposed Bill to make the Import and Export Control Act permanent a requirement that all subsequent regulations be subject to Positive resolution procedure and therefore debated. This offer was therefore made twice, first at the meeting between Peter Lilley and Gordon Brown and, secondly, and even more clearly, at the meeting between myself and Joyce Quin on 13 November. During that meeting, Joyce Quin said that she had had an opportunity to consider the issue of positive or negative Resolution procedure with Gordon Brown and she implied also with other Opposition figures, including perhaps Tony Blair. As I wrote in the letter I sent to the Scott Inquiry into the alleged export of arms to Iraq, dated 30 January 1995, the offer to include positive Resolution procedure was clearly rejected by Joyce Quin, 'somewhat to my surprise'. My view is that the Opposition decision to reject the offer was in part because of the difficulties the Labour Party always has had about anything to do with arms exports. They had, perhaps sensibly for their Party politics, concluded that the less said on the subject, the better.

I find it somewhat surprising that Sir Richard Scott cast doubt upon my evidence on this point but did not bother to call me for verbal examination as a witness. That was even stranger as I was the only minister involved in the affair who had served in the MoD, the FCO and the DTI, all the three departments under scrutiny. I was led to believe that Gordon Brown and Joyce Quin were both greatly upset to be the only Opposition figures even mildly criticised in the Scott Report. However, in the furore around the debate on the report focusing on the role of William Waldegrave, this aspect of the matter was overlooked.

The Supergun and chemical precursors did lead to my only appearance before a Select Committee. Select Committees carry out very important and often under-rated functions of Parliament. An appearance before them can be very nerve-racking occasions for ministers, civil servants and others. Luckily, I had been very well served by my department in respect of putting right what had previously not been very good in regard to record-keeping and procedures in dealing with applications for export licences. In consequence, in reply to the question from Dr Gilbert, the chairman of the Trade and Industry Select Committee, I was able to list a whole series of improvements, adjustments and amendments we had made to help exporters deal with what I identified as 'export orders for destinations which were of a "curious nature"' which would justify further scrutiny. As a result, I received an unusual compliment for a minister appearing before a Select Committee: Dr Gilbert said, 'That is one of the most comprehensive answers I think I have ever listened to, thank you very much.' So I escaped unharmed from that encounter, but there was a more dramatic and major issue to come.

A clever piece of investigative journalism by the *Sunday Times* Insight team led to the publication on 2 December of a major article alleging that exports by United Kingdom companies of military and defence-related equipment to Iraq had been surreptitiously encouraged by officials in the Department of Trade and Industry and, worse still, by Alan Clark, when he had been Minister of Trade. British troops had been part of the United Nations force that in Operation Desert Storm had driven the Iraqis out of Kuwait. This made the allegations in the *Sunday Times* of great significance. It was not as if the exports, which it was alleged had been encouraged, had merely been fuel to the long-running war between Iraq and Iran, there was a direct British interest. There had been British casualties, albeit a very small number, as a result of Operation Desert Storm, and the Opposition were not slow in taking up the case and proposed a Private Notice Question. I was therefore summoned to Number 10 early on a Monday for a small meeting chaired by John Major, who had hardly got his feet under the desk as Prime Minister before being faced with these charges of ministerial misbehaviour. Robin Butler, head of the Civil Service, had interviewed Alan Clark, who had 'strenuously denied' the allegations made against him. It was therefore decided that I should make a statement in the House that day about exports to Iraq.

My statement was perhaps quite accurately described by Martin O'Neill on behalf of the Opposition as being 'an insignificant statement'. The most important part of what I said was that 'My Honourable Friend, the Minister for Defence Procurement [Alan Clark], strongly denies the interpretation put on the remarks alleged to have been made by him in the *Sunday Times* article.' Alan Clark was sitting beside me on the front bench throughout the forty minutes or so which my statement and subsequent Questions lasted. Throughout, he was encouraging me to reject as strongly as possible the attacks of the Opposition. Subsequently, he made a sworn statement preparatory to the evidence he would be asked to give in the forthcoming trial of the directors of Matrix Churchill. It was only later, when he was cross-examined by the defence during that trial, that he admitted at long last that he had indeed encouraged the directors of Matrix Churchill to describe the end-use of the machine tools they were hoping to export to Iraq as being of a civilian nature, although they knew that they were going to be used to machine fuses for shells.

Not surprisingly, the prosecution collapsed. After Alan Clark's admission, the prosecution decided that the case was no longer tenable. This led to a mass of press and media coverage and political attacks on the Government led, cleverly, by Robin Cook. It was he who managed to attach the title 'Arms to Iraq' to the whole affair, which led most observers and commentators to believe or to suggest that what was involved was not machine tools, which were clearly capable of civilian and military use, but arms of a more direct nature that would clearly be for military use. Robin Cook's clever but unscrupulous campaign kept the matter at a high profile until the subsequent Report of the Scott Inquiry came to be debated in the House on 26 February 1996.

In his inquiry, Richard Scott ranged very widely over the whole issue of the export of defence-related equipment, but also the degree of accountability and openness by Government on that subject. In my view,

Some visits abroad were more dangerous than others. My protection team
during a visit to Colombia, 1992

he failed as a lawyer to understand that guidelines are simply guidelines
that have to be applied on a case-by-case basis. When applying guidelines, clearly a whole range of issues has to be taken into account. Those
matters will change as circumstances change, and international relations
are one of the circumstances. Sir Richard's Report effectively acquitted
the Government of two main charges. First, that there was a plot secretly
to arm Saddam Hussein; secondly, that there had been an attempt to sup-
press documents that could have led to a miscarriage of justice. However,
he did allege that the House had been misled on a change to the guidelines and consequently the debate which took place on a Motion for the
Adjournment was in effect, a vote of censure on William Waldegrave.
I spoke, by then from the back-benches, defending William and rejecting
the allegations in the Scott Report. The vote proved to be a very close-run
thing. John Major's Government had been steadily losing its majority
and the vote on the motion for the Adjournment was only rejected by
1 vote, 320 to 319.

The 'Arms to Iraq' issue had carried on after I had retired as a minister.
That part of my role, trying to stop illegal exports and dealing with the
fallout of some that had occurred, took up a surprising amount of my
time. But promoting exports remained my prime job. That called for a
lot of travel. I had already been in two ministerial roles which involved

a certain amount of overseas travel. When it came to going overseas, Minister for Trade was something else. During my two years in the job, I made over twenty overseas trips visiting some thirty different countries, in addition to numerous visits to Brussels for trade councils. Most of the Brussels visits were for one day and usually if they went to schedule, I would be back in London in time for dinner. However, all too often, ministerial meetings did not go according to schedule and overran, sometimes until late in the evening. This was very inconvenient because there was no dinner provided. It meant that on one occasion when I had hoped to be in England celebrating my cousin David's fiftieth birthday, I was instead stuck in Brussels making do with a baguette and the lucky find of a quarter bottle of Côte du Rhône. It was a very poor substitute for the dinner Susie was enjoying at Le Manoir aux Quat' Saisons.

Occasionally, a Brussels visit included a scheduled stay at the residence of our Ambassador to the European Union. In 1990, the Grand Residence opposite the Royal Palace was still occupied by the Ambassador to Belgium. The more important post of Ambassador to the European Union had a residence in a reasonably large house quite close to the centre, but nothing like as impressive as the Ambassador's residence. This meant that on one occasion, Tristan Garel-Jones, who was also in Brussels, and I were sharing a bathroom, which was between our two bedrooms. When I was using the bathroom after Tristan, there was suddenly a shout from the adjoining room, 'Tim, come here and see what I've found on the tele.' I assumed that I was going to see something provocative and indeed I did, but it was not what I had anticipated. It was the bullfighting equivalent of goal of the month. I don't know whether it was entitled 'kill of the week', but Tristan was very excited to find that his favourite entertainment was being shown on Belgian television.

The serious business of trade councils was often focused on trying to persuade the French to accept a more open trading system, and a more or less hopeless quest to persuade them that they ought to relax the extent of agricultural protection to which they were greatly attached. The French would have liked to have had what was described as 'fortress Europe', with their industries protected by high external tariffs. It is interesting that they did not succeed in that objective and even back in the 1990s, the European Union's external tariffs for industrial goods were relatively low and, for many countries in the developing world, were set at zero.

On one occasion, when I returned to the Ambassador's residence at about 11 p.m. at night after an extremely boring and unproductive discussion on tariffs, I found that Douglas Hurd, who had been at a much grander ministerial meeting of foreign ministers, had already returned to the residence. His meeting had ended with a dinner at which only the foreign ministers of the twelve member countries had been present, together with representatives of the Commission, so he was briefing our outstanding Ambassador to the EU, John Kerr, now Lord Kerr, as to what had been discussed or agreed at the dinner. When I entered the room, Douglas looked up and said, 'Hello Tim, how did it go?' I replied it was the usual story, 11 against 1. Douglas paused only for a few seconds before saying 'Ah, so the French were isolated, were they?' That had indeed been the situation, as it was quite often, so far from Britain being the country out on a limb, when I was involved in trade discussions, it was frequently France that was in that position.

In those days when there were just twelve members of the European Union, ministerial meetings took place in a large room in which each country was allocated three seats in the front row at the table and three more seats in the row behind. On one occasion when it was a rather grand council which Douglas Hurd was attending as well as myself, the French had three ministers in the front row: their Foreign Secretary, their Europe Minister and their Trade Minister. While we were listening to Leon Brittan speaking in English on behalf of the Commission, I noticed that two of the three French ministers did not have their headphones on and were listening in English, rather than to the simultaneous translation into French. John Kerr said to me that even a few years earlier that would have been unthinkable, as, however good a French minister's English was, he or she would always listen to an English-speaking commissioner in French via the headphones. This confirmed what I had already noticed, that English was gradually becoming the dominant language of the European Union. When there was a lunch during or after a meeting of trade ministers which I attended, the simultaneous translation was only available for English, French and German. I noticed during the four years during which I spent a lot of time in Brussels, that gradually more and more participants were listening and speaking in English. It seemed that the French had reluctantly accepted that theirs was no longer the language of diplomacy.

Many of my other overseas trips took me to more distant parts of the world. One of my first was to Hong Kong and Indonesia in September 1990. Susie accompanied me on that trip. In Hong Kong, we stayed in the Governor's palatial residence and were startled to find that I was allocated a valet and Susie a lady's maid. They were constantly asking us what we planned to wear for the next part of our programme so that those clothes could be whisked away and immaculately pressed or prepared. We were not surprised to be told that allegedly the Queen had said to David Wilson, the Governor, 'It appears, Mr Wilson that you live in greater state than I do.'

Later that year I went to West Africa, visiting Nigeria and Ghana. In Ghana, it was hoped that I would be able to have a meeting with Jerry Rawlings, who was then the Chairman of the Interim Revolutionary Council. He was effectively a dictatorial ruler of the country for the second time. As a junior officer in the Air Force, he had led a coup against the corrupt government on an earlier occasion, and then handed back control to the Parliament. He then led a second coup when that group of Parliamentarians proved to be as corrupt as their predecessors. My brief included the instruction that, if I did have the opportunity to meet him, I was to urge Jerry Rawlings to once more install a properly elected democratic government. Shortly before I was due to leave Ghana, I was told that the Chairman could see me and I had been allocated half an hour of his time. Our meeting eventually lasted nearly two hours, a lengthy and interesting discussion about the state of the world, the state of Ghana and democracy. During the latter part of the discussion, Jerry Rawlings said something to the effect that he had studied all forms of democracy. He added that, in his opinion, if you gave people the vote, they voted for taxi drivers. He said this with great scorn. Not long after my visit, democracy did return to Ghana and the country has remained a democratic state since. One of the few in Africa where an election resulted in a win for the Opposition which was allowed to take over without any delay and without seeking to imprison, or worse, eliminate, its predecessors.

During 1991, when I seemed to spend a lot of the year out of the country, one of my more unusual visits was to the Republic of Ireland. My programme in Dublin included a tour of the Guinness brewery. The following day I flew down to Cork where I started my visit with a call on the Lord Mayor. He was a bit upset that I didn't accept his offer of a small whisky at about 10.30 in the morning, but did explain to me with the greatest good humour that the two portraits on either side of his desk represented somebody who had starved himself to death in protest against the British and the other I think we shot, or hung. I later went on to a hotel to address a meeting of the Chamber of Commerce. It was the only occasion when on arrival I was told not to get out of the car until security had indicated that it was safe to do so. I am glad to say that I returned to Britain untroubled by anything other than the friendly welcome and warm hospitality throughout my visit to the Republic.

Later that year, I paid my only official visit to an Arab country. I went to Kuwait, and from there on to Bahrain. We arrived late, after dark in Kuwait, and the next morning when I looked out of my bedroom window, there were blue skies. It was not long after the end of Operation Desert Storm, which liberated Kuwait from Iraqi occupation, and there had been a great deal of publicity about the pollution coming from all the oil wells which the Iraqis had set on fire when they retreated. Our Ambassador, Michael Weston, commented that it was the first day when the smoke was not a predominant feature in the sky. There was as usual a dinner, for which Michael had gone to a great deal of effort to obtain a case of white wine. Unfortunately, he concluded that it had been left on arrival at the docks unrefrigerated; ten of the twelve bottles proved to be undrinkable. I travelled down to Bahrain with the Kuwaiti Minister for Trade. We were both planning to attend the opening of a large trade fair. We were accommodated in what I took to be the best hotel in Bahrain, each being allocated a palatial suite at either end of a corridor. I was amused to note that each of us had a guard outside our room. The Kuwaiti minister's guard was dressed in full Arab robes, mine was in a western suit.

My next visit in 1991 was perhaps the most interesting and important I ever made. It was a week in the Republic of South Africa during the period of the transition government before the first fully democratic election in the Republic's history. I was the first British Minister for Trade to visit South Africa for over twenty years, as the move to democracy allowed us to promote trade and direct British investment in South Africa. It was a long, eight-day, visit including a weekend off which we spent in a cottage we had been lent by the sea. It included numerous meetings and several speeches. One of the meetings with trade unionists, members of the ANC, enabled me to have a short encounter with Nelson Mandela. The *Cape Times* declared me to be Businessman of the Week. The article which accompanied this statement involved being interviewed by a lady who said her name was Mrs Le May. I asked if by any chance she was related to a history don at Worcester College of the same name. I got the somewhat surprising reply, 'I was his first and much the nicest of his wives.'

Undoubtedly the high point of the visit was a meeting with President

F. W. de Klerk. It was arranged at quite short notice but the President clearly thought it went well, as he arranged an impromptu television and radio press conference on the steps of the presidential building in which we both took part. After my return, I received a very nice letter of thanks for what I had done from John Major. I concluded that the reports back must have been satisfactory, the many potential banana skins avoided.

One of the incidental responsibilities I acquired as Minister for Trade was for the development of the British Pavilion at the forthcoming World Expo in Seville. I was assured that this important project was being well managed, as it was being supervised by a particularly talented young civil servant. Our pavilion was extremely well sited, as it looked down the principal avenue in the exhibition grounds. The main feature was the front, which was an entirely glass wall with water spilling down it, a feature designed by the sculptor William Pye. Not long after I had become Minister for Trade, I was told by the civil servant in charge of the project that a satisfactory contract had been found for the supply of the glass in the façade. When I asked who was to be the supplier, I was told it was St Gobain. I was astonished and felt like using the McEnroe expressions 'You must be joking,' or 'You can't be serious.' To have the main feature of the British pavilion provided by a French company was quite unacceptable. I was told that the price from the French company was less than that provided by the British company, Pilkington's. Luckily I had met Alistair Pilkington, who ran the company, and said to my Private Secretary, 'Get him on the telephone.' I said to him, 'I need a sharper price.' In due course that was provided, and so it was a British company that provided the glass for the façade. Not much later, I was told that a satisfactory contract had been negotiated for the provision of the uniforms for all the guides who would take people round our pavilion. I asked who was providing the cloth, and was told it was a very good Italian company. So I had to go through the same procedure to ensure that the cloth came from a British company. It seemed to me that both instances were typical examples of the political insensitivity of most civil servants.

During 1991 there had been continuous speculation about the timing of the next General Election, ever since John Major had taken over as Prime Minister in November 1990. The election had to be held by July 1992. Throughout 1991, the economy refused to show much sign of recovery from the recession. Not surprisingly, the polls showed Labour with a considerable lead. By 1992, the situation was getting slightly better, certainly in respect of the opinion polls, but when John Major decided

The *Cape Times* 'Businessman of the Week'. Cartoon by Colin Daniel, 1991

to call the election immediately after the Budget had been announced, the outlook was still fairly gloomy. Many forecasters said the best result that could be expected for the Tories was a hung Parliament. With an election under way, I discovered another difference between being a Parliamentary Under Secretary of State and Minister of State. As Minister for Trade, I was given a tour to go to various constituencies to speak or attend an event in support of the Conservative candidate. So I spent a lot less time in Hove during the 1992 Election than in any other of the six General Elections in which I fought.

The opinion polls on election day were still indicating a very close election result, very few forecasting a Conservative victory. On election night, Susie and I did not go early to the count in Hove because the constituency was notoriously slow in counting the vote and the result was usually only declared at, or after, 2.00 in the morning. Even before we went to the Town Hall, the first results coming in were more encouraging than we had expected. Once we arrived at the count, it became more difficult to get definite information, but as information trickled through, we realized that we were doing much better than had been expected. When all results had been declared, there was an overall Conservative majority of twenty-one seats.

I had held Hove with a reduced majority of 12,268, 49% of the total vote, the only time since the by-election when I got less than 50%.

18

MINISTER FOR INDUSTRY

B ack in London (after the Conservative victory in the 1992 General Election), I started wondering about my position. The Cabinet appointments had been announced, numerous new appointments and moves of Ministers of State and Parliamentary Under Secretaries were being announced, but I had heard nothing about myself. Eventually, when all Government appointments seemed to have been made, I rang my office, or what had been my office, to ask what my position was. The reply I received was that as far as they knew, I was still Minister of State in the Department of Trade and Industry and they suggested I should come into the office to find out what was happening. This I did. I already knew about, and very much welcomed, the appointment of Michael Heseltine under the title President of the Board of Trade to head the DTI in place of Peter Lilley.

When I arrived at the department, I soon discovered that Michael had decided to divide responsibility for the trade side of the department into two. I retained responsibility for trade policy, including the Uruguay round of GATT, while Richard Needham became Minister of State for Trade, concentrating on national trade and export promotion. As Michael described it, I remained responsible for the conduct of trade negotiations, the time-consuming agenda of the trade councils in Brussels. Richard, whom Michael accurately described as a natural-born salesman with indefatigable energy and irrepressible enthusiasm, was able to concentrate on the export promotion side of the department. Energy policy was once again part of the DTI. Tim Eggar was Minister of State for Energy, so there were three Ministers of State and also three Parliamentary Under Secretaries of State in the DTI : Edward Leigh for Technology, Neil Hamilton for Corporate Affairs, and Jean Denton, our lady in the Lords.

As Minister for Industry, there were three strands to my work. The first was supporting Michael Heseltine's competitiveness agenda. He was rightly concerned about the declining competitiveness of much of British industry. He established a 'Competitiveness Unit' in the DTI. I supported its work, particularly the creation of a network of business links, bringing together all those parts of Government and other agencies supporting business, especially smaller businesses. Secondly, there were issues concerning specific industries, of which the most significant was the aerospace industry. Not only was it a major employer, employing over 100,000, but also a major exporter and an industry where exports often required political intervention and offset agreements. These happened when a British company, or the Government, decided to buy an aircraft or aerospace product from an overseas supplier, usually the USA, and as part of the purchase there would be a side agreement that the foreign company would make arrangements to obtain certain supplies and create an agreed amount of employment in Britain. Discussing those matters took me to Seattle to see Boeing, and the interesting experience of going to what at the time was the largest building in the world in terms of space covered and seeing 747 jumbo jets being assembled.

Aerospace was the one private industry for which the Government provided specific financial assistance in the form of launch aid. The justification was the very high cost of developing new aero engines, and the long period of development involved. It had proved impossible for Rolls Royce to obtain private sector finance. I was able to persuade a reluctant Treasury to continue to provide launch aid. In 1983, it was for the new three shaft engines, with 8,000lb thrust. The launch aid payments were loans and a steady stream of repayments were received. Even the Treasury recognised the value of the employment and exports that resulted from Rolls Royce, being one of only three world-class aero engine manufacturers.

The third strand, which was perhaps the most important of my responsibilities and which, together with the trade negotiations, produced the most work, was our regional industrial policy. That role gave me the job of presiding over the re-drawing of the map delineating the areas eligible for national and European regional aid. That required negotiation with the European Community in Brussels. Having produced our proposals based on an analysis of all the available data for the various areas of England, we then had to get it agreed by the Commission, who had the duty of ensuring 'a level playing field' for all members in respect of any aid to industry. The unemployment rate in Brighton and Hove meant that the area was on the borderline of those that might qualify for Regional Selective Assistance. Not including my own constituency area in the map helped me persuade the EU that the list must be fair. I got the impression that they expected other countries to be less scrupulous.

I had done three successive ministerial jobs which involved a lot of overseas travel; my new role involved a great deal of travel around England. The main purpose was not visiting factories, but going to the areas which were to be included, or perhaps not included, in the new map of eligibility for Regional Selective Assistance. These visits were unusual for a Conservative minister, as I would find myself meeting all the interested parties in an area. They would try to persuade me that their area should continue to be eligible, or should become eligible. Since many of the areas were in more depressed parts of the country, the Members of Parliament and council leaders who were in the reception committee were very often from the Labour Party. Representatives of the local TUC and the CBI and Chambers of Commerce would also be present, all of whom were very polite.

Throughout my ministerial experience, I found that a junior minister in London was of little, if any, interest to the media. In Birmingham or Manchester, it was possible there might be an interview by the local media. When it came to visits to the remoter parts of the country, the media reaction was very different. In Cornwall or Cumbria, it was 'hold the front page'. Not only were the local media anxious to get an interview, but they were unfailingly polite and friendly, and I was not subject to awkward questions. It could be said that this was not the ideal training for having to appear in front of Jeremy Paxman to defend the BMW takeover of Rover. That was an occasion when Michael Heseltine was very ready to leave the media work to one of his Ministers of State. It was fortunate that he was unavailable, as he was in Australia promoting UK exports. Michael was less ready than I to accept the change of ownership. It meant that I had to make a statement in the House followed, as I recall, by eleven media events. Both the statement in the House of Commons and the various media events were easier than might have been expected. There were no immediate job losses and the investment and expertise coming in offset the ownership going out.

21 June 1993 was the first day of the Wimbledon tennis fortnight. As a debenture holder for many years, I was planning as usual to attend on the first day. Over breakfast we heard the extremely worrying news that Michael Heseltine had had a heart attack in Venice and was in hospital. Initially it was very unclear as to how serious the heart attack was. I spoke with our excellent Permanent Secretary at the DTI, Sir Peter Gregson, as it seemed likely that I would be regarded as the most senior minister in the department, being a Privy Councillor and having been in the

department longer than the other two Ministers of State. Sir Peter agreed that there was nothing we could do until we had better information, and so we agreed to keep in touch by my phoning him once or twice from Wimbledon. This was before the days of mobiles, which enable us to maintain instant communication at all times. Happily, it soon emerged that Michael's heart attack was not too serious and it was not long before he was evacuated back to Britain. He was photographed en route looking really quite cheerful.

When it became clear that it was going to be some time before Michael would be able to return to his ministerial responsibilities, I was appointed a temporary member of the Cabinet. As well as attending the weekly Cabinet meetings, I was invited to a number of Cabinet sub-committees, both formal and informal. I was amused to find that when standing in as the official replacement for a Cabinet minister who is temporarily absent, you sit in his place at the Cabinet table for Cabinet meetings. Since Michael was a very senior Cabinet minister, ranking number 5 in the pecking order, it meant that I sat right in the middle of the long table at Number 10, nearly opposite the Prime Minister and next to Ken Clarke, the Chancellor of the Exchequer. While I wasn't silent, I do not recall making any significant contributions at Cabinet meetings which I attended, other than on one occasion when a special meeting was called to discuss the situation in the former Yugoslavia. The issue was essentially whether we should bomb Serbian artillery and tanks, particularly those involved in the siege of Sarajevo. Drawing on my experience in the MoD, I expressed the view that such an intervention would be effective, as the military tended to be very reluctant to lose their favourite weapons, particularly when they are relatively few in number. I was a lone voice with that view, and the Foreign Office view, favouring further negotiation, prevailed. Later when the allies did bomb Serbian positions, it led fairly rapidly to a ceasefire.

To my surprise, I discovered that even as a stand-in member of the Cabinet, unusual efforts would be made to make sure that I could attend. On one occasion, I had engagements in Cornwall lasting until late in the evening, and an aircraft was provided to fly me back to London to be ready for the Cabinet meeting the following morning. As the sole passenger in the small plane, I felt the whole exercise was somewhat extravagant.

While Michael was recovering, I did, however, have to take on some extra responsibilities for matters including becoming the de facto chairman of the morning meeting of ministers. All my fellow ministers, other than Neil Hamilton, were helpful and co-operative in keeping the department operating smoothly. The most important task I had to take on was to agree with Michael Portillo, the Chief Secretary, the department's budget in the forthcoming public expenditure review. Sometimes these discussions could be very contentious and lead, in the absence of agreement between the Treasury and the department concerned, for the issue to be sent to a Cabinet sub-committee for resolution. Luckily I was able to reach quick agreement with Michael and on a basis that was regarded as quite satisfactory by our Permanent Secretary. The concession I had made was to agree a sizeable increase in the cost of the standard postage rate. This reduced the deficit of the Post Office and therefore saved Government subsidy and reduced the overall costs of the department.

The most important Parliamentary occasion for which I had to take responsibility was to make a statement on the revisions to the map of areas eligible to receive Regional Selective Assistance. This was a fairly high-profile issue. There would be MPs bitterly disappointed at their constituency, or part of it, losing eligibility or not being upgraded to become eligible. Some would be Tory, but most of the areas affected would be in Labour seats. The Opposition would be led by Robin Cook, which made our Whips' Office nervous; he was a formidable debater. Labour Members, whose constituencies were involved and who asked questions after my statement and Robin Cook's response, included Gerald Kaufman, Neil Kinnock, Peter Shore and Alan Milburn. I was helped by supportive questions from Michael Alison, Michael Jopling and several other colleagues. William Powell even managed to make a positive contribution, commenting on his constituency losing assisted area status being good news, as it showed that local unemployment rates were lower. Thanks in no small part to the excellent work done by my Parliamentary Private Secretary, Angela Knight, what could have been a difficult occasion went extremely well, and the Whips' Office, who had been anxious, were able to relax. The Commons sketch in the *Daily Telegraph* wrote of my performance, 'It was as close to game, set and match as the Tory Party has been since Maastricht.' A compliment at the time, but sounding rather dubious later.

There was one nasty moment when I thought I would have to take over preparing the Government's response to a major inquiry into the gas industry. This would have involved me having to read a very large amount of background material on a subject about which I knew very little. I was saved by an unexpected discovery: the Permanent Secretary told me that I would not be able to do that job because Sainsbury's had, much to my surprise, submitted evidence to the inquiry. I was very grateful to the company. I was not entirely surprised to find that, in the absence of Michael, another department made a power-grab for part of the DTI's responsibilities for regional industrial policy and this came from the Department of Employment, in the person of David Hunt. I felt he should have known from our time in the Whips' Office together that I was not one to fall for his tactic.

On one occasion, I had to go to a small informal meeting at Number 10 with John Major and four very senior ministers discussing an issue with a European dimension. I cannot now remember exactly what was involved but I do recall that, to me, the issue seemed extremely straight-forward. I was surprised that we spent nearly two hours under John's patient guidance discussing the matter. At the end of the discussion, all five or six present agreed and John Major took me on one side and said, 'Tim, it's not always like this; I just wanted to make sure that all those involved had accepted the decision which, as you might have guessed, seemed to be fairly obvious.'

The House rose at the end of July as usual. I stayed as Duty Minister during August before we went on our holiday in September. Before leaving, I wrote a letter to Michael Portillo, the Chief Secretary, about the looming problem of further pit closures. I had been informed that another list of closures was going to be announced shortly. It seemed clear to me that we needed to do a lot more by way of special assistance to ameliorate the problems that would be created in the areas where the pits were due to be closed. I wrote a letter marked confidential to the six key ministers and the Prime Minister, who needed to be involved. My main point was to ask for additional funds and expenditure to be agreed by the Treasury. I also asked that we might access some European Commission funding. I then departed on holiday with Susie on our lovely boat, *Fair Lady*, to cruise the Turkish coast. While there, I heard that my letter had been leaked and a copy had found its way to the *Guardian* and to Arthur Scargill, President of the National Union of Mineworkers. The leak had produced headlines in the *Guardian* and a brief flurry of pub-licity but, in the absence of most of the principal players in Government, the Opposition and the media, all away on holiday and awaiting the return of Parliament, the row quickly subsided. I suspect this led to the Government under-estimating the reaction when the announcement of more pit closures was eventually made. By then, Michael Heseltine was back in post and I was not much involved in the subsequent arguments about the future of the mining industry.

Before leaving on holiday, I had gone to Michael's house at Thenford to discuss the situation in the department and the outlook for my areas of responsibility. The occasion also gave me the opportunity to see how Michael was getting on. He was clearly making very good progress and was looking forward to an early return to full responsibilities. It did, however, seem clear that he was unlikely to be ready to make a speech at the Party Conference during the debate on DTI matters. During our discussion, I told him that I had decided not to stand again at the next General Election and that I would ask John Major to relieve me of my ministerial responsibilities, probably during the following year. Michael found this very strange, as he couldn't really understand why anybody involved in politics at a senior level should want to give up while they were still well able to carry on. I felt that I had done as much as I was likely to do at a senior level in Government and, since I would be approaching sixty-five by the time of the next election, if I was going to take up any new activities, preferably in the arts world, it was the right time to retire. In addition, I must admit that I was finding that the routine responsibilities of being an MP and dealing with constituents' problems was becoming more time-consuming and less interesting. However, I did have one more unusual experience just before going on holiday. This was being called to a meeting with Ken Clarke, as Chancellor of the Exchequer, about a Budget matter, which meant that the meeting was just between Ken and me and one of his officials. The issue was the proposed introduction of a tax on insurance policies. Since the insurance industry was a DTI responsibility, he needed to consult with the DTI and secure my agreement to the idea. I accepted that it seemed a very logical way of bringing in a little extra revenue and was, in a sense, a minor form of wealth tax, since the better off had more of value to insure and would be likely to be able to pay the higher premiums. Indeed, many of the least well off would have no insurance policies at all, and therefore would not be affected by the tax. The tax was introduced and the rate has been increased several times since.

My final task as Michael's stand-in was to make the speech at the Party Conference, on 8 October 1993, in response to the debate on trade and industry. Although Michael's doctors had advised that he should not take on the responsibility, he was able to be present on the platform sitting beside me while I made the speech. At the end of the speech, he got up and we stood together to receive an enthusiastic standing ovation which I am sure was more for the Party faithful being so glad to see Michael's return to health than appreciation for my adequate, but not in any way brilliant, speech. As Michael observed, it was the only time he got a standing ovation for not making a speech.

One evening early in 1994, I went round to the flat above Number 10 for a drink and a chat with John and Norma Major. I told him that I would like to retire at the time of his next reshuffle, which we both expected to be shortly before the House rose for the summer recess. At the time, John was still confident of winning the next election. During our discussion, we talked about the possibility of his retiring as PM during the next Parliament. At that time, neither of us knew what lay ahead with the revelations about the abuse of expenses, nor the ever-growing divisions in the Party on the subject of Europe. Those factors, combined with some very effective campaigning by Tony Blair, would lead to the Labour landslide in 1997. Not the least unexpected feature of that remarkable turn of events was Hove becoming a Labour gain.

19

EUROPE

The House of Commons voted for the United Kingdom to join the European Economic Community, as the European Union then was, on 28 October 1971. The United Kingdom joined the Community on 1 January 1973. It was only nine months later that I was involved in the high-profile and much publicised by-election in Hove during which we had no less than seven public meetings. I do not recall that at any of those meetings Britain's membership of the EEC was raised. At that time, the Conservative Party was regarded by many as 'the Party for Europe', whereas the Labour Party were generally against membership of the EEC. However, there were a number of Labour Members of Parliament, and also clearly many Labour Party members, who were supporters of membership, sometimes very committed and enthusiastic supporters. Some of those MPs had helped the Conservative Government to get the necessary legislation through Parliament at the beginning of the 1970s.

So when Labour, somewhat to their surprise, came to power in 1974, Harold Wilson had a dilemma: how was he to resolve the commitment in the Manifesto for the February election to 'seek a fundamental re-negotiation of the terms of entry'. Although the negotiations were started during 1974, there had been very little progress before the second 1974 election. The Labour Manifesto for October pledged that 'within twelve months of this Election, we will give the British people the final say, which will be binding on the Government'. The 'final say' took the form of a Referendum on 5 June 1976. The electorate expressed strong support for continuing EC membership, with 67.23% voting in favour, on a national turnout of 64.67%. It provided a clear answer to the question that had been posed: 'Do you think that the United Kingdom should stay in the European Community (the Common Market)?'

There was an interesting and fundamental difference between the campaign fought by 'the Remainers' in 1975 and that on 23 June 2016.

The 'Keep Britain in Europe' campaign was an all-Party affair. It was organised and supervised by non-Party committees in each area. For my constituency and the two neighbouring constituencies in Brighton, there was a Brighton and Hove Keep Britain in Europe committee. It was led, I think, by the Vice-Chancellor of the University and included various luminaries from the TUC, the CBI, local industry, sport and the arts. The three local MPs were not members. The literature for the campaign and the meetings which were held were deliberately non-Party political. In Hove, there were two meetings, one in Portslade in the western end of my constituency, organised by the Liberals, and the other in the eastern end, organised by the Tories. At each meeting there were three speakers, one from the Conservatives, one from Labour and one from the Liberals. The remarkable feature of the Hove meeting, which gained a mention in *The Times*, was that it was the only occasion that my father and myself appeared for the same cause on the same platform speaking for different Parties. My father spoke on behalf of the Labour campaign for Europe, I for the Conservatives, and my Liberal opponent in the second 1974 election spoke for the Liberals. He had been somewhat surprised during the campaign when I lent him my Range Rover on a day when I was not able to go out canvassing, for him to do so using my car and my loudspeaker equipment. That was further evidence of the extent to which the Remainers were fighting a non-Party political campaign and that proved to be exceptionally effective. The Leave side featured Enoch Powell and Tony Benn fighting for the same cause. I found it quite an effective way to persuade reluctant, often elderly, Conservative supporters in Hove to vote Remain by saying, 'Surely you don't want to be on the same side as Tony Benn and Enoch Powell.'

I was then and remain an enthusiastic supporter of British membership of the European Economic Community. Securing the post-war peace in Europe was the predominant motive. However, I did see the economic advantages, particularly for a trading nation like Britain.

European matters did not play a significant part in my political life until I was made Minister for Trade by Margaret Thatcher in the summer of 1990. By then, the work to turn the Common Market, which had been created when the EEC started, into a Single Market, was well under way. Margaret Thatcher had sent Arthur Cockfield as the British Commissioner to Brussels to lead the drive to update the Union's trading arrangements. His brilliant work had led to a treaty, the 'Single European Act', which, by allowing qualified majority voting, enabled the rules and regulations of the Single Market to be agreed. The Single Market came into effect on 1 January 1993, saving British exporters having to fill in about 3 million forms every year. I had been working on trade policy for the two and a half years before the Single Market started, and continued to do so for the first eighteen months of its life. So I was able to see the immense benefit it brought to trade with our largest and nearest market, benefits that have led over the years to the introduction of 'just in time' trading and integrated production with our European partners, particularly in the motor industry.

My frequent trips to Brussels also showed me at first hand the problem the EU has with the media. After a Council of Trade Ministers, I would usually be questioned about what had been decided or discussed by a BBC journalist and sometimes, others. Very occasionally, there would be a press conference or statement for the press. If there had been agreement, it was likely that nothing would be reported. It seemed that only disagreement was news. The underlying assumption was often that Britain was the only country that obeyed the rules. The Commission, with Britain's enthusiastic support, was continually striving to achieve a 'level playing field' for all companies and countries. They slowly achieved success in reducing and sometimes eliminating operating subsidies, especially those to State-owned companies in other EU Member States. They also attacked any agreements designed to restrict competition. On one occasion, in February 1994, the Commission announced fines on sixteen steel companies in six EU States, including British Steel. The Private Notice Question tabled by Robin Cook, to which I had to reply, led to my having a very uncomfortable forty minutes when most of the questions ignored the fines on the fifteen steel companies in other States and the benefits to UK industry, including steel users, of achieving that level playing field.

There was a time when tariffs on industrial goods were a major obstacle to trade. The Common Market had done away with those tariffs in trade between the members of the Common Market. However, non-tariff barriers, all those rules and regulations affecting consumer protection, health and safety, labelling standards and rules of origin, had become the major obstacle to trade in goods. Twenty-five years later, the widespread adoption of just-in-time delivery is evidence of the effectiveness of a Single Market, which enables goods to move between the different countries of the European Union with a minimum of paperwork. I believe that many of those opposed to British membership of the European Union fail to appreciate the significant difference between a Common Market and a Single Market. One of the last things I did as a Government minister was to sign on behalf of the British Government the treaty which brought into existence the World Trade Organisation,

Signing the Treaty which established the World Trade Organisation, April 1994

the WTO. Negotiations since 1945, originally under the aegis of GATT, the General Agreement on Tariffs and Trade, since 1994 under the WTO, have meant that for the vast majority of industrial goods, tariffs are no longer a significant barrier to trade. They remain a major obstacle for most agricultural trade but for industry it is the non-tariff barriers, all those rules and regulations, which can make trade difficult or, in some cases, impossible.

The European Union became a major part of my political life when I became Minister for Trade. I lost count of the number of times that I caught the early flight, known as the Red Eye special, to go to Brussels for some form of meeting, most often for a Council of Trade Ministers. I also became more aware of the deeply ingrained Euroscepticism, and in some cases Europhobia, of some members of the Tory Party. They included the Secretary of State, Peter Lilley, and two of his ministerial team in the DTI. His reservations about Europe seemed to be mainly concerned with his reluctance to accept any form of regulation or Government interference in the economy, or indeed anything else. Edward Leigh was Eurosceptic and remains so, but was always charming and friendly in dealing with those like myself who had contrary views. That could not be said about Neil Hamilton, who managed to convey the impression that he actively disliked members of his own Party who were of the One Nation/pro-Europe wing. That obviously included myself.

It is now nearly thirty years since I became Minister of Trade and first experienced directly the economic advantages of our membership of the European Union and a year later, of the Single Market. It often seemed to me that the Eurosceptics undervalued the economic benefits of the Single Market. I recall one conversation with a hard-line Eurosceptic when I said, 'If you carry on promoting your ever stronger views, you will split the Party.' The surprising reply I received was, 'That would be a good thing, we could get rid of a few people like you.' At the time, in the early 1990s, the Europhobe wing of the Parliamentary Party was very much a minority, and even among Party membership, the Eurosceptics were a minority. Since then, the Europhobe and Eurosceptic members of the Parliamentary Party have grown in number and, with the diminished and ever more elderly membership of the Party in the country, Euroscepticism has become the majority view.

It seems to me that one of the reasons why it is so difficult to reach a compromise between the opposing wings of the Party is that they are actually concerned with different issues. The leavers, the Brexiteers, worry about sovereignty. They dream of a time when Britain could happily go it alone and seem to overlook the way that the world has become ever more integrated. The major issues which face Britain and indeed Europe and the world today can only be tackled by countries co-operating with each other. That must be true of fighting international terrorism, responding to climate change, or drug trafficking. Immigration is another issue which is essentially a multi-national problem.

The Remainers' prime concern is the strength of our economy. They emphasise that it is always easiest to trade with your nearest neighbours. The advantages of geographical proximity have been greatly increased as the creation of the Single Market has removed not just the tariff barriers, but all the non-tariff barriers with our nearest and largest market. That is why Remainers value membership of what is in effect the largest and best free-trade area in the world. It has always seemed eccentric, to say the least, to abandon membership of that enormous free-trade area on our doorstep and search for replacements in more distant, more difficult and smaller markets.

My penultimate speech as an MP was during a two-day debate on the European Union, in December 1996. My first sentence seems even more true now than it was then: 'If the debate has done nothing else, it has reminded the House and, I hope, a wider audience of the extent of the differences of view about Europe on both sides of the House.' My final remarks summed up my views on the European Union, which I held then and still hold: 'Therefore, for trade, for inward investment and for so many other reasons, our membership is overwhelmingly in the national interest, but we shall not gain membership's full benefits if we stay on the EU's sidelines. We must show a willingness and a commitment to play a full and constructive part in the EU's affairs if we are to gain those benefits. If we do that, however, we shall continue to see the economic benefits. They will continue to grow. I therefore urge my right hon. Friends to negotiate with that end in mind, because it is jobs and our economy that are at stake.'

POSTSCRIPT

So we have left the European Union. We have discarded our membership of the Single Market, the world's largest and most comprehensive free trade area, the one on our doorstep; the one that is with by far our most important trading partner; the only one from which goods can come and go by road; the one with which over the last forty-five years we have developed such close industrial and commercial relationships, often involving the complexities of 'Just in time' delivery. Instead we are going to try to agree free trade deals with markets that are smaller, more distant and more difficult. It is no wonder that so many regard it as the most egregious act of economic self-harm; a view with which I agree.

In some ways it is almost worse that our children and grandchildren will no longer have the right to study, work, live in or retire to the twenty-seven countries across the Channel. It is hard to find a silver lining to this cloud.

20

REFLECTIONS ON MY CAREER IN PARLIAMENT

An MP has a job like no other. All 650 have one aspect of their work in common: they represent a constituency in the UK. This gives every MP a 'Territorial Link'. It means that not only does every voter in Britain have an MP who they can lobby, but also every school, business, hospital or doctor's surgery has an MP. It is a two-way relationship which I found of great value. Visiting schools in Hove, talking to businesses based in my constituency or doctors practising there, as well as numerous individual voters, is the best way of understanding how Government policies work on the ground.

This territorial link is the strongest argument against introducing Proportional Representation instead of our first-past-the-post system of election. PR would mean either that there were two categories of MPs, those with constituencies and those without, or that there would be much larger constituencies, each with a number of MPs. The other often proposed alternative, a 'single transferable vote' system, would mean that the result of an election could depend on the second choice of those who voted for the least popular candidate.

There are other reasons to reject PR. Any PR system is likely to result in coalition Governments. The policies it will implement will not be those of any Party Manifesto; so nobody would get what they voted for. There is also the likelihood that Parties with extremist views will win a few seats, which would encourage the creation of Parties on the far right or left with the risk that they might hold the balance of power and wield an influence quite disproportionate to their size. So my first reflection on twenty-three-and-a-half years as an MP is that we should steadfastly reject the siren voices claiming our electoral system is unfair and stick to our tried and tested first-past-the-post system, even if it does not always result in one Party having a working majority.

My second reflection is that 650 MPs is far too many. When I was elected, there were 630. In October 1974, the figure increased to 635. Since then, we have created a Scottish Parliament, a Welsh Assembly and increased the size of the House of Commons to 650 Members. A reduction of at least 10% to about 600 would be sensible. There is a plan to implement the change but a noticeable reluctance to legislate for its introduction. I suspect that there are also too many ministers, both junior and Cabinet. A reduction would save both money and space.

When I was first elected, the office space for MPs was totally inadequate. My desk was in a building well away from the Palace of Westminster, and I learned to use one of the desks in the Library as a pop-up office. On one occasion, I found a vacant space, and had only been sitting there for a minute or two before somebody said, 'You can't sit there, that's Enoch's desk.' Apparently Enoch Powell never had an office and answered all his constituency correspondence in longhand from his chosen desk in the Library!

The arrival of the internet has changed drastically the life of a Member of Parliament. When I started, most Members shared a secretary, many of whom worked part-time. A privileged few shared a research assistant. Now, most MPs have at least three members of full-time staff; although there has been a massive increase in the number of communications, the vast majority of them are emails, many stimulated by lobby and pressure groups requiring identical email replies. These are frequently dealt with by staff. In spite of the considerable increase in the number of secretaries and researchers employed by MPs, the House of Commons now has adequate, some would say more than adequate, office space. My secretary only worked in the same building as my office during my last three years. That is a problem solved.

But there is a very major problem outstanding. It is now, at long last, starting to be addressed. It is the modernisation of the Palace of Westminster. Decades of neglect have left behind a building with crumbling external stonework, a dangerously outdated electrical system, inadequate ventilation and very little air-cooling, antiquated plumbing and telephone systems. It is going to cost a lot of money and take quite a long time, but at least there is now recognition that the work can no longer be delayed and that the only sensible way to tackle it is for both the House of Commons and the House of Lords to relocate while the work is being carried out. My third reflection is: for goodness sake, get on with it.

My fourth reflection is that there is a growing problem in attracting enough candidates with the ability, not just to serve as good constituency MPs but, when required, to be ministers at every level from Whips and Parliamentary Under Secretaries of State, to Prime Minister. The role of an MP used to be one that carried a degree of recognition and respect in the community. Now it seems to make the holder the target for excessive media scrutiny of every aspect of their life and even, to some extent, that of their family. Even worse is the growing unpleasantness of online abuse and incidents and threats of physical violence. The problem has increased noticeably since the Brexit Referendum. The growth in the use of aggressive language in the House of Commons has made it worse. During my time as an MP, in general, relations between Members in different Parties were amicable, even when the language used got more exaggerated. I recall an incident when Tony Banks called me a 'Yankee lickspittle'. As we left the Chamber, I said to him, 'That was going a bit far', to which he replied with a smile, 'Only business dear boy, only business.' Now relations between Members, even sometimes between those in the same Party, are all too often disagreeable.

If the aspiring candidate is prepared to accept the life in a goldfish bowl, which seems to be expected of today's MP, there are some other issues which he or she and their family will need to consider. The first is the question of where to live. Nearly all MPs will want to have a home in or near to their constituency. Although the hours of Parliament have been much changed since I retired, and there are very few late-night sittings, there are still votes at 10.00 p.m. and occasionally later, so living within what would normally be regarded as commuting distance becomes difficult, if not impossible. That means that many MPs will also need a London as well as a constituency home. So most MPs with families representing constituencies outside London have two homes. The MP is faced with a difficult choice if they have a family with school-age children. Do the children go to school from the home near to Westminster, or they go to school from the home that is located in or near their constituency? And of course it isn't only the children. Their spouse may also have a job and faces a choice of trying to find employment in the London area or in the constituency area. Either choice is disruptive of family life. Since the constituency work takes place mainly at the weekend, most MPs representing seats outside London will choose to have their home in or near their constituency. That of course, means there will be three or four nights a week when the House is sitting when the MP will be away from home.

Weekends are a time for relaxing and leisure activities or spending more time with your family, but, if you are a Member of Parliament, that opportunity is severely constrained. Fridays are the main day for visits in the constituency, but some can be made on Saturday or even Sunday. The advice sessions or constituency surgeries, as they are variously called, will normally be held on Fridays and Saturdays. In the internet age, it is not just the telephone calls or encounters in the street that can be vexatious to a Member. There is the ceaseless stream of social media and internet communications. I suspect that few Members, before they get elected, fully appreciate the extent to which weekends get occupied by Parliamentary and constituency business.

It is a change from the nineteenth century, when Gladstone never went to one of the constituencies which he represented in his long Parliamentary career. Another long-serving MP, when asked when it would be convenient for him to come to the constituency to accept a presentation to mark his twenty-five years as its representative, replied, 'It is never convenient for me to come to the constituency.'

Another obstacle to attracting enough good candidates to be MPs is the uncertainties which are a feature of Parliamentary life. The first challenge for anybody seeking to become a Member of Parliament is to get chosen by their Party as a potential candidate. Next they have to be selected to fight a seat. After that, sometimes the biggest challenge is to get elected. That done, there are a number of hazards ahead that can disturb or bring to an early end a Parliamentary career. The first and most obvious is losing your seat at the next election. It is now clear that more seats than previously are vulnerable to big swings at election time. A factor making the seat more or less secure that is entirely beyond the candidate or Member's control is redistribution. The boundaries of their constituency may be altered.

The three seats in what is now the city of Brighton and Hove are a good example of this. Hove in the 1970 election had been one of the twenty safest seats held by the Conservatives. The eastern side of Brighton, Brighton Kemp Town, was always regarded as a Conservative marginal. Andrew Bowden won in 1970 and held the seat with varying, always small, majorities, until 1997 when he was defeated by Labour's Desmond Turner. The Brighton Pavilion seat, including all of central Brighton, was a Conservative seat which became increasingly marginal throughout my Parliamentary career. The redistribution of the 1990s which came into effect in the 1997 election meant that one ward, bad from the Conservatives' point of view, in Kemp Town was transferred to Brighton Pavilion. This tipped the balance and turned what had been a marginal into a relatively safe Labour seat.

All three seats had been subject to demographic change and one additional factor, an ever-increasing number of students. The latter point particularly impacted Brighton Pavilion, which, having been won by Labour only in 1997, was won by the Greens in 2010 and has been held by them as their only Parliamentary seat since. Before the 1997 election, Andrew Bowden said he had spent his Parliamentary life successfully holding a Conservative marginal and he looked forward to an easier passage in the 1997 election, having acquired a good ward from Lewes and passed a bad ward on to Pavilion. Sadly for Andrew, the landslide of 1997 was of such a proportion that even those changes could not save him. Kemp Town was won back by the Conservatives in 2015 but with a majority of less than 1,000. In 2017, it once again fell to Labour, and was held by Labour at the 2019 General Election.

Meanwhile, Hove, where I once had a majority of over 19,000, fell to Labour in the landslide of 1997. Until 2017, it was a Labour Conservative marginal, held by Labour in 2001 and 2005, regained by the Tories in 2010 and once again falling to Labour in 2015, who held it with a much increased majority in 2017. In 2019, Hove having voted to remain in the Referendum, Peter Kyle, the pro-EU, moderate Labour MP, retained the seat with a majority of over 17,000. I held the seat for over twenty-three years, and in the twenty-two years since I have retired, there have been four other Members of Parliament for Hove. Now of course, Brighton and Hove, like the rest of England, faces a dramatic and much needed re-distribution, reducing the number of MPs to 600. This will probably mean that instead of three seats in Brighton and Hove, there will be only two. It is quite likely that both will be marginals.

Another contemporary problem is the pressure on MPs not to have any other job or responsibility that produces any income. To my mind, this is absurd. There are often, justified, complaints that MPs do not have enough experience of the outside world. But then it is made difficult or nearly impossible for an MP who does not have ministerial or front-bench responsibilities to have any outside interests. This is counter-productive. It is also another obstacle to attracting into and retaining in Parliamentary politics the best and the brightest.

Next there is the most contentious issue, remuneration. The misuse of the expenses allowances was encouraged by all Parties to make up for the collective and long-lasting failure to address the pay of MPs. The exposure of the scandal by the *Daily Telegraph* was very damaging to the image of an MP. It reinforced the view, cultivated by the tabloid press, that MPs are overpaid. But there are many who would agree that it is absurd that the Prime Minister is only paid £158,754.

In April 2019, the annual basic salary paid to a Member of Parliament was set at £79,468 by the Independent Parliamentary Standards Authority and paid to every MP. Ministers receive an additional salary, and Opposition front-bench Members also receive additional remuneration. However, although that salary is a lot higher than average earnings, it is considerably less than the likely pay of the manager of a department store or large supermarket, or large supermarket or a head teacher of a secondary school, a doctor and most senior managers in industry and of many who work in the service economy. So if somebody who has enjoyed a successful career starts being an MP in their late thirties or forties, when they have acquired some real experience of life outside Parliament, the likelihood is that they will have to accept a reduction in salary. That is perhaps the biggest obstacle to getting people of ability and integrity to seek to become Members of Parliament.

There is no easy answer to this dilemma, but I have two suggestions which might help. First, there could be more activities in Parliament, like membership of a Select Committee, which could carry an additional salary. This would reflect more accurately the variation in the workload of MPs. The second is more contentious: ministerial salaries should be increased considerably, taking into account their responsibilities and the extremely hard work which is required of ministers. They are actually doing three jobs: minister, constituency representative and their Parliamentary duties. In the nineteenth century, ministerial salaries were in real terms much greater than those of today. While it is recognised that we do not want people to seek to become MPs purely for the salary, it is unfortunate if people are put off seeking to become an MP when they have the ability and the wish to become an MP but are reluctant to accept the scale of the financial sacrifice which they and their family would have to make. So my next reflection is there is an urgent need for a Prime Minister bold enough to increase ministerial salaries, including their own.

The Chamber of the House of Commons is a confrontational setting for debate. The Government is on one side and opposite are the Opposition Parties. When matters come to a vote, the choice is Aye or No. But looking back on twenty-three years of debating and voting, it seems to me that most of the time, most MPs are seeking to obtain the same objectives. The differences lie in the method which they wish to use to achieve those objectives. Housing is a good example of the Parties sharing a recognition that much needs to be done to make it more affordable and provide more social housing. Socialists tend to believe in rent controls as a way of ensuring or helping to ensure a supply of modestly priced accommodation and ensuring that landlords do not profit unreasonably. On the other hand, Conservatives view rent controls as being a major deterrent to landlords or any other body to provide rented housing in the first place. My own belief is that rent controls are counter-productive to the shared objective of providing more and better rented accommodation, and that is one reason why I became a Conservative, housing having been one of the most important issues in politics in the 1960s and 1970s.

Similarly, Socialists are very strong supporters of local-authority-provided accommodation, council housing. On the other hand, Conservatives believe that it is better for people to own their own. We believe that councils are usually very bad and inefficient managers of housing stock. That view for me was strongly reinforced by my experiences in Liverpool with Michael Heseltine after the Toxteth riots.

As well as being badly managed, council house stock is seldom allocated in the way which is most effective for relieving housing problems. There is no incentive for a tenant under-occupying their council house to move to something less costly to maintain. Often council house tenants may remain as subsidised tenants regardless of the changes to their personal circumstances. There will be a number of occupiers in council-owned property who do not need subsidised accommodation, while most areas have long waiting lists of those who do. In an era when most people expect to change their jobs, and sometimes their occupations, several times during their working career, council houses are a very inflexible form of housing. While in theory it is possible to swap council housing from one area to another, in practice it is extremely difficult.

As well as disagreeing about methods, Parties will also disagree about priorities. Conservatives believe in the overwhelming importance of wealth creation. They hold that only by enlarging the cake will it be possible to give everybody a bigger slice. It often seems to us that the Socialist approach to taxation in the pursuit of fairness and equality ignores the risk of damaging enterprise, hard work and job creation.

When I retired in 1997, I did feel that much had been achieved in the previous twenty-three years to improve the quality of life and the working of the economy. In 1973, the inefficient, loss-making nationalised industries were a burden not just on the taxpayer but on the rest of the

The three family members of the Houses of Parliament when
my brother John, *left*, took his seat, joining my father in the
House of Lords, 1989 (Universal Pictorial Press Agency)

business world. They included British Telecom, British Rail, the steel industry and ship-building. Penal rates of taxation acted as a deterrent to investment and entrepreneurship. The labour laws encouraged irresponsible trade unionism. Nearly a third of the nation's housing stock was being mismanaged by local authorities and all too often allocated to the wrong people. By 1997, all those issues had been addressed.

My younger son said to me shortly after the 1997 election, 'Daddy, when you became an MP the country's problems were largely economic, I would have been a Conservative. Now the problems are largely social and that's why I am not a Conservative.' I recognised a lot of truth in what he said, although I did not entirely agree with his conclusion.

Most MPs would agree that being in Government is more interesting and rewarding than spending all your time in opposition. My first five years in opposition were useful in enabling me to get to know my colleagues and more about the way the House of Commons worked and, in some respects, did not work. For the first fifteen of my last eighteen years in the House I was part of the 'payroll'. My progress up the ladder was slow and step by step. I started with four years as a PPS before spending four years in the Whips' Office, three more years as a Parliamentary Under Secretary, followed by four years as a Minister of State in two different roles. All my ministerial jobs were interesting and involved a great deal of travel. I largely avoided those jobs which tied ministers down in lengthy committee proceedings or involved a massive workload of correspondence with fellow MPs about their constituents' problems.

Finally, I retired from ministerial office at a time of my choosing, when I felt I had done enough and wanted to spend the last couple of years of my Parliamentary career slowing down. This meant that I never experienced that unhappy meeting with the Prime Minister when you are told he or she wants your job. I also avoided the other somewhat ignominious end to a Parliamentary career by retiring from my constituency before the electors threw me out.

A final observation on my Parliamentary career is how I should reply to the question I was often asked both during and since my time in the House: 'Did you enjoy it?' My reaction was to say that that was the wrong question. It is the right question to ask of someone who has been to the theatre or to see a film or a sporting event. The question to ask an MP should be, 'Did you find it worthwhile?' and I would have been able to answer, 'Yes.' There were occasions when Parliamentary life became frustrating and times when you wondered what you were doing when being asked to vote at 3 o'clock in the morning on a matter of little or no importance. But, on the whole, the answer would have been, 'Yes.' If I made a contribution, however small, to the strengthening of the economy, the reduction in poverty and the general improvement in the quality of life, I feel that answer is justified.

.

PART IV

21

MY THIRD CAREER

Career may be a misnomer for the miscellaneous activities and interests I have had since leaving Parliament. I retired as a Member of Parliament aged sixty-five so as to leave time for taking on serious, albeit very part-time, activities. I wanted these to be mainly in the charitable or third sector. Philanthropy through grant-making charities was to become a significant part of my 'third career'. Although I retained an interest in politics, I have largely avoided any time-consuming participation in Party political life during this period.

My first involvement with charities went back to the mid-1950s when I started work at JS. Christchurch Blackfriars was surrounded by various Sainsbury's headquarters buildings. It had been bombed during the war, and rebuilt while I was first working at JS. The vicar persuaded me to become a Trustee of the local Church of England primary school. This was to prove my only involvement in the education sector during my life, other than as a parent. A change in the demographics of the area meant that the school, which had once had over 900 pupils, was reduced to less than half that number when I became involved. There was a gap between the ambitions of the children and the preconceptions of the parents as to what constituted a proper job. Most of the parents were, or had been, involved in some form of manual labour, many in riverside warehouses, quite a lot in 'the print', still in those days mostly located in the Fleet Street area, where jobs were passed down through the family. The offices which were proliferating in the area created job opportunities which some of the parents regarded as 'not proper work'. The number of pupils was steadily decreasing; the school buildings were old and multi-storey. It was not long before the school closed, but the vicar found another activity for me.

I was introduced to a nearby youth club in Walworth, run by a charismatic Church Army captain, Peter Simmonds. It was located on the lower floor of another church which had been rebuilt after being destroyed during the war. One of the problems experienced by the club was that most of the locals with ambition or ability, including those who helped at the club, tended to move away from the area. So there was always a need for volunteer helpers from outside the neighbourhood and I became one of those. I used to drive to the club and park outside; I was advised to be sure to lock the car doors. However, an interesting insight into the changing pattern of local life was that I was told that, until comparatively recently, people in the area did not bother to lock their doors because they had nothing worth stealing. Now the situation was changing. Television sets were appearing in more and more households, which were portable valuables, so that criminals living in the area actually sometimes stole from their neighbours.

A longer-established local charity, of which I became a Trustee, was Marshall's. This had been endowed in the seventeenth century by a wealthy local inhabitant. Its headquarters were based just off Borough High Street in Southwark. My father had been a Trustee before me. It had several different strands of work. One was helping to maintain churches in Kent, Surrey and Lincolnshire, the three counties associated with John Marshall, its founder. The largest area of activity was called 'the Relief of Poor Livings'. Originally this involved giving a better income to vicars and curates in parishes where the stipend was otherwise very modest. With the incumbents no longer being dependent on local funds, Marshall's devoted its quite considerable income to helping provide central heating, double glazing and sometimes office space in vicarages and rectories in relatively poor parishes. This early experience of a substantial grant-making charity enabled me to see how important it was for a charity to receive good advice on financial management and have a competent administration. I also realised how conservative trustees could be when it came to looking at their investments. Marshall's had a large holding of shares in Woolworth's. When I suggested that this was not a good investment, the reaction was that they couldn't sell it because they would be selling it below the price they had paid.

Becoming a director of JS in 1962 meant that I received a substantial holding of Sainsbury's shares from trusts which my father had established in the 1950s. This enabled Susie and me to establish our first grant-making charity, which we named after where we had our cottage in the country, the Hazeley Trust. The endowment of the trust was a holding in JS shares. However, during the 1960s, these shares had a very low dividend. The company was still unquoted and all its resources were needed to finance the change from counter service to self-service. At the beginning of the decade, only 10% of stores were self-service; by the end of the 1960s it was 50%, and the profits of the company had doubled.

It was only after flotation of the company in July 1973 that dividend payments became significant. We established our main grant-making charity, which is still in existence, after the flotation. We named it after where we had built our new home in the country, the Headley Trust. Its annual report is published. It explains that the Trust makes its donations in five categories: Arts and Heritage UK, Arts and Heritage overseas, Developing Countries, Education, and Health and Social Welfare. The Trustees allocate an indicative percentage of the available funds to each category to help the executives in bringing forward proposals for support to a meeting of the Trustees.

It is hard to write about philanthropy except in general terms. The decision on how much to give, the choice of charities you donate to and the method used for giving are all very personal issues. Furthermore, there is good guidance to be found in Matthew, chapter 6, verses 2 and 4: 'When you give alms sound no trumpet before you' 'so that your alms may be in secret'. False modesty should, however, be avoided. So I am not writing anything about specific charities which our charitable Trusts have supported, with the exception of three projects with which I was involved as a Trustee and the building with which the family name is most often connected, the National Gallery Sainsbury Wing. What follows are some comments on how we allocate the income that our two charitable trusts have between different areas, and how we organise and administer the donations.

There are a number of benefits from establishing a grant-making trust rather than just giving money to various charities each year. The first is that it does enable multi-year grants to be made, and the recipient to have confidence that they will be received. Secondly, it simplifies the administration, as neither party has to apply for Gift Aid as the grants are made tax-free by a registered charity which itself pays no tax. The third, and most important, advantage is that the trust can employ executives to manage not just the administration, but also research, and report on possible beneficiaries.

When JS became a public company, the prospectus for the flotation had made it clear that the company would follow a normal dividend policy. The continued success growing profits and increased dividends that followed increased greatly the income of our trust and of the charitable trusts established by the third and the other members of the fourth generation members of the family. The increasing scale of their grant-making clearly required staff to provide advice, do research on possible beneficiaries and administer the giving and accounting for the grants, so the organisation, now known as the Sainsbury Family Charitable Trusts (SFCT), was established. Initially it was run by Hugh de Quetteville and Tim Riviere, both old friends of the family, and had only a handful of staff. As the income and grant-making of the family charities grew, there was a steady increase in the size of the office of the Sainsbury Family Charitable Trusts. The number of grants being made, the amount of research and reports being produced increased as the resources of the various trusts grew. Those established by the third and fourth generation were joined later by trusts established by eight members of the fifth generation, including our four children. At the time of writing, the SFCT has its headquarters in Victoria and the staff, who number around ninety, are providing the administration, financial management, advice and research to sixteen active family charitable trusts.

As we were making an increasing number of donations to promote the Christian religion and support the work of Christian charitable organisations, in 1982 we decided that it would be sensible to have a separate Christian trust which could have its own trustees. We therefore divided the Headley Trust in two, and Susie had the brilliant idea of naming our Christian charity the Jerusalem Trust. These two trusts have been the vehicle through which we have made the vast majority of our charitable donations. They also produce a workload which is both rewarding and quite demanding. The trusts have eight grant-making meetings a year, each of which is accompanied by a large volume of material, analysis reports and recommendations to read. Between meetings, we have papers about smaller grant applications, which do not need to be considered at a full meeting of the Trustees. In addition, there are meetings to review the investments of the trusts, and sometimes visits to possible beneficiaries or charities already in receipt of grants. Not surprisingly, there is much correspondence from friends and others enquiring about the possibility of obtaining a grant for a cause with which they are involved.

When my father established his grant-making charity in 1953, charitable bodies, including grant-making trusts, were, as now, exempt from tax. However, there were few of the current tax incentives for giving to charity. The most important new incentive is Gift Aid, which was introduced in 1990. It has made it so much easier to give small grants to many charities. There had been, in the 1970s, reservations about private charities in left-wing circles. Some felt that they were doing things which were better done by the state and its agencies. This view was particularly prevalent in the arts, where there was a widespread belief that arts organisations should be fully funded by Government. The 1970s was also an era when marginal tax rates were 80% or more, so individual giving from disposable income was less likely. The introduction of Gift Aid reflected both the wider acceptance of the value of the voluntary sector, and lower rates of personal taxation.

By far the biggest innovation in the funding of the third sector has been the National Lottery. It is John Major who deserves much of the credit for its introduction in 1994 and the near £40 billion it has raised for charities since. It is established by the 2006 Lottery Act that lottery funding does not act as a replacement for Government funds, so that near £40 Billion is new money. As it is normal for Lottery funding for many projects, particularly those for museums and galleries, to be dependent on other funds being raised from the public, trusts and foundations and sometimes local authorities, the existence of the National Lottery has been a stimulus to raising a great deal of extra money for good causes.

My father had expressed the wish that, if and when the company started paying dividends, his children would allocate some of their income to charity, possibly using a trust of their own. It is part of the Judaeo-Christian tradition that those who can, should make charitable donations from their income. It is also well established for those who have much, that those donations ought to be substantial. There are, of course, great examples going back into the nineteenth century and earlier, when many almshouses, schools and hospitals were established by gifts. The Marshall Charity was an example of a wealthy individual establishing a trust to help with specifically Christian charitable objectives. Being a trustee of Marshall's Charity and working as a volunteer at the Church Army youth club are examples of the other, often even more valuable, work that can be done in the voluntary sector, that is, giving one's time, experience and expertise to help in the work of a charity. Nearly all charities, whether they be operating within health and welfare, education, arts, religious or sporting activities, rely on an army of volunteers. In the last twenty-five years, I have been lucky enough to be able to be, I hope, a useful volunteer with a succession of major organisations: first the Ashmolean Museum in Oxford, secondly the Somerset House Trust, and thirdly, the V&A, with which I still have a small commitment as Trustee of the V&A Foundation, of which until recently I was chairman.

My third career includes some commercial activities. In late 1994, we bought a motor yacht, a classic launched in 1927. She was in very bad condition and needed a very major refit. This was done by the Pendennis shipyard in Falmouth in 1995 and 1996. I later became the non-executive chairman of the company for seven years. This was after I had taken part in two 'rescue' operations to relieve cashflow problems at the company.

The site of our house in Hampshire came with some eighty-five acres of grazing land. Shortly after moving in, we acquired a neighbouring farm. I would never dare to claim to be a farmer, but nowadays, a farm owner has a role in strategic planning, particularly when property is involved. Over the years, the farm has steadily grown and now has a turnover approaching £1 million a year from arable crops, a prize-winning suckler herd of Limousin cross cattle and property rents. Helping the business activities of friends has at various times involved me with businesses operating Art and Archaeology tours for small groups, selling agricultural machinery, modern British paintings, and designer furniture. I also became chairman of a long-established but very small company making, importing and selling, ceramic tiles.

As I had hoped, all these activities and interests still left more time for leisure and pleasure than during my first and second careers. Our family, increasing to include twelve grandchildren and, at the time of writing, two great grandchildren, had first claim on that time. We did a lot of travel, much of it on board *Fair Lady*. There are not many islands in the Mediterranean that we have not visited, and she took us as far as St Petersburg, through the Caledonian Canal and out to the Hebrides. Visits to museums and galleries have been more frequent, as have ballet, opera and concerts. We have added a few more paintings and sculptures to those which I first started acquiring in 1956 when I bought a William Scott. British twentieth-century works predominate with St Ives-based artists, particularly Peter Lanyon and Barbara Hepworth well represented. In the last twenty-five years, David Bomberg has become one of our favourites. We were delighted that one of the three self-portraits by him that we own featured on the cover of the recent book on his life and work by Sarah MacDougall and Rachel Dickson.

Since I retired from Parliament, it has been the third sector that has been my main third career activity. However, while I was still an MP, I was able to give quite a lot of time to the project with which the family name is most often associated: the extension to the National Gallery.

22

THE NATIONAL GALLERY – SAINSBURY WING

The idea that the three Sainsbury brothers should together make a large and high-profile charitable donation came from my brother John. It was his brilliant leadership of the company which had led to the value of the shares increasing very greatly over the decade since the flotation. John had no difficulty in persuading Simon and me to support his idea. However, the choice of giving the National Gallery a building on the Hampton site, to accommodate the outstanding early Renaissance collection and provide a temporary exhibition space, a restaurant, shop, educational facilities and other working spaces that they desperately needed, was a project about which I was somewhat hesitant.

The Hampton site had had a very unhappy history, culminating in the disastrous mishandling of the architectural competition for a building which would have, on one floor, galleries to exhibit the Renaissance paintings. The other floors were to have been commercial development which would finance the development. It was a sad commentary on the commitment of successive Governments to the arts that although the site had been acquired by the Government for the expansion of the National Gallery in 1958, for twenty-five years no Government had been prepared to fund a new building. The site had remained unused. Eventually, at the end of 1981, Michael Heseltine, then Secretary of State for the Environment, announced that there would be a competition to select a developer and an architect for the Hampton site. The architect would produce a design that the developer would construct. The developer would use the commercial part and the National Gallery would get the main floor. The applicants who produced designs for the competition faced an extremely difficult task in that they had to satisfy two clients: the commercial developer and the National Gallery. In addition, the design they produced would be subject to scrutiny and possibly criticism from a wide range of other bodies, ranging from Westminster City Council through the Royal Fine Arts Commission, the Government itself, to HRH The Prince of Wales.

The winner of the competition was Trafalgar House as the developer, with Ahrends, Burton & Koralek as the architect. Their initial plans were eventually rejected, and they were asked to come back with a revision. In my view, the revised plan was much less satisfactory than the original. The revised plan was the one that attracted the most criticism from a number of sources, HRH The Prince of Wales memorably describing the proposed building as 'a monstrous carbuncle on the face of a much-loved and elegant friend'. What was described as 'a well-intentioned but misguided scheme' had gone badly wrong. The National Gallery Trustees decided that the only thing they could do was to see whether there was a possibility of finding a private sponsor who would provide a new building entirely dedicated to the National Gallery. So clearly providing that building was an obvious choice for the brothers' 'big donation'. However, I was concerned that, in view of the recent difficulties in finding an acceptable scheme, we ran the risk of being involved in a high-profile controversy, possibly ending with our proposed building being rejected on aesthetic grounds.

I was eventually persuaded to go along with the proposal that John, Simon and I offer to fund the building for the National Gallery for two reasons. The first was that, as we would be funding the whole building, we could collectively be closely involved in the choice of architect and design. The second was that we were not proposing to hold an open competition, or indeed a design competition. Our proposal was for there to be a limited competition to select an architect rather than a design. In practice, it is almost impossible to hold an architectural competition for a design for any prominent site that would not attract some objectors, and sometimes rather high-profile objectors. Choosing an architect instead of a design reduces the scope for objections even if it does not entirely eliminate them.

When the gift was announced in March 1985, it was made clear that the selection of the architect would be done by a committee which included both the donors and representatives of the Trustees. The selection committee was advised by two consultants who had expert knowledge of contemporary architecture and had help from staff of the National Gallery. There was a six-month period of interviews, discussions and visits, by some or all of the members of the selection committee, to France, Germany and Denmark. The longest and most comprehensive visit was to the United States. Happily, I was at the time of the trip a Whip and it is a characteristic of the work of the Government Whips that they have very little, if anything, to do other than their constituency responsibilities when the House is not sitting. I was able therefore to take part in the US visit in September 1985. By October, there was unanimous agreement by the committee in choosing six architects, four from the UK and two from the USA, who were to be invited to put forward proposals for a building on the Hampton site.

In January 1986, the selection committee and its advisers met for three days over a weekend in London to consider the ideas put forward by the six selected architects, and to interview each of them and receive from our advisers a technical assessment of each entry. Somewhat to my surprise and, I suspect, to the surprise of some of the others involved, we were unanimous in reaching a decision as to which of the six architects we should choose. One factor which I regarded as of importance was whether a scheme brought visitors into the new galleries at the same place, irrespective of whether they arrived by lift, by stairs or came over from the existing National Gallery building. James Stirling was expected by many critics to be the winner. Interestingly his scheme, which was rejected on other grounds, had visitors arriving in three different places; at either end of the gallery floor, and in the middle. It would have made it extremely difficult to produce either a chronological or thematic hang of the paintings. Venturi, Rauch and Scott Brown was the only practice of the six architects whose ideas brought the visitors into the new galleries at the same point, whichever method they used to get there. The second and very important point in favour of the Venturi scheme was the magnificent staircase which not only provided a suitably impressive approach to the gallery floor, but also allowed a view of the new galleries on one side and the existing building on the other, together with a glimpse back into Trafalgar Square. All members of the selection committee were particularly impressed by Bob Venturi's ideas for the layout and design of the galleries themselves. We were also impressed by his skill in fitting into what was quite a limited site all the spaces that had been requested, including a new temporary exhibition space in the basement.

The unanimous selection of an architect was a major achievement. Maintaining unanimity during the design development stage would prove challenging. Overseeing the process, it was agreed that there should be a 'Client Steering Committee' consisting of donors, Trustees and members of the Gallery staff. The most important decision was that the meetings should be chaired by my late brother, Simon. He gave an immense amount of time to the work and successfully smoothed out the minor disagreements that emerged during the design development stage; even the three brothers did not always agree with the architect's proposals. On one occasion, John was arguing for dark treads on the grand staircase while Simon wanted light. I did not contribute to the argument other than to suggest unhelpfully that maybe half the staircase could be one, and half the other. Eventually agreement was reached, and the staircase with its light treads is now an outstanding feature of the design. Another occasion when the brothers were unable all to agree with what was proposed was the inclusion of several large columns in the interior design of the entrance floor. John had an aversion to columns in general, from his experience with supermarkets. He had always wanted large supermarkets to be built without any columns in the sales area. He objected to the fact that two of the columns in the National Gallery entrance area were not structural, but purely decorative, and insisted that inside one of them there should be a time capsule containing a note that he objected to this unnecessary feature.

The comparison between the design development stage for the National Gallery and that of the National Theatre is interesting. The National Theatre Committee quite quickly achieved the unanimous choice of an architect, Sir Denys Lasdun. But then they had a great deal of trouble, many disagreements and spent a very long time in reaching an agreed design. One reason for this has been recorded as 'the appallingly weak and unprofessional chairing of the building committee' by the no less a luminary than Sir Laurence Olivier. Chairing such a committee was clearly not his forte.

The final, and by no means least important, stage was implementing the detailed design that had been agreed. The Client Steering Committee continued to oversee this, helped by a project manager, Eric Gabriel, whose previous experience of project management had been largely confined to major petrochemical projects in the Saudi Arabian desert. He had decided that before he retired, he would like to do something different and, in some ways, more worthwhile. He made an outstanding contribution to achieving completion of the building, very nearly to time, and not far over the original budget. It was a time of relatively high inflation: in 1987, the figure was 4.2%, rising to 4.9% in 1988, and by 1989 the inflation figure had reached 7.8%. The brothers had originally agreed that £10 million of Sainsbury's shares would be contributed by each of us. Happily, although the eventual cost was more than £30 million, the value of the Sainsbury shares had risen sharply during the period of design

The three brothers at the opening of the Sainsbury Wing of the
National Gallery, 1991. We are seated in front of Raphael's
Ansidei Madonna, which features St Nicholas of Bari with his
attribute of three bags of gold

and construction. At the end, there was a significant sum left over which
I allocated to a special section of my charitable trust which we called the
'Museums, Galleries and Libraries Fund'. It was not finally fully expended
until the millennium projects came along in 2000.

The Prince of Wales laid the foundation stone for the new wing in
March 1988. Her Majesty The Queen opened the Sainsbury Wing three
and a quarter years later, in July 1991. During the six years since the

short-list of architects was announced, the project had attracted much interest in the press and from architectural critics. By the autumn of 1990, as the façade was gradually revealed, the volume of comment steadily increased. It is notable that the early press comment was at best luke-warm: 'No carbuncle but just a weak spot.' Some were highly critical: 'A disaster behind the gauze.'

When the commentators were able to see the interior and the galleries displaying the early Renaissance paintings, the balance changed. Most comments were at least favourable and some almost ecstatic. Simon Jenkins wrote in *The Times*, 'The Wing is a marvel' and 'No praise is too great for the most exciting new galleries I have ever seen.' There were still some who remained dissatisfied. In the same paper, on the same day, Gavin Stamp wrote, 'The cruellest disappointment I have ever suffered as an architectural critic.'

In my view, this reflects a weakness in both the public and the press comments on new buildings. Too much attention is focused on the exterior and too little on the interior, and how well the building fulfils its purpose. The main function of the Sainsbury Wing was to provide galleries to display the superb paintings. Nearly all critics were agreed that Venturi, Rauch and Scott Brown had met that objective brilliantly, though most were more restrained than the *Saturday Telegraph* magazine, which wrote of 'The miracle in Trafalgar Square'.

23

SOMERSET HOUSE TRUST

In 1997, as the moment when I would no longer be an MP approached, I was looking for opportunities to become more active in the third sector. By a happy coincidence, the ideal opportunity came up. Somerset House was built between 1776 and 1801 to designs by Sir William Chambers, on the site of the decrepit royal palace originally erected as the London home of the Duke of Somerset, 'Protector Somerset'. It was planned to accommodate nearly all the departments of Government together with the recently created learned societies, the Royal Academy, the Royal Society and the Society of Antiquaries.

In 1780, Sir Joshua Reynolds, President of the Royal Academy, delivered his biennial discourse for the first time in Somerset House. He said, 'This building in which we are now assembled will remain to many future ages an illustrious specimen of the architect's abilities.' Edmund Burke declaimed that 'Somerset House did honour to the present age who would render the metropolis of Great Britain famous throughout Europe.' It survived the Second World War with hardly any damage and, being Government-owned, had been spared the possible depredations of developers. It is one of the great public squares of London. In the 1990s, however, it was no longer a 'public' square. Although the Strand frontage had become the home of the Courtauld Institute, most of the rest of the building was occupied by Government departments, mainly by the Inland Revenue. Worst of all, the wonderful courtyard was a car park for Inland Revenue civil servants. It was described as 'London's forgotten architectural masterpiece'.

In 1971, a campaign was started by Simon Jenkins, then a young *Evening Standard* journalist, to open up the courtyard to the public. That required money and, at the time, nothing happened. The creation of the National Lottery by John Major changed the situation. Jacob Rothschild was chairman of the Heritage Lottery Fund, part of the National Lottery, and he saw an opportunity to persuade Sir Arthur Gilbert, born in Golders Green but resident in California, to bring back to Britain his splendid collection of silver, micro-mosaics and gold boxes. Arthur wanted a prestigious location for his collection and had become dissatisfied with the way it was displayed by the Los Angeles County Museum. He was, I understand, offered the Queen's House at Greenwich as the home for his collection. Surprisingly, he turned it down as 'not central enough'. He was, however, persuaded that Somerset House was central and grand enough for his splendid collection. Lord Rothschild was able to find £10 million to finance the conversion of the lower floors of the south building to house the Gilbert Collection and, somewhat exceptionally, he also found another £10 million as an endowment for the collection. The arrival of the Gilbert Collection was the key that unlocked Somerset House. All that was needed was action by the Government, both owner of all and occupier of most of Somerset House, to hand it over to a trust to carry out the work and create there a centre for culture and the arts.

Michael Heseltine, Deputy Prime Minister and Secretary of State for the Environment, had been a supporter of Simon Jenkins's campaign in the 1970s and had long wanted to get Somerset House back into public use. He was able to persuade his Cabinet colleagues that the building should be handed over to a trust and Michael found it very easy to persuade me to take over as the first chairman of the trust. It is interesting to reflect that in those days there was no advertisement for the job. I was asked to do the job, and I said yes. I was appointed and asked to go and find my fellow Trustees. This I did, and, using contacts and friends, we assembled an excellent group of Trustees including Sir David Rowland, the architectural critic Giles Worsley, Dr Ros Savill, the director of the Wallace Collection, Sir Mark Potter, a judge with good contacts in the Blair administration and Sir Jeremy Isaacs with his knowledge and contacts in the arts world. Simon Jenkins was also a Trustee during our first year. When the Blair Government took over in 1997, I went to see Chris Smith, the new Secretary of State for Culture, and he said, 'Carry on.' This I did, and recruited as our first director Duncan Wilson, who left the Civil Service to begin a prestigious career in the arts. He is now the chief executive of Historic England. We got ourselves a portacabin which we put in the courtyard at Somerset House, found a secretary, and started the transformation of London's most splendid square.

Somerset House Trust was a long way short of a full-time job, but for five years it was the main activity in my third career in the third sector. While we did not achieve everything I would have liked to have achieved in those five years – at the time, we did not get the Inland Revenue out of the new wing or the west wing – nevertheless much progress was made in the transformation. The Gilbert Trust Collection was safely installed

The Queen Mother signing the book at the reopening of Somerset House, 2000

in the south wing and opened by HM Queen Elizabeth, The Queen Mother, on 25 May 2000. We recruited further Trustees, including Tony Elliott, founder of *Time Out*, and Ricky Burdett from the London School of Economics, whom I credit with being the first to suggest that we might have a winter ice rink in the courtyard. We finally got the Inland Revenue cars out of the courtyard, and we were able to transform it by the installation of the fountains and the first of the many winter ice rinks that are now to be found across London. There was so much scepticism about the finances of the ice rink in the first year that it had to be supported by Jacob Rothschild and myself through our charities. In subsequent years, it has got bigger and bigger and more and more successful, and has been heavily sponsored, making money for the Trust.

In the first few years of the Trust, Jacob Rothschild was constantly looking over our shoulder and trying to tell us what we ought to be doing. He wrote me numerous letters and memos, and had papers prepared which were circulated suggesting outsourcing various activities, creating various other bodies and working with others including, for no very good reason, the South Bank. At one stage, I was getting two letters a month with suggestions, comments or criticisms, all of which required a reply. I eventually wrote to him saying, 'I do feel we should avoid trying to do each other's job. Whilst I greatly value the many contributions you have made to the Somerset House project, it is not helpful when

Above, Somerset House courtyard as an HMRC car park, 1997, and *below*, later, as a public space with Safra fountains, 2006 (The Lutyens Photographic Archives, photo © Ben Hatherell; The Edmond J. Safra Fountain Court, photo © Jeff Knowles)

you give the impression that you are Chairman of the Somerset House Trust.' I am glad to say that we have both now moved on from that prickly relationship. At the time, I believe Jacob was worried that the Gilbert Collection would open with no progress having been made on the rest of Somerset House. Admittedly progress was relatively slow, but it was steady and had to contend all the time with getting the Civil Service out of the spaces we wanted. I also suspected that Jacob foresaw the problem which eventually led to the closure of the Gilbert Collection at Somerset House and its removal to the V&A. However magnificent a collection of silver, micro-mosaics and gold boxes is, it is only likely to attract the ordinary visitor once. The collection did not have any significant temporary exhibition space, so there was nothing to bring back the generalist for a second visit, a problem only temporarily addressed by the opening of the Hermitage Rooms on the ground floor of the South Building. So visitor numbers to the Gilbert Collection, which were well over 100,000 in year one, rapidly tailed off towards 20,000, which was a totally uneconomic number for a collection which needed such high security. I suspect Jacob foresaw some embarrassment in having invested some £20 million of Lottery money in supporting the Gilbert Collection and its move to Somerset House and it not proving to be the success he had anticipated. Looking back, I think the justification was that the Gilbert Collection proved to be the key which enabled us to unlock Somerset House and open it up for the public.

In 2018/19, Somerset House attracted over 3 million visitors to thirty-three different exhibitions, live music and outdoor cinema at night, and the ice rink operating for nine weeks. In the same year, seventeen new businesses joined the 'creative community'. Any visitor now will find that it fully answers the original challenge to create there a centre for the arts and culture. I congratulate my successors for what has been achieved and how Somerset House is now such a splendid public space and centre for the arts. It also has some pretty good restaurants and cafés.

THE ASHMOLEAN MUSEUM

While still chairman of the Somerset House Trust, I became a Visitor, that is a Trustee, of the Ashmolean Museum. It is at the St Giles' end of Beaumont Street in Oxford. At the other end of the street is Worcester College. The route from the college to activities in other parts of the university, whether academic, sporting or social, usually went past the Ashmolean. So in each of my three years at Oxford, I must have passed on foot or on a bicycle, or occasionally in a car, the entrance to the museum several hundred times. I regret to say that only on two or three occasions during those three years did I enter the museum. Rather to my surprise, I was not encouraged to do so by any of my tutors, so it is only in the last twenty-five years that I have got to know some of its many pleasures and outstanding collections.

After I retired as a minister, I was able to give more time and thought to the activities of the Headley Trust. When the Dutch had the presidency of the European Union, they had a trade council which I attended, held in The Hague. After the Council Meeting, they hosted a dinner in the Mauritshuis. In addition to an opportunity to enjoy a private view of the magnificent collection of paintings, I saw what could be achieved by using the basement and forecourt space to improve the facilities of a museum. This gave me the idea of doing something similar at the Ashmolean.

In the 1980s, the museum was evolving from being an institution which was somewhat inward-looking, not particularly seeking out or encouraging visitors, even those who were members of the University, and becoming a more normal museum. The Ashmolean lacked a proper shop and catering facilities which could both generate income and attract visitors. There was a need for much more space for education and an outreach department which had, until then, been only a minor activity. So in 1984, the Headley Trust made a substantial donation to fund what became known as the forecourt development at the Ashmolean. We selected Alan Stanton of Stanton Williams to be the architects. Interestingly, this was the first of a series of projects which the practice carried out for trusts within the SFCT umbrella. The other projects included the sterling prize-winning plant research building at Cambridge, funded by Gatsby, and the Simon Sainsbury building, an extension to the Judge Business Centre at Cambridge, funded by the Monument Trust.

Stanton Williams produced an excellent scheme which provided the museum with a proper shop, a great improvement on a small space largely under the stairs, a proper café, a much enlarged and improved space for the education department and a lecture room, something which the museum had not had at all hitherto.

The Trustees of the Ashmolean were known as the Visitors. The Visitors were mostly ex officio members of the University, such as the Senior Proctor and the Lincoln Professor of Classical Archaeology, who had a particular interest in the splendid cast collection. As part of the evolution of the museum in the 1990s, the first non-University Visitors were appointed, one of whom was Anne Heseltine. In 2001, I was invited to become a Visitor and served for five years, overlapping at the beginning with my chairmanship of the Somerset House Trust, and for the last two years with my becoming a Trustee of the V&A. It was a very interesting experience because, among other things, it made me far better acquainted with the complexities of university funding and the work of the Higher Education Funding Council (HEFC). I discovered that there seemed to be nearly as many organisations identified by their initials in the university funding world as there were in the MoD. During my time as a Visitor, I helped the steady evolution of the Ashmolean from an inward-looking university department to a museum, seeking not just to conserve but also to display to a wider public its superb collections.

We have often found that grants to an organisation can encourage others to make grants to the same organisation to enable it to improve and expand its work. For the Ashmolean, the Headley Trust attracted the attention of the Linbury Trust, set up by my brother John, also a graduate of Worcester College. He offered to be the lead donor for a much more substantial development of the museum. Behind the splendid façade and the relatively narrow buildings that were built in the nineteenth century, there was a set of buildings about 100 years old which were erected as a temporary home to house the collection of Minoan treasures brought back from Crete by Sir Arthur Evans. Indeed, it was he who coined the word Minoan, as he connected the site at Knossos that he was excavating with the Minotaur. I believe the Headley Trust can take some credit for inspiring the museum to seek a major development involving replacing those temporary buildings and modernising the displays in the rest of the museum. This became a very large project, designed by Rick Mather, costing about ten times that of the forecourt development. At this time, I decided to retire as a Visitor and leave the field to my brother, and to concentrate on my recent appointment as a Trustee of the V&A.

25

THE V&A AND MUSEUM CHARGES

The V&A, the Victoria and Albert Museum, was founded in 1852 as a 'Museum of Manufactures'. It is, in effect, a museum devoted to displaying the design of man-made objects of any period, including the contemporary. Its collections include ceramics, metalwork, jewellery, furniture, woodwork, sculpture, textiles, paintings, drawings, prints, architecture and books. However, it was none of these which sparked my special interest in the museum.

The museum had chosen the American architect Daniel Libeskind to design a new building on the vacant site known as the Boilerhouse Yard. The director at the time was an old friend of ours, Alan Borg. Libeskind produced a remarkable design for what would have been an iconic building. At the time, I felt that the construction of such a building in London would be a significant mark of the importance we attached both to our museums and to modern architecture. With the benefit of hindsight, it is probable that the building would have been remarkable to look at, interesting to go round, but extremely difficult for the museum to use effectively.

At the time, my enthusiasm for promoting modern and iconic architecture led me to support the development of the design with a substantial donation from the Headley Trust and to try to encourage others to support the proposal. Eventually the museum had to abandon the Libeskind design for lack of that other financial support, particularly from the Heritage Lottery Fund, although it had received planning approval from the Westminster City Council.

It was the support that the Headley Trust had given to the proposal that contributed to my being asked to become a Trustee of the Museum at the end of 2003. So in the same way that my becoming a Visitor of the Ashmolean had overlapped with the end of my time as chairman of the Somerset House Trust, my eight years as a Trustee of the V&A overlapped with the end of my five years as a Visitor of the Ashmolean. Shortly after my appointment, Alan Borg retired as director, to be succeeded by Mark, now Sir Mark Jones. This was the beginning of a decade during which the V&A was totally transformed when gallery after gallery was remodelled and modernised.

The ceramics galleries had been opened in 1909, and 100 years later were largely unchanged, with the original display cases and lighting. During my time as Trustee, the major Headley grant to the museum was towards the total redesign of the ceramics galleries. New galleries opened to great acclaim in 2009, and the designers, chosen by the museum, were Stanton Williams, whom we had chosen for the forecourt development at the Ashmolean. More recently, the Headley Trust was a lead donor for the Exhibition Road development.

Each Trustee of the V&A is given one or two departments in which to take a particular interest. My main department was ceramics and glass. During the period when the ceramics galleries were closed for the rebuild, a touring exhibition of the 100 best objects was put together and went, among other places, to Japan. At that time, in 2008, Damascus was the Arab City of Culture and the Foreign Office view was that the Assad regime was possibly trying 'to come in from the cold'. The thought was therefore that it could be a useful bit of cultural diplomacy to send the V&A 100 best objects as a touring exhibition to Damascus. This was agreed.

I was asked if I would like to go to Syria to attend the opening, which I did. The exhibition was under the patronage of Asma al-Assad, the President's wife. The evening before the opening, the V&A team were invited to a reception at the presidential palace to meet her. We were told to assemble not at the palace but at a hotel from where we would be taken by presidential cars up to the palace for the reception. I was warned to be aware that all the cars were bugged and not to say anything which might be misinterpreted in any way as a criticism of the regime. When we arrived at the palace, I thought that the scale and luxury of the building, a fairly recent construction, was totally inappropriate to a relatively poor country. To get to the area where the reception was being held, guests had to walk quite a long way along a red carpet through a two-level hall. On either side of the carpet, about every five metres, there was a lady, so there must have been at least a dozen of them, none of whom were wearing headscarves. There were three groups present for the reception, one American, one from the V&A, and one other – Asma al-Assad went from group to group and did as good a job as you would expect a member of the British Royal Family to do at a similar occasion.

Above, the Victoria and Albert Museum: the Ceramics Galleries as they were
from 1909 until 2007. *Below*, The redesigned galleries in 2009
(Victoria and Albert Museum)

The following day, I took her around the exhibition, which she had just formally opened. During the course of my time with her, I remarked that their own National Museum needed considerable improvement because it had some wonderful exhibits but they were all displayed in a very old-fashioned and dull way, to which Asma al-Assad replied with a smile, 'We need a Sainsbury.'

During my time as a Trustee, another activity which I was asked to be part of was the selection committee for choosing a new chairman of the Trustees to succeed Paula Ridley. I was the only Trustee on the Committee; the other members were all either chosen by the Department for Culture, Media and Sport, or were from the department. One of the latter's sole interest in and knowledge of the Museum seemed to be whether the candidates were sound on diversity. None of the others had any close connection or involvement with the V&A, and certainly none had ever been a Trustee of a National Collection.

The surprising composition of the selection committee reflected a dilemma that successive Governments have yet to resolve. The buildings that house the National Collection – the Tate, the National Gallery, the Science Museum and the others, together with all their contents – are owned by the Government. Fifty years ago, they were to all intents and purposes entirely funded by the Government. Successive expenditure rounds, and the reality of the pressure on public expenditure from the NHS and the ageing population, education and social services, has gradually reduced the grant in aid.

Catering and shops must now make a significant contribution to revenue, with more from Friends or Members schemes, venue hire and publishing. Charges for admission to temporary exhibitions have steadily increased as a major source of revenue. The modern reality is that major acquisitions, extensions to, or the modernisation of buildings or galleries, have to be funded by private sector donations, with a great deal of help from the Heritage Lottery Fund and sometimes the Art Fund. So in effect, the national museums have become a kind of public-private partnership. One of the major functions of the Trustees, particularly the chairman of the Trust, is to promote the fund-raising aspect which enables the museum or gallery concerned to make acquisitions and improvements to displays which otherwise would not occur. This is to some extent reflected in the composition of the Trustees but as yet sits uneasily as far as the Government is concerned with Government ownership.

One solution that helps to some extent is to create, as has been done by the V&A, a separate 'foundation' whose members reflect the donors and supporters rather than experts on the museum and its role as conservators and curators. However, there is no doubt that becoming a Trustee of the National Gallery or the V&A is a major recognition of support and a more recognised one than becoming a member of the 'foundation'. In my view, consideration should be given to expanding the number of Trustees of these national museums and galleries while making it clear that some of the Trustees are involved mainly in fund-raising and support, and others in more academic aspects.

There is one aspect of the finances of our national museums which many consider should remain off-limits, and that is the long discussed and always controversial issue of museum charges. Just before I became a Trustee of the V&A, I had written an article which the *Spectator* indicated they might like to publish, advocating the merits of charges for admission to our national museums and galleries. On being appointed a Trustee, I withdrew the article as clearly it was incompatible with the policy both of the Government and of the Trustees of the V&A. However, I continue to believe that the reality of the financial situation of the arts and the Government indicates that fresh consideration should be given to this controversial issue.

Charging for admission to our national museums has been a contentious issue for over sixty years. Indeed, for many in the museum world, free admission seems to be an article of faith. However, at a time when there is at long last recognition that no Government is going to provide all the funding needed for those museums – in the decade to 2017 public spending on museums and galleries fell by 30% in real terms – it must be worth asking two questions. First, who benefits most from free admission? Secondly, could there be a better use for the money?

It had been hoped that free admission would encourage a more diverse mix of visitors. However, the reality is that the composition of those in our museums has hardly changed. Nearly half of all UK adults never visit any museum in a year. Those who are not students or pensioners, who would continue to have free admission under any likely charging scheme, are predominantly middle-class; not those most in need of support from the taxpayer. Visitors from overseas are the other main beneficiaries of free admission. Over 60% of those crowding into the British Museum during the average weekday are tourists. They are about 50% of those who visit the V&A. They come from countries where British visitors would have to pay for admission to museums. The British taxpayer might well question why they are required to fund this indiscriminate subsidy.

Some would suggest that free admission is a great attraction to overseas visitors. There is, however, no evidence that having to pay for admission to our wonderful museums would reduce the number of tourists who come to Britain. Indeed many of those coming from overseas, particularly North America, are surprised to find that they are not asked to pay. It used to be argued that the cost of collecting entrance fees, and the delay caused by the collection of those fees, made them not worthwhile. However, the modern need for security control means that collecting an admission charge would scarcely increase costs and delays. They would undoubtedly be a great recruiting sergeant for Museum Friends' schemes, which offer those who join free admission at all times to the museum and any temporary exhibitions.

Opponents of museum charges often suggest they would mean everyone would pay. Far from it, as a sensible charging regime should minimise the deterrent to British visitors while maximising the amount received from tourists. To that end, I would suggest that there should be free admission to all British pensioners and students at all times. Next, it would probably be sensible to have time with free admission for everybody. Bank Holidays would be the most suitable times, as then the British visitors have more leisure time. Another possibility would be a period of free admission in the late afternoons on one or more days of the week. It is noticeable that the prime times for tourists are the morning and the early afternoon; not so many come later in the day.

Advocates of museum charges are often accused of seeking to charge to see our national heritage. The reality is that few of the paintings in the National Gallery had a connection with Britain prior to being acquired, sometimes in rather dubious ways, by the British mainly in the nineteenth century. The organisation which looks after the most British part of our national heritage is the National Trust. They do charge, and have always charged, and have over 5 million paying members.

There would be no shortage of applicants for the income from the charges. The charging institutions should keep the receipts. A reduction in the grant-in-aid to museums would allow the Department for Digital, Culture, Media and Sport to increase grants to other areas. More funds for curatorial posts should be a big priority. Art education at every level should be a priority. This might require some transfer of funds to the Department of Education. The desperately under-funded local authority and other regional museums should get more help. Local authority funding has decreased by nearly a third since 2010, causing a severe loss of curators. Conservation of our heritage, from archaeology to cathedrals, deserves a share. All these areas seem more deserving than a subsidy to tourists and the middle class.

The proportion of visitors from overseas is likely to continue to increase. The grant-in-aid from Government is more likely to reduce in real terms than maintain even its current value. The operating costs will probably continue to increase faster than inflation. It is surely time that free admission is reconsidered.

26

PENDENNIS AND *FAIR LADY*

Being chairman of a yacht-building company was the largest commercial activity of my third career. In 1984, we decided to try something new for a family holiday. We chartered a 62ft motor yacht, *Maharissa*, for a ten-day cruise along the Turkish coast, starting and finishing in Rhodes. We were first-time charterers, but what we hadn't realised was that the owner of *Maharissa* was also chartering his yacht for the first time and acted as his own captain. The holiday was a great success but it did include a few minor dramas brought about by mutual inexperience. We went aground on several occasions. Once, the owner attached a stern line to a tree and then put the boat into forward too fast and pulled the tree straight out of the ground. On another occasion, towing the tender across Fetiye Bay, we looked back to find there was no tender, it had broken loose. Amazingly, sailing back across the Bay we managed to find and retrieve the boat. As a result of that first experience, we decided that chartering yachts for family holidays was very enjoyable.

We next tried it in 1986 when we chartered a Greek-built reproduction of a Turkish-style gulet, this time starting off from Athens but again heading for the Turkish coast and ending in Rhodes. The boat we chartered, *Kyma Alpha*, did have sails but they were only put up to enable us to photograph the yacht under sail. Two years later, we had a third family holiday on a chartered boat, this one called *Lady Hoo*, and sailed to a new area, the Adriatic, cruising down the coast of what was still Yugoslavia. At that time, this was a very under-developed tourist area with some great architecture and fascinating islands.

There was a four-year gap before we next tried a charter. It was August 1992, after the Conservative victory at the General Election when I had become Minister for Industry. I was Duty Minister in the early part of August, and when we left for our holiday I thought the economy was in a reasonable state and did not expect there to be any dramas. We were once again cruising the Turkish coast and, in those days, communication depended upon the BBC World Service. On 16 September 1992, we were astonished to be told by the captain that interest rates had come down to 12%. In trying to find out what had happened, I discovered that they had risen to 15% in a failed attempt to protect Sterling against the disaster of Black Wednesday. I realised that Parliament was bound to be recalled, but thought it would not be until the following week, so we carried on enjoying the holiday and the superb weather. On returning to Britain, it was to find the Conservative Party's reputation for financial competence had taken a severe blow from which it would not recover for a decade.

The boat we had chartered on that occasion was called *Fair Lady*. She had been launched in 1927 by Camper & Nicholson and was designed by Charles Nicholson. Unlike most boats of the era, she had not been drastically altered and retained many of her original features. After having been owned for nearly fifty years by a Frenchman, some of whose family lived in Spain and Argentina, she had been bought in 1983 by a Canadian who had modernised her, but not extensively or very well. As charterers we were not aware of the fact that she had two separate electrical systems, one relying on a DC generator, originally installed in 1928. Early in 1994, having told John Major of my wish to retire as a minister at the next reshuffle, we had started thinking about acquiring a holiday home. At first, the idea we had in mind was to find a villa somewhere between Florence and Siena. However, we had received various brochures about boats we might charter, and one of them showed that *Fair Lady*, which we had liked so much, was now for sale. The price quoted was not as absurd as that for some other boats. As our four boating holidays had been so successful, we decided to investigate the possibility of buying the boat. We asked the broker who had arranged our charter in 1992 about the implications of ownership. She told us that the owner was very anxious to sell and would very much like to meet us. When I asked where he lived, I was told to my astonishment that he had a cottage just outside Kingsclere, two miles from our home at Hill House. I said I would like to meet him when the House rose for the summer recess, knowing that by then I would no longer be a minister and would have much more time available to discuss matters like buying a yacht. When we met at his cottage, he spent a long time telling me how wonderful *Fair Lady* was, so I asked why he wanted to sell her. His honest reply was, 'I am not as rich as I thought I was.' It should have been a warning. So we started the negotiations which led eventually to our purchase of *Fair Lady*.

There was a family visit in October to Paris to celebrate my mother-in-law's eightieth birthday. Afterwards, Susie and I went down to the south of France to spend thirty-six hours on *Fair Lady* to enable us to discuss our purchase with the Captain. Eventually a price was agreed, and on

19 December 1994, I became the owner of a seventy-seven-year old motor yacht. By then we knew she was in pretty poor condition and lacked a lot of basic equipment. However, we decided to do the minimum over the winter of 1994/95; strengthening metal was added and important items like a new radar were acquired, along with a carpet and some new curtains. Meanwhile we started discussing with a naval architect, John Winterbottom, who was originally brought up in Hove, and John Mumford, the designer, about how best to modernise *Fair Lady*. I was very keen that the work should be carried out in England, and in the light of my recent involvement with Cornwall as an area suffering from high unemployment, a recipient of Regional Select Assistance, the idea of having the job done by Pendennis, based in Falmouth, was attractive.

Pendennis had been started in 1988 by Peter de Savary when he mounted a challenge for the America's Cup. In 1995 there was a management buy-out. It was quite a small company, operating mainly from one construction shed. They were one of six companies invited to bid for the work. The initial tender they submitted was far too high. Perhaps reflecting a somewhat uncommercial approach, they had submitted their bid several days before the due date. I contacted them to say that if they hoped to be successful, they had to take a red pencil to their price. This they did, and we got down to two final bidders; one was two shipyards operating jointly based in Portsmouth and the other, Pendennis. They were asked to submit their best and final offers and the Portsmouth companies, who were very confident they would get the contract, put their price up whereas Pendennis put their price down. I didn't realise at the time that this was going to lead to the most significant commercial activity of my retirement. *Fair Lady* came over to Falmouth in November 1995 and remained there being substantially re-built until August 1996. We found the staff of the company to be both competent and friendly and were delighted with the work, which was eventually completed in time for us to use her for a short time at the end of the summer of 1996.

Before we had been involved with Pendennis, the company had experienced a disastrous fire which had burnt out their main construction hall, including a boat which was half built. It had been caused by a painting sub-contractor whose insurance company went bankrupt, leading to years of complex negotiations between various insurance companies and an insurance industry arrangement to cover insured parties against the bankruptcy of an insurance company. The complications meant that on a number of occasions, just when Pendennis thought they would get the money from the claim, they learned that yet again there was some legal objection which meant further delay. As a result, the company, which like most that have been subject to management buy-outs, was short of capital. It was not long after they had completed the work to *Fair Lady* that they asked some of the owners for whom work had been done at Falmouth whether they could inject some capital to keep the company going. This rescue I was happy to support.

However, it was only a few months later when I got a call from Henk Weikens, the CEO, asking if he could come and see me in London. I said, 'of course, when would he like to come' to which he replied 'this week'. I realised immediately that there was a major problem. It was cashflow again, and I was told that unless they could see a realistic chance of putting together a rescue package by the weekend, the shipyard would have to call in administrators because otherwise they could be accused of trading while insolvent. So those who had originally contributed to the first rescue plan were asked to contribute again, which I was prepared to do. One major supporter was George Lindeman, an American who was the owner of a yacht named *Adela*, which had been beautifully rebuilt and restored by Pendennis. When he got the telephone call from the company to ask for help, he cut it short by just saying, 'How much?'

Pendennis's bankers were NatWest, and indeed they still are, and at the time the chairman of NatWest was Sir David Rowland, one of my very oldest friends. I was able to ring him up and say, 'Please don't get involved yourself, but can you make sure that somebody who can look at the situation realistically, realise how important and sensitive this sort of matter is in Cornwall, and is capable of taking decisions, be sent to look at the matter?' This was arranged, and bankers, who so often get berated for their failure to support small companies, played a major part in helping to put together a rescue package. George Lindeman said to me, 'Tim, these guys aren't commercial enough, one of us has got to take over as chairman. I'm in Florida, you're in London, it's got to be you.'

So, much to my surprise, I took over as non-executive chairman from Terry Vernon, who had had a distinguished career in yachting, but was, on his own admission, not very commercial. So I became chairman of a struggling company, employing about 130 people, nearly all in skilled jobs. As non-executive chairman, my main function was to chair a quarterly board meeting. I also kept in fairly close contact with what was happening, and was able to make a contribution by making four suggestions as to how results might be improved. The first was to insist that no variations should be accepted or carried out until they had been costed and signed off by the owner or agent concerned. I said this against a background of knowing that when we had asked for an extra porthole for *Fair Lady*, I never got charged for it. The next, more significant comment was to point out that on the whole, building new boats, while very rewarding, did not result in a profit, whereas carrying out refitting work nearly always did. This is because when a boat comes in for a refit, perhaps with half a million pounds' worth of work for which the yard has tendered, there will almost invariably be a lot of other work which would be done on a cost and materials basis. It is very difficult to lose money on the cost plus part of a contract. Also, the main competitor yards in Europe were much more interested in new builds. There was an ever-increasing market for refits and repairs. In the 1990s there had been a dramatic increase in the number of super-yachts, those in excess of thirty metres in length. Two hundred or more such yachts were under construction in various parts of the world every year. Having identified a significant market opportunity, Pendennis has gradually become Europe's leading shipyard specialising in refits and repairs. During the winter of 2017/18, there were no less than twenty yachts in the yard for refit work.

My next contribution was to support enthusiastically the idea of starting an apprentice scheme. This was managed by the wife of Mike Carr, the joint managing director. Pendennis's training schemes have since won national awards, and the work of Jill Carr has been recognised by the award of an MBE. By 2018, the thirtieth anniversary of the buy-out, about one-quarter of the 450 employees were previous or current apprentices.

My fourth, and in some ways most substantial, contribution to the development of the company was to propose that they took advantage of being in Cornwall in an area eligible for Regional Selective Assistance. Our analysis showed that with the current workforce of about 130, the company was not viable. It could stabilise itself as a smaller company just concentrating on perhaps one or two jobs at a time. This would be a high-risk approach, and would anyhow involve the loss of some fifty jobs. The alternative was to expand and create at least another fifty jobs by developing the ability to handle more refits. This would require investment, primarily in converting the wet dock into a usable dry dock by restoring the gates and pumps and covering it so that it would be an ideal workplace for refits. With the help of consultants, Pendennis put forward a proposal to the DTI, and I led a delegation to London to the Ministry

Above, Pendennis Shipyard in 1999 and *below*, as now in 2020

to argue the case for a grant. That section of the DTI was always headed by an accountant seconded from one of the leading accountancy firms. When we had the meeting in London, I could detect that the very competent lady accountant thought it was somewhat strange that the chairman of the company applying for a grant had been the minister responsible for approving such grants only a few years earlier. Anyhow, we made our application, we were successful, we got our grant and converted the wet dock into a usable dry dock. Over the next fifteen years, the company obtained a number of grants, both from the Government's Regional Selective Assistance and from the European Union, which enabled the yard to be totally rebuilt, and it is now the best-equipped refit yard in Europe. I became the non-executive chairman in 1999, retiring in 2007 when I reached seventy-five. I remain an interested shareholder in a company which now has over 500 employees.

27

REFLECTIONS ON MY THIRD CAREER

Everyone should have one. That is my first reflection on my third career. Getting interested in and involved with activities outside family and business is best started before that morning when you no longer have to go to work. Giving money to or helping a charity is a lifelong act. Giving that often equally valuable thing, time, becomes easier and more worthwhile after retirement. You can be a volunteer helper, a part-time employee, a trustee or even a non-executive director; there are a myriad of opportunities available to help keep active, both physically and mentally. The challenge is to find the ones that suit you best, and to get the timing and the workload right.

So my second reflection is some thoughts on achieving that balance of activities. A year after I retired as a Member of Parliament, I realised I had got it seriously wrong. An audit revealed that I had taken on nineteen interests, each requiring action and most of them meetings. They ranged from helping to raise money for the 'Faith Zone' of the Millennium Dome, working with Peter Mandelson, to chairing the Somerset House Trust, and being a non-executive director of JS. As well as not taking on too many new activities too quickly, scepticism about what you will be expected to do is advisable. All too often, something that is presented as requiring half a day a month can become a day a week. I had not realised the extent of the difference between being on a committee and being the chairman. He or she not only has to attend every meeting and deal with queries and questions between meetings, they are expected to read all the papers for the meetings. Sometimes, the most difficult part of the role is to stay alert, or even awake, throughout the meeting. It is in some ways more difficult to chair a voluntary organisation than a commercial one. Your fellow members of a corporate board will recognise and usually respect the authority and leadership of the chair. Those around a charity board table are giving their time and knowledge freely. If they are long-winded, they must be heard and will resent not being asked for their opinion. I have learned that it is wise to exercise the prerogative of the chair very gently in the third sector. So I recommend careful consideration before agreeing to take on even what at first sight might appear quite minor commitments and be ready sometimes to say, 'No, thank you.'

Variety is said to be the very spice of life, and it is certainly a valuable element in a 'third career'. Being involved in activities in different areas means meeting people with a variety of backgrounds and experiencing various challenges. So having some commercial interest will often help an understanding of the worries and complaints of the business world. There is even a lot to be said in favour of including a bit of politics, national or local. Too many of the retired take the easy option of complaining about politics and politicians from the sidelines. All political Parties would benefit from having more members so that they are not left in the control of extremists.

My next reflection is to express my admiration and thanks to all those who give of their time and money to enable the third sector to achieve so much. There is no shortage of charities. Indeed, in some areas, especially health, there are perhaps too many, some overlapping or even duplicating the work of others. Both the Headley and Jerusalem Trusts have tried to use their influence to encourage amalgamation of charities that seem to be working in the same area. Even more often, the Trusts have questioned the need for a new charity to be established when there is another, or sometimes several others, already working on the same issues. In their commendable enthusiasm to do good, people often seem to underestimate the inevitable overhead costs and administrative time required for even the smallest charity.

The Trusts have usually declined to support appeals to raise money for a charity to acquire real estate, most often for a new office. Money tied up in the freehold of an office is money that is not being spent on a good cause. My early experience of the property world gave me some useful insights into some of the risks of property ownership. First, the building that seems just right for the needs of a charity at one time may soon be found to be too small or even too large. Secondly, there are costs, often seriously underestimated, in having to maintain and sometimes modernise a property. Being a tenant does mean that there is a quarterly or monthly rent bill to pay, but it also means that occupancy costs are predictable for a three- to five-year period. Someone else, the landlord, will have to pay the bill if the roof starts leaking or the boiler needs replacing.

Avoiding wasteful duplication and tying up money and management time in owning property are two aspects of the greatest challenge in philanthropy, achieving 'effective giving'. At a basic level, handing a fiver to the beggar holding a sign saying they are hungry or homeless may make the donor feel better. Sadly, it is very unlikely to be 'effective giving'. There is a risk that the money will be wasted on drink or drugs and it is also quite likely that the recipient is a professional beggar, neither hungry nor homeless. It would be more effective to take the beggar to a place where you could buy them a cup of tea, and a sandwich, or direct them to a food bank or hostel. At the other end of the scale, trusts and foundations should have clear objectives, shared and discussed with those they are supporting, and seek to evaluate outcomes.

There are three ways that our trusts have sought to make their giving effective. Quite often, we have been told that an organisation is able to attract support for projects or programmes, but struggles to finance its central administration. Many charities explain that donors expect their money to be spent directly on services to individuals in need. They find it difficult to elicit support for programmes and work whose impact is less directly visible. In response, we have been prepared to allocate funds to do that rather unexciting-sounding work, instead of backing something to which the Headley or Jerusalem name could be attached.

Innovation, trying out new ways to address a problem such as reducing re-offending or helping the elderly or infirm remain living in their own home, is another type of appeal that often finds it difficult to attract funding. It may not work and the funder then has to accept that that particular grant was not effective. But being prepared to fund outside a trust's natural comfort zone and accept occasional failure may make possible other successes. It has to be accepted that innovative ideas may be quite costly to implement, test and evaluate. There may be occasions when giving can be more effective when done jointly with others. Different Sainsbury family trusts will often work together. Partnering with others in researching where need is greatest, or in evaluating how effective giving is, will often be worth considering. Joint action will be most necessary on those few occasions when making representations to central or local government. We have found that Government, when amendments to charity law are proposed, usually overlooks the difference between charities which raise money from the public and foundations which use the income from their capital, and seek to impose inappropriate regulations upon them.

There are other activities after retiring from a full-time job that are not strictly part of a career but can contribute to the objective of keeping active physically and mentally. Golf, which I have never tried, is strongly recommended by many friends as an enjoyable way of taking exercise that can carry on into the eighties and beyond. Tennis and swimming share that attribute. I referred to my interest in bridge during my time at Oxford. It has carried on ever since. My skill may not improve but it is a game in which you can always go on learning.

My final reflection is that often, especially in the later stages of a third career, the most useful and effective action can be encouraging others to get involved and sometimes indicating ways that they can do so. I suggest that it is sensible to start planning for that third career in good time, and accept that it will be wise to slow the level of activity over time. Maybe one way of encouraging the next generation to give more time or money could be by writing about a third career in a book.

ACKNOWLEDGEMENTS

I am grateful to my publisher, David Campbell, and to my copy editor, Annie Lee, for the contribution they made to the final version of this book. My special thanks go to my editor, Eleo Carson, for her considerable help. Others who have made useful comments include Duncan Wilson on the chapter on Somerset House and Martin Hatfull on my time in the FCO. **I must emphasise that any** errors in those or any other chapters are entirely my fault. Michael Heseltine, a friend and colleague for over forty years, has not only given advice, but also provided the Foreword, for all of which I am particularly grateful. As I also am to Elizabeth Johnston, now my part-time PA, but earlier my Parliamentary Secretary, for her skill in turning incoherent dictation and indecipherable manuscript into a coherent text. My wife Susie has encouraged and endorsed my efforts for nearly four years, and it is to her I dedicate this book.

INDEX

Numbers in *italics* refer to photograph content or captions.